Between Sacred and Profane

Researching Religion and Popular Culture

EDITED BY
GORDON LYNCH

LONDON · NEW YORK

Published in 2007 by I.B.Tauris & Co Ltd
6 Salem Road, London W2 4BU
175 Fifth Avenue, New York NY 10010
www.ibtauris.com

In the United States and Canada distributed by Palgrave Macmillan,
a division of St Martin's Press, 175 Fifth Avenue, New York NY 10010

ISBN: 978 1 84511 540 1

A full CIP record for this book is available from the British Library
A full CIP record for this book is available from the Library of Congress

Library of Congress catalogue card: available

Printed and bound in Great Britain by TJ International Ltd, Padstow, Cornwall
From camera-ready copy edited and supplied by the author.

WITHDRAWN

Between S⸱ ⸱ne

This is an excellent introduction to and assessment of religion and popular culture studies. The volume's attention to theories and methods is unique and much needed in this expanding field of research. This is an essential text for the academic and theological study of religion, media, and popular culture.

Sean McCloud, University of North Carolina; co-chair of the Religion, Media and Culture Group of the American Academy of Religion

In *Between Sacred and Profane*, Gordon Lynch brings together leading scholarly voices in the religion and popular culture interdiscipline. The contributors argue that the study of popular culture *does* matter for the study of religion and theology, and they demonstrate *how* it matters. This is a significant contribution to a still-emerging field and it makes the case that popular culture simply cannot be ignored in any comprehensive understanding of religion.

S. Brent Plate, Texas Christian University and author of *Blasphemy Art that Offends* and co-editor of *The Religion and Film Reader.*

Anyone interested in religion, media and popular culture will find this book indispensable reading. Its contributors form a who's who of scholars working in the area. Their analyses and projections will surely provide much of the agenda for future work in the field.

Robert K. Johnston, Fuller Theological Seminary and editor of *Reframing Theology and Film: New Focus for an Emerging Discipline*

Contents

Introduction

Gordon Lynch

As the following chapters in this book attest, the study of religion, media and popular culture is a maturing discipline. Interest in the constructive study of the 'popular arts' (Hall & Whannel, 1964), associated with the creation of the Centre for Contemporary Cultural Studies at Birmingham University in 1964, pre-dated the emergence of the study of religion, media and popular culture in the 1970's, and to some extent scholars interested in this latter field are still playing catch-up with leading edge theoretical and methodological advances in disciplines such as film studies, cultural studies and media studies. Over the past thirty years, though, there has been considerable consolidation and increasing sophistication in the study of religion, media and popular culture, with the work of scholars trained in theology, religious studies, and the sociology and anthropology of religion, being valuably complemented by contributions from scholars trained in other disciplines such as media, cultural and communication studies, media anthropology, film studies, popular music studies and art history. The chapters by Lynn Schofield Clark and Jeffrey H. Mahan in this book give a more detailed discussion of the highlights and achievements of this growing literature.

This field has become arguably one of the most interesting areas in the study of contemporary religion – reflecting the wider turn to practices and resources of everyday life in the study of religion (Ammerman, 2007) – not only because it offers the possibility of deepening our understanding of the meaning and significance of religion and the sacred in relation to cultural life, but because it also provides an exciting and challenging framework for advanced inter-disciplinary research in theology and the study of religion. As David Morgan comments in his chapter, scholars working in this field typically find themselves working not so much within a particular academic discipline, but within an academic 'inter-discipline' – forced to engage with theoretical and methodological resources from a range of relevant disciplines. This raises issues such as the academic identity and training of scholars working in this field, which have a concrete bearing on where graduate students choose to pursue this kind of research and where they are likely to be employed (or not be employed) when they complete their doctorates. The study of religion, media and popular culture therefore provokes difficult and important questions, both about the world in which we and others live, but also about the nature of our work as academic practitioners and what it means to pursue valuable and rigorous research in this field.

This book is an attempt to pause for reflection on this emerging field. As Lynn Schofield Clark observes in her chapter, there have been a number of edited volumes on religion, media and popular culture published over the past ten years. This current volume is trying to do something rather different to these previous texts, however. Where as previous edited books have generally been collections of specific case studies, occasionally including broader theoretical or methodological reflections, *Between Sacred and Profane* attempts to offer a more sustained moment of reflection on the current state of this field. This project began its life as a panel discussion for the Religion and Popular Culture Group at the annual meeting of the American Academy of Religion in November 2005 in San Antonio, TX, on 'Exploring the research agenda for religion and popular culture'. Drawing on contributions from Lynn Schofield Clark, David Morgan, Tom Beaudoin, Jeffrey Mahan and Anthony Pinn, this panel focused on a range of theoretical and methodological challenges faced by research in this area (Lynch, 2006). Following this panel, a number of other writers were invited to add to this process of reflection by contributing to this book.

In writing their chapters, the contributors have sought to address a wide range of questions:

Why does research in religion, media and popular culture matter?

What is the role of the study of religion, media and popular culture in the context of wider debates about religion, culture and society, and what distinctive contribution has the study of religion, media and popular culture made (or could make) to these wider debates?

How might the study of religion, media and popular culture inform broader concepts of religion and the sacred?

How can we understand the range of disciplinary interests and approaches that make up research in this field, and what are the particular challenges raised by developing inter-disciplinary research in this field?

What have been the strengths, weaknesses and omissions, of the previous literature on religion, media and popular culture, and what questions and approaches should be given more attention in the next phase of research in this area?

What do we bring to this field as researchers in terms of our assumptions, interests and motivations, and what role can reflexivity play for research in this area?

In addressing these questions, the following chapters fall into four different clusters. Chapters 1-4, by Lynn Schofield Clark, David Morgan, Jolyon Mitchell and Jeffrey Mahan offer different overviews of this field. Schofield Clark discusses the rationale for undertaking research in religion, media and popular culture, and provides an overview of key literature in this field to date. David Morgan similarly makes the case for the importance of work in this area, discusses the particular challenges of inter-disciplinarity and suggests an approach to future research which takes both issues of cultural production and consumption seriously. Jolyon Mitchell poses five questions which form an important research agenda for the study of religion and media, and Jeffrey Mahan reflects on both past achievements and future challenges for the study of religion and popular culture. Chapters 5-6 have a more explicitly theological focus, as Elaine Graham and Pete Ward explore the recent 'cultural turn' in the study of theology (particularly practical theology). Graham's chapter discusses the nature and significance of this cultural turn in theological study, whilst Ward uses the example of the ritual of the Eucharist to demonstrate how the cultural turn and concepts from cultural studies can inform theological reflection on this particular example of religious practice. Chapters 7-8 address the issue of reflexivity. Tom Beaudoin argues that we should pay greater attention to the motivations, cultural location and discursive formation of ourselves as researchers in the study of religion and popular culture, arguing that work in this field can be undertaken as a self-consciously spiritual exercise. Robert Beckford's chapter offers a concrete example of this kind of reflexivity, as he reflects on the cultural gaze that he adopts through his work as a black theologian and film-maker commenting on contemporary culture. Finally, chapters 9-10 explore how the study of religion, media and popular culture might inform broader understandings of religion and the sacred. In my chapter, I argue that the study of religion, media and popular culture can make a valuable contribution to the contested debate about the nature of 'religion' by exploring the nature and significance of sacred objects within human cultures. Anthony Pinn argues that African-American religious studies has typically operated on the basis of limited notions of conversion and the religious life, borrowed uncritically from Christian theology, and that attention to the work of rap artists, Tupac Shakur and Snoop Dogg, provides an alternative way of conceiving of conversion and the religious life as a form of existential orientation to the world.

The questions that have driven this book are important and complex, and the chapters are intended not as the final word on these subjects but as provocations for future discussion. At the end of the book, I offer my own concluding reflections, as one interpretation of the preceding material. But the value of this book will lie in the extent to which it is able to stimulate different kinds of reading and response, and to encourage a new degree of self-awareness and areas of focus in future scholarly work in this area.

Editing this book has been an enjoyable experience, and I'm grateful to the friends and colleagues who have contributed chapters to it. My thanks also go to the Religion and Popular Culture Group within the AAR for providing the opportunity for this discussion to develop, and to Alex Wright, Jayne Hill and everyone else at I.B.Tauris, as well as Matthew Brown at Bookcraft, who has made the subsequent production of this book possible.

1

Why Study Popular Culture?

Or, How to Build a Case for your Thesis in a Religious Studies or Theology Department

LYNN SCHOFIELD CLARK

A young scholar had just finished presenting the final paper on a panel exploring the intersection of popular culture and journalism. The setting was an international conference of journalism and mass communication educators, and the audience included a mix of graduate students and junior to more fully established scholars. When the time came for the panelists to entertain questions from the audience, one of the senior scholars in the audience stood up and addressed the young scholar. 'What you've said about video games related to the television program *Buffy the Vampire Slayer* is very interesting. It also seems like a fun topic to study. But how does this speak to any of the recent developments in theories of journalism and media?' Her sample size was 'anecdotal' and too small for generalizability, he continued, noting that the data were too slim to build a case of media effects (e.g., that the media *cause* certain people to behave in certain ways). And despite the fact that she also seemed interested in how media were shaping public opinion, she didn't reference either framing or agenda-setting theories, which explore how the news media, in the endlessly quoted words of researchers Maxwell McCombs and Donald Shaw (1992, p.176), tell us 'not what to think but what to think *about*.' How did this research contribute to our understandings of society and the role of the media within it, then, this senior scholar wondered?

The young scholar was understandably flustered. The senior scholar had not asked these questions in a way that was visibly condescending, but for everyone in the room it was clear that these were not completely inno-cent questions, either: they spoke to the differences in paradigms that currently undergird studies of the media within the field that is professionally devoted to the study of the role of media in society. A more senior scholar on the panel jumped in and explained that the young scholar's work was framed within the interdisciplinary theories of cultural studies and thus spoke to those theories and concerns rather than to those of more mainstream journalism and media effects theories. Unfortunately, this senior scholar did not explain what those theories and concerns of cultural studies actually *were*. And the junior scholar, emboldened by her co-panelist's comments, added (with the slightest *harrumph*), 'I guess if you don't know why cultural studies would be valuable, I don't know how to explain it to you.'

As I sat in the audience, I thought about the young scholar's statement. I could imagine her spending many hours after this exchange pondering, 'what I *should* have said...' But I also wondered: why does it seem to be so difficult to explain to more traditionally-schooled scholars the value of the study of culture, and the embrace of a cultural studies framework, specifically in the study of mass mediated popular culture? And I wondered: how would *I* advise junior scholars to explain why their studies of popular culture and their embrace of a cultural studies framework are useful and important? It seems to me that this kind of exchange is just as likely to happen among religious studies and theology scholars as among media scholars. Of course, among the latter, one would need to argue not only why the study of culture is important, but why the study of popular culture and mass mediated popular culture in particular is relevant to concerns within the fields of religious studies and theology. Thus, I begin this chapter with those questions in mind.

To begin, I will offer an explanation of what the term 'popular culture' refers to and how it has been studied in the past. I will then address this issue of why the study of popular culture is interesting and important for those in the fields of theology and religious studies, and why it has met such resistance, concluding with observations about how it is currently being studied in the fields of religious studies and theology.

What is Popular Culture?

I believe that the broadest and simplest reason for the study of popular culture in theology and religious studies is that the study of popular cultural artifacts can lead to insights into issues that transcend popular culture itself. In order to understand how this works, we have to understand how popular culture works – and that, inevitably, leads us to address why people have such distaste and sometimes even disdain for it. Even within media studies, the study of popular culture has not been free of this disdain.

Until the 1960s, the study of popular culture within the field of media scholarship had been undertaken primarily in relation to an 'effects' paradigm in the U.S., exploring how popular culture – and popular media in particular – could influence the behaviors of vulnerable populations such as immigrants and youth. This is generally considered the 'mass communication' perspective within the study of media in society. The 1960s inaugurated a turn to what has been termed 'uses and gratifications' studies, marked by Elihu Katz's famous recommendation that scholars should spend less time pondering what the media do *to* people and more time considering what people do *with* the media, thus placing on the research agenda the various uses to which media were put and the gratifications people received in consuming it. This focus on the everyday uses of media and the meanings people made from them echoed the emergence of what has been variously termed cultural history, new history, or in France, the *histoire des mentalités* in the fields of history. Scholars in this tradition were (and remain) interested in popular cultural practices and phenomena of non-elite groups, and seek to reframe naturalized understandings of history by uncovering these accounts and practices of the non-dominant majority. Similarly, in literary studies the 1960s saw the emergence of reader-response theory, which foregrounded the role readers played in constructing the meanings of literary texts. And also during this same time period, the interdisciplinary field of cultural studies was emerging in Britain and elsewhere in Europe, focusing on how media and other artifacts of culture helped to contribute to subcultural identity, especially among youth cultures.

Whereas the rising interest in 'uses and gratifications' approaches in America held some theoretical and methodological overlap with British traditions, most scholars who identify with the American tradition of media cultural studies consider themselves at some distance from the uses and gratifications paradigm and identify more strongly with the British cultural studies tradition. This is because whereas uses and gratifications largely builds upon existing theories within mass communication studies and often employs positivist methods for investigation, those within cultural studies traditions are committed to interdisciplinarity and a wider range of methodologies, thus employing in their analyses learnings from feminism, anthropology and interpretive sociology, critical race theory, neo-Marxism, and postcolonial theory. Those within media cultural studies have also been influenced by reader-response and cultural historical approaches, and some increasingly explore not only mass mediated artifacts, but aspects of popular culture that are commercially produced or mass mediated in some other way.

Although in the European tradition of media studies the psychological/behaviorist influence has never been as strong as in the U.S., like their counterparts elsewhere in the world the study of popular culture was considered rather less important than studies of high and middlebrow culture such as news reporting or the more traditional arts. Thus, the study of popular culture in the cultural studies tradition, with its emphasis on peoples' everyday lives and practices (practices that themselves have a history), is in many ways more closely allied *across* disciplines than within a particular discipline, sharing as it does a commitment to understanding everyday lives in order to reconstruct and reevaluate taken-for-granted notions of societal organization and individual experiences within it.

Today, the study of popular culture brings together three different, yet related, concerns: culture, the popular, and mass culture. *Culture* is the term used to denote a particular way of life for a specific group of people during a certain period in history. It also references the artifacts, narratives, images, habits, and products that give style and substance to that particular way of life. In an oft-cited discussion, Raymond Williams (1992) referred to culture as a 'structure of feeling', culture is something that informs the way that a group of people see and experience the world, even when they do not consciously recognize its collective organization or impact. *Mass culture* is a term that highlights the profit motive that directs the production of certain products made available for commercial sale. It refers to both these mass-produced products and the consumer demand for them that justifies their widespread production and distribution. *The popular* makes reference to 'the people' and *popular culture* therefore usually refers to those commercially-produced items specifically associated with leisure, the mass media, and lifestyle choices that people consume. Items of popular culture can include products such as reading materials, music, visual images, photos, film, television, advertising, video games, celebrity culture, professional sports, talk radio, comics, ipods, and items on youtube. But they can also include what we might call 'high culture' things such as live and performance theater, art, musical arrangements and performances, and museum installations designed for popular consumption. Popular culture also refers to a seemingly endless variety of goods, including modes of transportation, fashion, toys, sporting goods, and even food.

In short, popular culture is anything that can be successfully packaged for consumers in response to their desire for a means to both identify with some people, ideas, or movements, and to distinguish themselves from others (Bourdieu, 1984/2002).

In order to be successful and to receive widespread attention – in other words, to become a popular culture phenomenon – popular culture has to connect to something that holds meaning for people. Sometimes, popular culture expresses the *zeitgeist* of an era, speaking to deep-seated beliefs that are consistent with what we believe are the best qualities of our collective society. It is no coincidence that a rise in state support for civil unions and same sex marriages would occur in the same era in which a film like *Brokeback Mountain* attracts A-list movie stars and achieves box office success. While not exactly comporting with a specific political agenda, the film's appeal certainly was consistent with the growing desire on the part of many in the U.S. to embrace greater acceptance for gay and lesbian relationships even as past and current discriminations are acknowledged and mourned. But popular culture also reflects the unconscious, taken-for-granted views that we prefer not to admit to ourselves. Pepi Leistyna's (2006) work on representations of class in American sitcom television, for example, points to the longstanding pattern of portraying lower-wage working class men as bumbling, blustery, anti-intellectual subjects of humor, from *The Honeymooners'* Jackie Gleason and *All in the Family's* Archie Bunker, to *King of Queens'* Doug Heffernan and *The Simpsons'* Homer Simpson. Leistyna's argument is that in this time of increased economic disparity, job loss, and employment insecurity, such depictions reinforce the notion that lower-wage workers are to blame for their own situation, and that people in lower-wage jobs are therefore distinct in their interests from working people with higher wages. In this case, the study of media representations might serve as a wake-up call to the fact that such negatively patterned representations cannot change until we work to change social reality. A cultural studies perspective on this notes that it is not so much that people are convinced by television, therefore (the 'media effects' perspective), but that television's entertainment value rests on its ability to articulate what we believe without doing so in a way that threatens our very sense of who we believe ourselves to be (and we prefer to believe ourselves to be tolerant, humane, accepting, non-racist, etc.). Popular culture such as television and film, as well as novels, comedy clubs, fashion magazines, and more, are locations in which these contradictions and negotiations are constantly played out through narrative and representation.

That's what makes them interesting as objects of study. We need to remember, as Robert Thompson has pointed out, that 'escapism and relevance are not mutually exclusive' (Rose, 2004). Indeed, Australian journalist Catharine Lumby (2004) observed, 'where critics of cultural studies go
wrong is that they think the quality of thinking is somehow predetermined
by the cultural value of the object being analyzed'.

This takes us back to the issue of how studies of popular culture are
able to transcend concerns of popular culture itself.

Popular culture appeals to our emotions and our processes of identification, making it a prime location for communicating significant ideals and
ideas. This is a fact, of course, not lost on the public relations and advertising industries. Scholars in religious studies and theology may feel understandable frustration in the ways in which the popular cultural industries
have hijacked our identification processes for the purposes of profit. Most
of us resent the flood of advertising and marketing that greets us at every
point in our day in ever new and increasingly intrusive forms. Some of us
worry, with Neil Postman (1986), that we are a society 'amusing ourselves
to death.' And religion is increasingly getting into the act, employing
branding techniques in order to appeal to prospective parishioners, to
encourage giving in capital campaigns, or simply to increase awareness of
religious organizations or to evangelize within their communities. Meanwhile, advertisers themselves continue to borrow from the language and
imagery of religion, appealing to a sense of tradition and sentimentality, a
desire for transcendent experience, or a love of beauty and Truth in well-
crafted messages designed to invoke sales of everything from beer to running shoes. Politicians, too, increasingly see the benefit of what marketers
call the practices of product placement and celebrity endorsement in their
appeals. As an example, many were outraged to learn that a syndicated
broadcast columnist in the U.S. accepted a payment of $240,000 from the
U.S. Education Department to promote the No Child Left Behind Act in
columns supposedly devoted to his own opinions (Chaddock, 2005, p.1).
These and similar efforts are surely undertaken out of a tacit acknowl-
edgement in the role popular culture plays in informing public opinion.
When scholars study these specific instances, they can gain insights into
the role religion plays in politics, and in how the commercial marketplace
is shaping the way in which persons of faith literally and figuratively clothe
themselves in ways consistent with what they believe are a certain set of
religious (or even post-religious) commitments (Clark, 2007). Studying
popular culture in religious studies and theology therefore provides in-

sights into how commitments to faith communities and alternative communities are formed and maintained through connections to material goods, and what it might mean to be a faith participant, and a citizen and consumer in public life in a commercially-drenched world. Within a more historically informed perspective, studies of popular culture and religion can also demonstrate that such issues are not completely new, but in fact religious practices and beliefs have always existed in a context in which certain societal groups sought to persuade, influence, or sell something (Beaudoin, 2003).

Popular culture is also a fundamental part of our social lives and our interactions with others; it provides an especially emotive language through which we communicate with others about those things that are especially meaningful to us. When we talk enthusiastically about our favorite independent film, or when we choose *not* to talk about our favorite trashy television program, we do so both as a way to communicate something about ourselves and to join a conversation that's already structured with regard to a certain set of cultural expectations. It is through the stories, myths, narratives, sounds, and images of culture that we are able to make sense of our lives, both for ourselves and for others. By communicating with others through reference to popular culture, we are able to place ourselves socially and to ascribe meaning to our own actions. In this way, popular culture provides the framework through which understandings of religion can be shaped or maintained: it gives us a way to evaluate in the presence of others who we are, what we believe and do, and why. It provides us with a cultural repertoire, to use the language of sociologists of culture. Studying what becomes popular therefore gives us insight into why society is organized as it is, and what deeply-held beliefs might need to be challenged in order to bring about change in its structure (or perhaps, why such change may be just short of impossible). These are some of the compelling reasons that one might strive to undertake a study of popular culture within the context of theology and religious studies.

Why is it that popular culture is associated with triviality, then? The roots of this approach go back to the earliest critiques of popular culture.

Popular Culture: Trivial or Threatening?

The phrase 'popular culture' first came into use in the English language in the early nineteenth century, when for the first time, it was possible to manufacture and widely distribute cultural products with relative ease and speed (Clark, 2006). Prior to the emergence of a capitalist market economy with industrialization, 'the popular' was a term with legal and political meaning that derived from the Latin *popularis*, or 'belonging to the people.' The term was used as a way to draw distinctions between the views of 'the people' and those who wielded power over them. In the past, therefore, the term popular culture was used to reference the folk traditions created and maintained by the people outside of the purview of cultural authorities and away from the demands of labor.

As the working class that staffed the industrial landscape continued to grow in the 19th century, however, the bourgeoisie in industrialized Europe came to view the shared artifacts of working-class culture as evidence of both their unity and their inferiority. Early criticism of working-class popular culture therefore emerged in a context in which the bourgeoisie feared an uprising similar to that of the French Revolution. Known today as the 'culture and civilization' tradition, its first articulation appeared through the writings of Britain's famous poet, Matthew Arnold. In his book *Culture and Anarchy* Arnold argued that much of the problem of his generation lay in the emergent working class and their seeming refusal to adopt a position of subordination and deference to the elite and their culture.

The 'culture and civilization' tradition of popular cultural critiques found renewed expression in the writings of Frank R. and Queenie D. Leavis, who began writing about popular culture in the 1930s in England. Believing that popular culture provided a dangerous distraction to responsible participation in democracy, they advocated that public schools engage in education about the ill effects of popular culture on young people. In their writings, the Leavises promoted a mythic 'golden age' of England's rural past, in which they believed a 'common culture' (or 'folk' culture) had flourished. Their many treatises aimed to keep the expansion of popular culture's influence under control so as to maintain what they believed were the truly valuable aspects of England's cultural tradition.

A similar strand of thought has long been a part of U.S. approaches to popular culture. In 1957, Bernard Rosenberg and David Manning White published *Mass Culture: The Popular Arts in America*, a collection of essays that bemoaned the supposed dehumanizing impact of popular culture, particularly mass mediated popular culture. In the shadow of the Cold War, the contributors to the Rosenberg and White volume feared that a passive audience in the sway of popular culture could be easily brought under the influence of a totalitarian government.

A fear of totalitarianism animated the writings of scholars such as Theodor Adorno, Max Horkheimer, Leo Lowenthal, and Herbert Marcuse of the Frankfurt School, as well. Like their U.S. counterparts, their intellectual roots were in Romanticism, although much more firmly located within Marxist critiques of labor relations and the power of the bourgeoisie over the proletariat masses. Ex-patriates from Hitler's Germany, scholars in the Frankfurt school feared the manipulative potential of popular culture through the workings of what they called the 'culture industries'. Although often dismissed as overly pessimistic in that they saw little potential for change in the relations between the privileged and the disadvantaged in society, these scholars (of the 'critical school') inaugurated several important streams of thought regarding popular culture. Particularly influential have been the ideas of critical theorist Walter Benjamin, whose attention to both the mass production and ideological role of images in contemporary society has been influential in debates of art, politics, and postmodernism. Equally important, the critical school spawned the scholarly tradition of cultural imperialism, which came to prominence in the 1970s as it explored the flow of mass media across national borders. Latin American scholars of media and popular culture such as Antonio Pasquali, Luis Ramiro Beltran, Fernandez Reyes Matta, and Mario Kaplun, as well as Herb Schiller in the U.S. and Dallas Smythe in Canada, were concerned about the ways in which multinational media corporations were, through the organization of profit and commerce, able to dominate the development of media, and by extension popular culture and the commercial marketplace, in smaller and less wealthy nations.

In contemporary studies and critiques of popular culture, one often witnesses strains of thought from these earlier explorations, from a dismissal of popular culture as banal and threatening to western civilization, to a concern about its potential to narcotize and depoliticize, to the fear that western popular culture's ubiquity will undermine the authenticity and uniqueness of those cultures at some distance from Hollywood. By the 1980s, however, some scholars of popular culture began to question these often-undermodulated concerns about the popular culture and the implications of its incursion into everyday life.

Studying Popular Culture and Everyday Life

With the rise of reader-response theory in literary criticism, 'pop art' that questioned 'high culture/low culture' distinctions, and the prominence of feminism, black, and cross-cultural perspectives in the late 1970s and

1980s, a new school of thought regarding popular culture had begun to take root in North America, Europe, Latin America, and Australia. Building upon interdisciplinary social theory and critical theorists' interests in the role the mass media play in social organization, the cultural studies approach to popular culture had its beginnings primarily in literature departments in the USA and in departments of sociology in Britain, Australia, and Latin America.

In the UK much of the early scholarship in cultural studies approaches to popular culture arose in response to the Frankfurt school's pessimism and the Leavis's bleak outlook on the demise of English high culture. In the 1970s and 1980s, scholars in cultural studies in Britain sought to demonstrate that audiences were not passive consumers of the products produced for them by the culture industries. Drawing upon the earlier scholarship of British historical cultural theorists, notably Raymond Williams, Richard Hoggart, and E.P. Thompson, cultural studies scholars such as Stuart Hall, David Morley, Charlotte Brundsen, and those at the Birmingham School set out to demonstrate the importance of the 'decoding' rather than the 'encoding' processes of mass mediated popular culture, to quote an oft-cited essay by Stuart Hall (1990). Pointing to such factors as the vast numbers of heavily promoted popular cultural artefacts that failed to find a positive reception in the marketplace, cultural studies scholars argued that popular cultural artefacts must meet the emotional needs of their audiences in order to succeed in the cultural economy (Fiske, 1989). Methodologies differed, although many embraced textual criticism, semiotics, audience reception research, and cultural history (Ang, 1995; Zelizer, 2000).

In the 1990s and the beginning of the new millennium, a reinvigoration of neo-Marxism through the emergence of postcolonial perspectives and critiques in anthropological methods, combined with a renewed interest in cultural history, everyday life, and issues of visual representation, redirected cultural studies toward its central concern with the ways in which specific narratives and representations contribute to maintaining power relations as they are.

The rise of interest in popular culture across scholarly disciplines is therefore intimately related to the emergence of 'grand theories' in the 1960s, 1970s, and 1980s. During those decades, scholars across the humanities and social sciences were reading the works of Roland Barthes, Michel Foucault, Jacques Derrida and Gilles Deleuze, and later Raymond Williams and Stuart Hall, each of whom foregrounded issues of representation, narrative, discourse, construction of meaning, and geographical contextualization in differing ways. Some in the social sciences began experimenting with what Clifford Geertz (1980) termed 'genre mixing', importing into scholarly narratives experimental forms of writing from the humanities while also borrowing from the humanities the metaphors of game, drama, and text as means to analyze social life and organization. Meanwhile, those in the humanities began more fulsome dialogues with the social sciences and the study of everyday life. After the 1960s, the field of theology began to move away from a model of a rational and reflective theological process to one that embraced a theology oriented not toward thinking but toward 'doing', 'experiencing', and practicing. Religious studies, too, followed this trend toward the everyday, while also seeking to depart from what Ninian Smart (1986, p.158) has referred to as the 'grip of the Christian establishment' on that field. This grip 'prevents an openness of approach, and means that interested agnostic, Jewish and other 'outsiders' are discouraged from taking up the subject.' After the 1960s, religious studies therefore became a more wholeheartedly 'secular' discipline, interested in exploring religion and the beliefs, behaviours, and institutions associated with it. Husserl's phenomenological approach became highly influential on religious studies, encouraging scholars to come as close as possible to understanding the 'meaning' of religious phenomena studied and to explore ways to communicate that understanding with as much depth as possible.

This focus on everyday life and on meaning is therefore central to an important argument for the study of popular culture in theology and religious studies, as Gordon Lynch has argued. Lynch notes that the study of popular culture should be seen within the context of the growing interest in the study of everyday life that dates at least to the end of the nineteenth century. It is 'part of a longer tradition in which the environment, practices, and resources of everyday life have been considered to be suitable subjects for critical academic study' (Lynch, 2005, p.15). As Lynch (ibid.,) continues, 'thinking about popular culture as the shared environment, practices, and resources of everyday life is a useful way of approaching this subject because it both helps us to maintain an open mind to studying whatever may be significant in everyday life and in a particular social context.' To the extent that scholars want to understand life as experienced from the ground up, popular cultural studies are going to be an inevitable and highly salient way for us to probe meaning-making practices of everyday lives.

Studying Religion and Popular Culture Today

Today, scholars are engaging in the study of religion and popular culture across a range of disciplines. The study of religion and popular culture is inherently interdisciplinary, drawing upon theories and methodologies from sociology, anthropology, philosophy, psychology, history, literary criticism, and media studies. Differences in methodology, concerns, and philosophical commitments tend to vary according to disciplines, and thus whereas the field (if indeed it might be called a field) will never be standardized, there are ways in which scholars might learn from compatriots who hail from different disciplines. The remainder of this chapter is therefore devoted to highlighting some of the most significant works in this area, categorizing them according to how they articulate their reasons for study.

Within the field of religious studies are several scholars who primarily see their work as speaking to others in religious studies, offering popular cultural analyses that shed light on pressing problems in the methodologies and theories of religion. Perhaps the most thorough explication of why scholars in religious studies and theology might want to study popular culture and how they might go about it can be found in Gordon Lynch's (2005) *Understanding Theology and Popular Culture*. This book explains roots of popular cultural studies in a way that complements and extends the argument presented here, while also modeling how one might engage in author-centric, reader-response, and cultural analytical approaches to the exploration of popular culture and religion. A similar approach is taken in Kelton Cobb's (2005) *Blackwell Guide to Theology and Popular Culture*.

Some of the most influential studies of popular culture and religion in recent years have come from historians of religion and material culture, such as R. Laurence Moore's (1995) *Selling God: American Religion in the Marketplace of Culture*, Colleen McDannell's (1995) *Material Christianity: Religion and Popular Culture in America*, David Morgan's (1998) *Visual Piety: A History and Theory of Popular Religious Images*, and Leigh Eric Schmidt's (1997) *Consumer Rites: The Buying and Selling of American Holidays*, all published in the mid-1990s. More recently, David Paul Nord (2004) has published what is sure to become a standard in exploring the role of the conservative Christian religion in the development of the U.S. media industries, called, *Faith in Reading: Religious Publishing and the Birth of Mass Media in America*.

Studies of religion and popular culture, and courses on this topic within religious studies and theology departments, began to proliferate from the mid-1990s to the mid-2000s. This led to several edited volumes on the topic, such as Eric Michael Mazur and Kate McCarthy's (2001) *God in the Details: American Religion and Popular Culture*, Bruce Forbes and Jeffrey Mahan's (2000/2005) *Religion and Poplar Culture in America*, John Giggie and Diane Winston's (2002) *Faith in the Market*, and David Morgan and Sally Promey's (1996) *Icons of American Protestantism*. Also included here but more specifically focused on religion and mass mediated elements of popular culture would be my edited volume, *Religion, Media, and the Marketplace* (Clark, 2007) and Birgit Meyers and Anneleis Moores' (2005) *Religion, Media, and the Public Sphere*, and the earlier edited volumes *Mediating Religion* (Mitchell & Marriage, 2003), *Religion and Popular Culture* (Stout & Buddenbaum, 2000), *Belief in Media* (Horsfield, Hess & Medrano, 2004), *Practicing Religion in the Age of the Media* (Hoover & Clark, 2002), *Quoting God* (Badaracco, 2004), *Star Trek and Sacred Ground* (Porter & McLaren, 2000), and *Rethinking Media, Religion, and Culture* (Hoover & Lundby, 1997).

By the middle of the first decade in the new millennium, several books on popular culture and religion modeled an approach that took seriously the experiences of religion in everyday life and the intersection of popular culture with those everyday concerns. Diane Winston's (2000) *Red Hot and Righteous* traced the ways in which the Salvation Army employed forces of urbanization and commercialization to its advantage but ultimately could not control the way the movement was portrayed in the media. Tona Hangen's (2001) *Redeeming the Dial: Radio, Religion, and Popular Culture in America* followed the evangelical use of radio from the early part of the 20th century, tracing how this movement experimented with uses of communication technology in order to build a coalition of like-minded believers. A similar book with a more theological orientation was Jolyon Mitchell's (1999) *Visually Speaking: Radio and the Renaissance of Preaching*. My own *From Angels to Aliens: Teenagers, the Media, and the Supernatural* (Clark, 2005) explored how popular culture's stories of the supernatural provided a framework for both religious and not-so-religious young people to think about religion, the afterlife, the supernatural, and the paranormal in a way sometimes remarkably similar to the evangelical/fundamentalist 'hellfire and brimstone' approach of two centuries earlier. Rebecca Sullivan's (2005) *Visual Habits: Nuns, Feminism, and American Postwar Popular Culture* similarly traced how representations of religious sisters shaped understandings and acceptance of jovial and traditional nuns even as their roles in society were dramatically shifting away from the peaceful to the activist and feminist-inspired sisters of today. Heather Hendershot's (2004) *Shaking the World for Jesus: Media and Conservative Evangelical Culture* offered an historically grounded exploration for why the Christian retailing industry had taken off by the end of the 20th century, exploring the dubious negotiations the creators of such popular cultural products underwent to make their efforts palatable to those outside the fold while satisfying their primary market of conservative Christians. And in *The Religion of the Media Age*, Stewart Hoover (2006) explored the growth of more individually-oriented religious practices in the U.S. and the development of an individually-oriented consumerist marketplace that both reflects and takes advantage of this new spiritual orientation.

By the middle of the first decade of the 21st century, religious studies scholars were also entering into this field with a host of manuscript-length contributions. In the book *Rapture Culture*, Amy Johnson Frykholm (2004), a professor of religion, literature, and cultural studies, sought to add a correction to the fact that whereas many in religious studies discuss the importance of understanding everyday life experiences and meaning making practices of religious practitioners, they rarely extend popular cultural studies to examinations of their reception. Frykholm therefore conducted a reader-response study of the popular *Left Behind* book series by Tim La-Haye and Jerry Jenkins. Frykholm's book illuminated why some people read the books and others find them appalling, shedding light on why the story of the apocalypse is found to be so compelling among conservative Christians in the U.S..

Frykholm's work built upon an earlier practice of exploring media texts as influential in the construction of religious social movements and their relation to mainstream U.S. culture. In Mark Hulsether's (1999) book, *Building a Protestant Left: Christianity and Crisis Magazine, 1941-1993*, a detailed history of a significant left-leaning religious publication provides insights into the religious support of peace activism, feminism, and civil rights, among other issues.

Similarly, Sean McCloud's (2004) book *Making the American Fringe: Exotics, Subversives, and Journalists, 1955-1993*, scholars in religious studies are introduced to the analysis of mainstream media reports in the exploration of how certain beliefs are portrayed as 'fringe' whereas others are taken for granted as reflecting the 'mainstream'. His book looks at important considerations in religious studies such as the role of emotions in religion, the different perceptions of normal versus 'abnormal' levels of piety in religious practice, and the role of the media industries in constructing religious understandings.

Complementing the study of evangelicals and their culture, the Protestant Left, and the study of the religious fringe, religious studies scholars such as Brent Plate (2003) have examined how films and popular cultural artifacts from various places around the world might be helpfully placed in dialogue with one another to illuminate key concepts in religious studies such as myth, memory, creation, and redemption. Employing writings by Walter Benjamin, Plate (2004) looks at developments in architecture, art, and film in light of religious developments around the world, thereby shedding light on religion as well as on the larger cultural textures that shape and reflect its sensibilities at particular moments in history. Also writing on film but from a more theological vein, John Lyden (2003) discusses the ways in which moviegoing performs religious functions in U.S. culture, and Tom Beaudoin (1998) has explored both the role of popular culture in 'Generation X' religious sensibilities and the rise of branding and its implications for the development of an economically-informed spirituality.

I have referred to these religious studies as 'brave', in that they have foregone the previous tendency in religious studies to explore popular culture as a dilettante or as a form of 'scholarly slumming'. For a long time, conventional wisdom held that those in religious studies in theology should attain expertise in something suitably ancient and respectable, only to 'dabble' in popular cultural studies after tenure had been safely secured. I have argued that those interested in the study of popular culture and religion should make it a point to read and cite works by these scholars, for their work represents a truly pioneering turn within the field of religious studies. I have also suggested that one way that scholars in this approach can build a body of work that is viewed as legitimate by the larger field of religious studies is to intentionally seek out ways to put popular cultural scholarship in dialogue with more traditional approaches, co-organizing panels in such American Academy of Religion divisions as the History of Christianity, Islam, Judaism, Buddhism, or Comparative Religion sections. In this way, those interested in popular culture can be in conversation with issues considered to be of key importance among religious studies scholars in these various sections and divisions. Similarly, I encourage those interested in legitimating the study of popular culture in the wider fields of religious studies and theology to invite those from other fields to participate in cross-disciplinary conferences, organizing panels including established scholars from other fields to the annual meetings of the American Academy of Religion, the Society for the Scientific

Study of Religion, and the British and American Sociological Associations, among others. Such efforts are likely to help to deepen relationships across disciplines, while also developing scholarship on popular culture and religion that will be of broader interest to those beginning to consider the topic.

Conclusion

The question that started this chapter, then, has multiple answers. Why should one study culture, and popular culture in particular in the context of theology and the study of religion? As has been discussed, the study of popular culture enables the scholar to transcend popular culture and reflect upon wider issues of religion's role in society. Such studies offer insights into how various religions might be represented and understood, how various popular cultural artifacts become adopted by religious subcultures as a means of establishing and reinforcing identity, how popular culture becomes a resource through which people can reflect and discuss with others their own views and practices, and how religious traditions might be meaningfully communicated to future generations through emotionally captivating stories, images, sounds, and rituals. The study of popular culture, therefore, does not need to have a particularly salvific aspect to it, or a politically motivated purpose that might lead scholars to better understand how to contribute to a social revolution that they (or we) may feel is necessary. David Morgan, one of the foremost scholars in the study of popular culture and religion, has explicitly argued against these politically-motivated aims. He writes (personal correspondence, March 18, 2007):

> I am wary of defending the study of popular culture (let alone any other forms of culture) on the basis that it will enhance people's lives or lead to greater social justice or pursue Truth. What it will lead to, it seems to me, is richer, more perceptive analysis and understanding of why people do what they do and how they build and sustain the imagined and lived worlds in which they exist.

The study of religion and popular culture may therefore be viewed as a particularly accessible way in which scholars can explore everyday life. Through its study, we may gain insight into how people construct and maintain the world in which they live, and how they are able to imagine a way in which to behave within that world.

2

Studying Religion and Popular Culture

Prospects, Presuppositions, Procedures

DAVID MORGAN

Scholars of religion are engaged by popular culture for many reasons. One in particular carries considerable weight. Such ordinary things as advertisements, tourism, and all manner of mass-produced media from the internet to baseball cards are the means whereby most people in the modern world spend most of their time constructing the selves and communities that define who they are. In varying degrees, these fuel the imagination of millions and deliver a shared stock of symbols that embody people's hopes, desires, fears, and hatreds. To ignore television, film, magazines, toys, fan clubs, souvenirs, or posters would be to miss fundamental aspects of religious behavior since these activities and experiences are the ingredients with which many, even most people religiously practice world-building and maintenance. But that raises an important question: given how pervasive these common forms of leisure, commerce, and entertainment are now, how widely shared they are, one must ask if 'popular culture' really means anything as critical nomenclature anymore? What's not *popular*? In fact, the category expanded because the object itself did so. It was not a band of wooly scholars who wrenched our attention from fine art; it was in the very bosom of the art world that popular and elite met to create what may be best referred to as common culture.

Since the mid-twentieth century in the United States and Europe, the study of popular culture has become inseparable from its looming other, elite culture, which has haunted every consideration of popular taste, commerce, consumer behavior, and 'the people.' This is understandable, given the genealogy of modern Western democracies, all of which emerged from the vertically structured societies of gentility, aristocracy, and royalty, whose political and social arrangements democracies have challenged, but also democratized, or better, popularized. Not long after the American and French republics established themselves, Romantic authors and compilers set to work to 'remember' (and invent) the fairy tales of preceding oral culture since these stories about princes and princesses, kings and queens, knights and damsels struck the new citizens of European and American societies as compelling stories of the human self. By psychologizing the class structure of pre-modern Europe, early Moderns transformed a static world of economic differences into the mythology of modern individualism and self-determination. But there was a price to pay. Gustave Flaubert's caustic account of the demise of Emma Bovary may be read as a meticulously forensic scrutiny of the presumptuousness of Modernity, which propels its enchantment with nobility and status with unbridled consumerism. Emma is what Emma buys. But, of course, nothing of the sort is true. She ends by consuming her own life in greedy mouthfuls of arsenic, then is deposited in a rude hole in the ground, where the pebbles falling on her coffin 'gave forth that dread sound that seems to us the reverberation of eternity' (Flaubert, 1965, p.247). An eternity of absolutely nothing, which is all Emma ever was beneath the paper doll clothing she fancifully, desperately cut from the yellowed pages of pious Romantic literature.

To grumble about my own guild, art historians have largely had use for popular culture only when it has been appropriated by avant-garde artists like Picasso or Matisse. To care about popular culture itself implied something altogether different than being concerned with fine art, that is, with important art—art that plunged toward the future. Sometimes Modernist artists expressed keen interest in whether the rest of the world followed the artist-genius. Wassily Kandinsky, for example, fashioned 'the life of the spirit' in his image of the movement of a 'spiritual triangle' as responsible for minting the new, which seems 'an incomprehensible gibberish' to the conventionally-minded, but inexorably becomes their 'true thought and feeling.' Kandinsky looked to folk culture and the art of children for a purer indication of where the uninhibited movement of the spiritual was to be found, and linked what he called the 'inner necessity' of such art to what he sought to accomplish as a painter (Kandinsky, 1912/1977, pp.6, 26). So he was able to elevate the marginalized or naïve to the status of the avant garde, not unlike the way that the Brothers

Grimm recounted the elevation of suppressed purity in the story of Cinderella or Snow White.

But others in the solemn temple of Modernist art repudiated any interest in popular culture, regarding it as the domain of the masses, whose group-think, directed by capitalism, represented a serious threat to the survival of true culture. Clement Greenberg bemoaned the appeal of 'kitsch' in Stalinist Russia and Western capitalist countries alike. The Russian peasant's preference for the realist art of Ilya Repin was no different than the American consumer's adoration of the art of Norman Rockwell. Both kinds of art were kitsch, which Greenberg defined as imagery one enjoys 'without effort' (Greenberg, 1939/1961, p.18). Good art was difficult art, art that demanded something from viewers, such as ongoing immersion the visual and critical discourse of Modernist art. In 1953 artist Ad Reinhardt issued his 'Twelve Rules for a New Academy,' in which he declared: 'The less an artist thinks in non-artistic terms and the less he exploits the easy, common skills, the more of an artist he is. The less an artist obtrudes himself in his painting, the purer and clearer his aims. The less exposed a painting is to a chance public, the better. Less is more' (Reinhardt, 1953/1996, p.86). In effect, Greenberg and Reinhardt and many others wanted to remove art from the pressures and insidious effects of the marketplace, and scorned any alliance between government and art as inevitably propagandistic. Purity meant disengagement from use or purpose beyond the immediate artistic act. Anything more amounted to a cooptation of art by the broader culture. This had been an abiding dream among American literati since the antebellum era, when Emerson and others issued calls for art and imagination to elevate national taste, to move Americans beyond their selfish, rude, and greedy penchant for commercial gain (Emerson, 2000).

The American avant-gardist sequestration of art came to an abrupt end with Pop Art, which luxuriated in the promiscuous intermingling of commercial culture and fine art, blurring any clear distinction as it may have been imagined by the hierophants of Modernism. But the post-war boom in the American economy created a marketplace in art that has not subsided, capitalizing fine art and virtually everything else that can be collected as an investment (see Hobbs, 1996, p.146-68). Art since the 1960s has not papered over the split between art world and common culture in the United States; it has simply stopped caring about the divide. The grandeur of the avant-garde has diminished as mid-brow culture has expanded. Accordingly, it may be more meaningful to speak of 'common culture' than popular culture.

But it is important to distinguish museum art from avant-garde. Bus loads of public school children tour the nation's leading museums each day. Secondary and university curricula commonly offer well-enrolled courses in the history of art. Public television airs well-received programming on world art. Bookstores thrive on the sale of beautifully produced coffee table art books and histories of everything from stoneware and the decorative arts to portraiture and Impressionism. It would seem that the contemporary world has witnessed a triumph of the middle-brow so great that the traditional stand-off between popular and elite is all but defunct. Virtually the only thing that reminds Americans of the bottomless rift between a once glorious avant-garde and the now universally regnant middle-brow culture is the occasional provocative gesture regarding sexuality and religion.

The cultural realm of entertainment—how life in a developed economy consumes the enormous amounts of leisure time that wealth allows—is so pervasive, so common, that rich, middling, and poor are not readily distinguished by their choice in music, food, film, or sport. These form a kind of cultural Esperanto, the common language of leisure that tends very much to blur distinctions that may have once been sharper, such as the practice of artistic taste. Avant-garde video art and television, cutting edge poetry and popular music, theological reflection and fishing are not worlds apart. Indeed, these distinctions tend to be either arbitrary or ideologically enforced. The mountainous volume of writing on such films as *Blue Velvet*, *Pulp Fiction*, *Blade Runner*, or *The Matrix*, for example, clearly shows how seriously many religion scholars take popular film, and how much such films as these reward serious consideration. These are films that were made for scholar and teenager alike. They are neither exclusively high nor low, but equally both.

Interdisciplinarity and Practice

An important need for the development of the field of religion and popular culture is ongoing reflection of its inherent interdisciplinarity. Lived religion is a complex and robust phenomenon (Hall, 1997). It is not simply about texts or images or dance or sound. It draws no boundaries, admits to few if any crisp lineaments that would allow the scholar to isolate this or that aspect for the sake of controlled investigation.

Moreover, the study of popular culture does not possess a long formation of disciplinarity that presses itself upon the scholarly imagination in order to cast a spell of factual or semantic stability. In fact, no object of human inquiry does so, but the cumulative effect of scholarly traditions is often a kind of intellectual circumscription or field-making that endows a welcome limit on analysis. Something as robust and mottled as religion is not easy to study. As a result, scholars of religion commonly find themselves adjusting their methodology by broadening their sights. For scholars of religion and popular culture this can mean they find themselves at an academic crossroads best called an 'interdiscipline,' to borrow a term used by W.J.T. Mitchell, who has done so much to illuminate the study of visual culture and its intimate relations of word and image (Mitchell, 1995).

Interdisciplinary scholars of popular religious culture face the constant stumbling block of being outsiders, interlopers among the prevailing norms of how historians or anthropologists or sociologists organize their own domains of research. Supposing, however, that the industrious researcher has attended to the literature and interpretive templates of a discipline and has thereby carefully avoided the nuisance of professional censure, other problems commonly arise. Who really cares about the work of interdisciplinary research if it does not fall squarely within the purview of a particular professional guild? Disciplines can be so consuming in their gravitational attraction that scholars find it difficult or even unattractive to look beyond the orbit of something as vast as a professional society of history, art, religion, or anthropology. And there is often good reason for scholars not to venture far from the boundaries of the guild: it is within the hold of every discipline that jobs are filled, mentoring is conducted, fellowships secured, journal articles reviewed and accepted, and professional recognition attained. Disciplines clearly serve an indispensable service.

So why even consider venturing beyond the well-paved road? There are really only two good reasons: because the subject of study demands it and because the audience for one's work welcomes it. The task, as I understand it, is to produce work that is a service to colleagues in many disciplines who agree that the nature of popular culture and religion stretches beyond the limits of any single discipline.

At the same time, it is necessary to recognize that interdisciplinarity is as problematic as it is alluring. How are students to be trained if not within the literature, methodology, and historiography of a discrete discipline?

Should we dismantle traditional disciplines of study and training in order to fit investigation more directly to its object? I think that would be a mistake. Real scholarly study already adapts itself to its object. Rigorous preparation in the matrix of a single discipline is not at issue as long as scholars resist the temptation to presume that any phenomenon may be exhaustively located within the parameters of one discipline. What we need, it seems to me, is well-trained historians, economists, linguists, sociologists, and ritualists who are willing to engage in meaningful conversation with colleagues on the other side of any of several disciplinary boundaries in order to frame research in a way that suits investigation to what is being investigated rather than the reverse.

Conversations that are one-sided are not conversations at all, but monologues in which the flow of information is unilateral. Genuine dialogue happens not when I as a scholar abandon my voice, but when I learn to speak from the depth of my discipline to the depths of another. Happily, it turns out, the job market is structured along disciplinary boundaries. It is precisely this resistance that allows us to push hard and productively against disciplinary inertia in order to conduct substantial exchange between disciplines. Lacking that resistance, our attempts might easily deteriorate into light-weight gestures in which nothing ventured would produce little gain. Students should identify their prevailing intellectual passions and select the appropriate discipline for graduate study. Only after mastering the practice of that discipline will they be able to transgress its boundaries in the interests of interdisciplinarity.

Interdisciplinary study is especially suited to the investigation of religion and popular culture because it is better able to respond to the fluidity and transience of popular culture, which is driven by markets, consumption, daily ritual, and all manner of human exchange. We need models for studying this, models that will help us describe the varieties of circulation of culture, or *culture as circulation*, in which religion is neither a fixed essence nor a merely economic behavior. The account of religion that will work best is the one that is practice-centered—able, in other words, to describe what people *do* in addition to what they *say* they believe.

Studying what people do means studying practices. This is something different from the more traditional approach of studying what people make—whether that is fine art or folk art. Object-centered studies undeniably teach us a great deal. Attending to the medium or materiality of an artifact is a vital part of the study of popular culture since people make choices about what they prefer in part on the basis of the sensuous features of a film or pair of jeans or the taste of a pizza. Scholars of popular culture make a serious mistake when they ignore medium by treating an artifact merely as the delivery of content, as a quantum of meaning that has no relation to its form or material structure. A practice-centered approach to the study of popular religious culture should not allow the object to be eclipsed, but should seek to enfold it as a material reality into the ritual or routine or daily habit that puts it to work in the world-constructing and maintaining behavior.

Speaking for myself, this is the real, the ultimate focus for my work as a scholar. I want to know how people use images to put their worlds together and to keep them working in the face of all the challenges that beset them. In order to do this, it is necessary to describe more than images as self-contained objects, as patently encoded with meaning or as illustrations of dogma. I find it important to trace the narrative life of an image from the mental schema, imagination, traditions, and commerce of making them to their purchase and display to the response they receive from one generation or context to the next. Meaning is a restless, forever unfinished thing. In knowing what an image does at any moment, we have one meaning, but an even greater need to know what it might do in the next moment. The study of religion is necessarily historical.

The Matrix of Study: Production, Distribution, Reception

Indebted no doubt to the study of genteel or elite culture, worlds of luxury commodities and their owners, humanistic studies have been deeply inclined to focus on either the maker of an object or on the object itself. As it is traditionally practiced, for example, art history attends to the genius of the artist and his or her life or to the style or formal features of the work produced by the artist. The interpretation or evaluation of a work of art, however, does not end when it leaves the artist's studio. In fact, since the meaning of a thing is continually reborn with each encounter with or use of the object, we must pay heed to the object's deployment and the responses of viewers as well as institutions such as temples or museums to it. That is what I mean by production, distribution, and reception as the proper matrix of analysis.

By distribution I have in mind the packaging, transmission, and display of an artifact—everything that happens to a commercial product after it leaves the manufacturer and before it is put to use in the consumer's hands. I will talk more about that below. Reception is a more varied area of study among scholars, and demands more attention here. I have often been asked what I mean by reception and how one, especially the historian, is supposed to do it. Simply put, by reception I mean what someone does with what she buys or receives as a gift, the significance she attaches to a ritual or photograph or film. Reception is an assignation of value and may be studied in many ways. Three are perhaps most familiar: scholars approach the study of reception quantitatively, as in the manner of a social survey (e.g. Marsden, 2001, pp.71-103); qualitatively, as in the case of ethnographic study, whether structured interviews or the freewheeling participant-observation (e.g. Hoover, Clark & Alters, 2004); and a mixed mode, integrating the statistical analysis of a survey with interviews (e.g. Wuthnow, 2003). But there are other ways. Historians of art, architecture, and archaeology are accustomed to conducting material and iconographical reception studies, in which they measure the impact of a technique, structure, or motif by tracing its successive impact on generations of artisans, or follow the history of a single monument over time, across the many lives of its career (Nelson, 2004; Davis, 1997; Kopytoff, 1986). A historical account of reception can be supplemented by making use of contemporary literary uses of a theme or topic, as Alan Trachtenberg did with fictional treatments of daguerreotypes during the 1840s (Trachtenberg, 1989). Literary historians in the 1970s and 1980s developed reader-response as another model of studying the reception of texts, scrutinizing how texts were read by certain readers given their gender, education, or the formal structure of the text itself (Hohendahl, 1977). Finally, there is the familiar method of historians who rely on anecdotal evidence to reconstruct the past. Anecdotal reception studies interrogate smaller, even singular samples of information that provide hints or clues to *mentalités*, class interests, or institutional motives that may help account for historical phenomena, the documentation for which is otherwise lacking. I offer below an example of this approach.

The consideration of reception is often what it takes to get scholars outside of their own heads, to throw themselves kicking and screaming into the minds and bodies of others. But reception studies are not a panacea. I do not wish to reduce the study of popular culture to the study of audiences, but to integrate the study of production with the examination of distribution and reception. We need to ask what a variety of consumers and users of cultural artifacts and practices gain from their activities and not just regard sit-coms or films or popular music for whatever about it seems interesting to us as scholars. And we need to ask what role the distribution or transmission of cultural artifacts plays in shaping experience. Popular culture is not a message-bullet fired by its producer. But the only way we will understand why is by finding out what it does for people and how they came to use it. So we need to scrutinize reception, even if that only means asking socially-minded questions of artifacts; we need to focus on practices rather than only on objects or texts; and we need to study the history of objects, genres, practices, and audiences. The *history* of religion and popular culture is perhaps one of the most under-studied aspects of the field. I join others who have called for its augmentation. We need to avoid the presentism that often accompanies the study of media, consumerism, fashion, and the latest cultural form.

But what do I mean by the study of reception, particularly with regard to historical analysis, where the documentation to support the study of how people reacted to an artifact or idea is gone, if it ever existed? I do not propose a full-fledged study of reception in every case of historical analysis, but rather an attempt to integrate the study of production, distribution, and reception. A study will inevitably privilege one or the other of these aspects, but interrogating the study of the production of something like religious tracts in antebellum America with consideration of how the tracts were distributed, who read them, and what those readers may have read and thought about them will only deepen the study of production by throwing certain aspects of it into relief. The scholar will be mindful that whatever an author, publisher, or an organization intended a tract to mean, readers of it were not limited to that intention. Scholars do not require dozens of instances of popular reception to register the range of meanings that might be assigned to a text. To judge from official accounts of tracts published by the American Tract Society, one would imagine that the ephemeral print that circulated in streets, stores, stage coaches, steamers, and railroad cars achieved miraculous effects, converting those who happened to pick up the tracts and read them. Such prospects pleased the Tract Society whose executives premised their organization's mission on the woeful inadequacy of the number of preachers and evangelists available to spread the gospel. Print was supposed to make up the gaping difference. The idea that a mere tract could take the place of a preacher was something the Society's leadership declared on more than one occasion. One finds tracts valorized and celebrated for their auratic presence in the mission field, carrying the word of God abroad, even operating with greater efficiency and effect than human speakers. It was a wholesale advocacy of print over the older culture of orality, endorsed by para-church organizations like the Tract

Society, the American Sunday School Union, and diverse mission societies.

But it is important not to be swept away by propaganda. The valorization of tracts was part of the Protestant ideology of print. Some historical records of how the Tract Society's hawkers or colporteurs were received, however, renders a more balanced account of the career of tracts and the interests of the tract distributors. Information about the distribution and reception of tracts to be gleaned from published and unpublished reports from the field offers very instructive insight. In 1841, the Tract Society began deploying traveling salesmen to hawk their wares. The colporteurs were both paid and unpaid and were assigned a district in which they sold books and gave away tracts (and some books) published by the Society. The colporteurs regularly tabulated the results of their efforts, making careful record of the number of items given out, the places they traveled, and the people with whom they spoke. The Tract Society gathered the reports and published the distribution data, sometimes including narrative or anecdotal accounts recorded by the colporteurs. Usually, such accounts are brief and calculated to illustrate the range of the colporteur's efforts and their success. But we learn a great deal from the reports, such as the sort of people they targeted—the poor, immigrants, Roman Catholics, school teachers, preachers seeking to ignite religious revival. We also learn a good deal about the method of the salesmen. D. H. Smith, colporteur at work in Virginia in 1853-54, relied on a standard technique among his colleagues to make progress working among Irish and German Catholics in the state: 'By giving books and tracts to their children and by treating them kindly they insensibly lose their prejudices against us and our faith.' Smith reported that he gave away more material among Catholics than he sold to them that year (Report of D. H. Smith, 1854, pp.71,104; also 121-22).

The colporteurs noted the appeal of tracts among children, the significance of which was not lost on the Tract Society. In 1854 a Methodist bishop estimated that 'one-half the entire net increase of the membership of the church' came from Sunday schools (Boylan, 1988, p.164). Children mattered, and the extent to which the Tract Society targeted them with their extensive list of children's literature comes through very clearly in colportage reports. Jonathan Cross, colporteur and superintendent of colportage in Virginia and the Carolinas, related that 'a pretty book given creates a desire that some one should be able to read it.' Yet another colporteur of the time observed that it was not uncommon 'for little boys and girls of eight and ten years to instruct their ignorant parents, who listen with all the earnestness of children' (Thirty-First Annual Report, 1856, p.89; Twenty-Eighth Annual Report, 1853, p.92; Morgan, 1999, pp.208-15).

But to anyone familiar with tracts by pious British authors like Hannah More or Leigh Richmond, both of whom enjoyed great success among Evangelical readers in antebellum United States, the power of the pious child is a commonplace in sentimental literature perhaps best remembered in the character of Little Eva in Harriet Beecher Stowe's blockbuster novel, *Uncle Tom's Cabin* published in 1852. The colporteurs found and represented what their publishers and readers were all prepared to accept as a bona fide portrayal of the way their kind of religion happened.

But what about occasions when their cherished view of matters religious met with resistance or even rejection? The published reports of the colporteurs do not offer much in the way of that kind of information. But an unpublished report of 1854 from a young man's tour in South Carolina has been scrutinized by Amy Thomas for its range of commentary (Thomas, 2002; Nord, 2004, pp.131-49). Micah Croswell was a student at Baptist Furman University in South Carolina in the fall of 1854, when he decided to supplement his income for several weeks by selling Tract Society publications. His fourteen-page report to Jonathan Cross records a range of encounters, not all of which glow with accounts of pious children and compliant parents. Croswell relates meeting an aged woman in Graniteville, South Carolina, who wept when Croswell 'spoke to her of old age and the short time she had left.' As proselytizing techniques go, that one seems manipulative indeed. The woman's adult daughter may well have thought so, and resented it, for Croswell dubbed her 'a very evil-minded woman' who told the young man that 'she did not & never would believe dancing was a sin. I replied it was not if we danced to the glory of God; for David danced. After an earnest conversation she said 'she had been a Church member & could shout and sing and enjoy it as well as any of them.' I spoke of the necessity of having the heart right; but found her a vain worldling & cruel to her mother' (Thomas, 2002, pp.122-23). Amy Thomas reports that Croswell encountered even more abrupt opposition from another citizen of Graniteville, a middle-aged man who objected sharply to the entire range of doctrines that the young Baptist encouraged him to ponder, as he offered a short tract: 'I shall believe what I damned please,' the man told Croswell, 'and drink what I damned please & no one can prevent me,' refusing to take the tract (ibid., p.120).

Another unpublished and unedited report by a Tract Society distributor, which has survived in the archives of the Historical Society of Rhode Island, documents a very unusual encounter in the annals of Evangelical print, one that ran counter to the prevailing Protestant culture, but which the honest worker must be credited for reporting as straightforwardly as he did. Dated February 1833, the hand-written account records that when the distributor working in Providence offered a tract to a man, the gift was declined because 'he had read the same tract the night before and there was nothing in it. He then began to read the tract to me remarking on it as he went along' (Tract Distribution Report, 1833, p.9). The man wondered why the tract carried no date or author or indication of the author's location. 'I soon found,' the report continues, 'that he wished to dispute with me and as he said he was going to convert me to his religion I very soon found that he was a Roman Catholic, and he began to reason with me to convince me that *that* was the only true religion.' When the tract distributor intervened with a stock objection, he was quickly and directly refuted: 'I asked him if it was true as was said that the Catholics were not permitted to read the Bible. He replied it was not, to prove which he would show me *two* bibles he had, and would lend me one if I wished, but he said it was not the same as my Bibles but was translated by Catholics. He also said it was not forbidden to any man to read the Bible only those who could not read' (ibid., p.10). The out-maneuvered Protestant offered up another Evangelical commonplace, insisting that religious denomination was meaningless 'without a change of heart,' but was immediately met with the Catholic man's hearty agreement. 'With this remark and an urgent request to call again,' we read, 'I left him.' With an abrupt escape, the deflated missionary closed his account with solemn indecision: 'Was there no influence exerted on that man's mind? The judgment day will show' (ibid., p.11).

We learn from such exchanges—in the pointed tone of individual historical voices—how the Tract Society's efforts sometimes aroused hostility; we also garner a direct sense of how invasive their methods could be; and we see the tables turned, the rhetoric and modus operandi of proselytic zeal turned back upon itself. For those who study the history of media, especially the allure of new media, this kind of resistance encourages a sobriety that quells the intoxicating romance of the new. On other occasions we learn something concrete about the priorities of those whom colporteurs encountered. When two young Princeton Seminary students, spending the summer of 1842 working as colporteurs in rural counties of eastern New Jersey, urged one man to purchase a bible, he replied, in students' words, that 'during these hard times he could scarce find money enough to buy rum, much less a Bible' (Colporteur Reports, 1940, p.10).

Another colporteur in New Jersey was disappointed to learn that a family to which he'd promised a bible 'had been repeatedly supplied [with one], and in every case it had been bartered for rum' (ibid., p.60).

Mothers told another group of Tract Society salesmen in the summer of 1843 that they would like to have bibles for the purpose of recording their children's names and ages in them (ibid., pp.39, 46). Reading them was another matter.

On the usefulness of considering reception, such information, though only anecdotal, can make the scholar mindful of the limits of studying production. Distribution and reception are the other sides of production if the scholar wishes to mount a robust study of popular culture. But how does one manage to balance the study of each of these with the demands of different fields and disciplines? Who can possibly master reception studies, theoretical critique, and disciplinary research as diverse as, say, art history, economics, and linguistics? Virtually no one. But the good news is that we do not have to do so. Team research is something that many of us have become engaged in over the last couple of decades. By combining the efforts of four or five scholars, colleagues can pool their respective strengths, teaching one another a great deal while mounting a much more comprehensive approach to the study of a cultural phenomenon. In this framework, studying the production and reception along with the theology, iconography, history, musicology, or economics of a cultural practice becomes both possible and deeply insightful. And this is something we can begin in the training of our students. We can focus on teaching them the virtue of collaboration and generosity. Not only will they learn to work together and benefit from one another's differences and respective strengths, they will in turn go on to reward us by demonstrating that academic research is a communitarian enterprise that makes our work even more pleasureful.

3

Questioning Media and Religion

JOLYON MITCHELL

What are the central questions raised regarding the interactions between media and religion? In this chapter I discuss five. Each of these questions is housed under a single defining theme, which provides the title for each section. I am not attempting a comprehensive description of all the major research questions raised in this area of study. This has been done elsewhere (Hoover, 2006, pp.32-44). Instead my aim is to consider critically some of the most significant approaches used by either those describing the complex relations between media and religion or those acting as religious communicators. In each case I begin with a simple central question to open the door onto a wider set of subsidiary questions and arguments. En route, I demonstrate how in many accounts of media and religion, produced by academics, critics and practitioners, there lie a number of assumptions. These are often understated or overlooked. By identifying these undercurrents the past, the present and the possible futures of this rapidly emerging field will become clearer.

Dangers?

What are the dangers or threats posed to religion by different media? This is not a new question. Plato was concerned that the invention of writing would undermine people's ability to remember well. Influenced by this account, several early Christians expressed a concern that writing would threaten the faith (Horsfield, 2003). The advent of printing in the fifteenth century may have been an 'agent of change', in Elizabeth Eisenstein's (1979) memorable phrase, but it was also perceived by some copyists of manuscripts as a threat to monastic order. While many embraced the new communicative technologies, over three hundred years later excessive reading was still not universally welcomed. In one 1795 tract it was predicted that too much reading will cause 'colds, headaches… arthritis, haemorrhoids, asthma… migraines, epilepsy, hypochondria, and, melancholy' (Spender, 1995, p.8). Behind such anxieties was a desire to control what was imbibed by the ploughman, the herdsmen and other members of the 'serving classes'. Increased literacy and availability of texts meant that the clergyman was no longer necessarily one of the most educated or best informed persons in the parish. The gradual democratisation of knowledge was threatening, and several different kinds of media played a significant role in this process.

In a similar vein, it is possible to trace critical responses by religious leaders to the telegraph, the camera, the electric light-bulb, the wireless, the cinema, the television set, and the internet. Technological change is often unsettling to the accepted order. It threatens monopolies of power and knowledge. Critical voices employ a range of resources for such criticisms, from religious imagery or sacred texts to theological beliefs or historical precedents. For example, in the early days of moving pictures there are a number of highly critical accounts of the dangers of cinema. Consider some of their titles: *The Devil's Camera* (1932), *What's Wrong with the Movies?* (1938), and *What's Wrong with the Cinema* (1948), (see Mitchell, 2005a). These early critical voices were not confined to the West, for example, in 1904 in Iran a leading clerical figure, Sheykh Fazlollah Nuri, 'attended Iran's first public cinema in Tehran and proscribed it, causing it to shut down after only one month of operation' (Naficy, 2002, p.27). Some of the arguments employed in Western critical texts against cinema sound strikingly similar to the criticisms made more recently against the new media of the internet (Campbell, 2005, pp.15-16). Similarly, anxiety among writers about the detrimental effects of television resonates with many of the early concerns expressed about the dangers of going to the cinema. The main difference is that television was seen as an invader of the home, a 'plug in drug'. The 'electronic hearth' or the 'box in the corner' makes an interesting case to reflect in more detail upon. When watching television was the dominant media consumption habit of the day in the Western world, it also attracted a barrage of criticism from different quarters. Let us consider three critical voices in particular.

First, Neil Postman (1985), the author of the much cited *Amusing Ourselves to Death,* has been the standard-bearer for those who are critical of television's impact on society or religion. Ironically his iconoclastic analysis of a televisual culture is itself extremely entertaining. For Postman, television promotes 'incoherence and triviality' and 'is transforming our culture into one vast arena for show business' (ibid., p.80). His thesis has been summed up as the belief that television provides 'corrosive amusement' (see Jensen, 1990, pp.44-50). Behind Postman's fear of the corrosion or trivialising of politics, education and religion by television, lies a nostalgia for the printed word and the logical, linear world which it upheld. In Postman's eyes 'television has gradually *become* our culture, the background radiation of the social and intellectual universe' (ibid., p.79). Postman balances such contextual arguments with specific criticisms, such as that on television God is:

a vague and subordinate character. Though His name is invoked repeatedly, the concreteness and persistence of the image of the preacher carries the clear message that it is he, not He, who must be worshipped. I do not mean to imply that the preacher wishes it to be so; only that the power of a close-up televised face, in color, makes idolatry a continual hazard. Television is, after all, a form of graven imagery far more alluring than a golden calf. (ibid., pp.122-3)

Postman, coming from a Jewish background, clearly wishes to shatter that 'golden calf'. His primary tool is education, but he himself often falls into the trap of caricaturing television in order to support his own case (see Lynch, 2005, pp.78-82).

A second highly critical voice comes from the French sociologist, Jacques Ellul. He believes that 'the iconoclasts were right. But they were defeated' (Ellul, 1985, p.106). In so far as he is also deeply suspicious of our visual culture, and in particular of television, he represents the European counterpart of Postman (ibid., p.213). His justification, however, is more theologically grounded and is most clearly expounded in *The Humiliation of the Word* (1985). In his eyes it is disastrous for the church to mimic the 'technique' of an image based culture and make television programmes. He believes that by 'allying' itself 'with images, Christianity gains (perhaps) efficacy, but destroys itself, its foundations and its content' (ibid., p.203). His polemic fuses together a post-Marxist critique with a theology influenced by the Swiss theologian Karl Barth.

Malcolm Muggeridge's *Christ and the Media* (1977) represents a third iconoclastic voice. Like Ellul he is writing from a Christian perspective: 'In the beginning was the Word, and the Word became flesh, not celluloid...'(ibid., p.88). Unlike Ellul, Muggeridge focuses the spotlight less on the idea of the word heard and more on the person of Christ encountered, contrasting the fantasy created by television with the perceived reality of Christ. For Muggeridge, part of the inherent danger of a communicative environment shaped by television is the potential, at all levels, for it to 'draw the people away from reality' (ibid., p.60). On this basis he believes that television is not simply incompatible with, but is even destructive of, Christianity. He constructs a now famous imaginary fourth temptation for Christ, a prime time chat show which 'would launch him off on a tremendous career as a world-wide evangelist....' (ibid., p.37). Christ rejects this dazzling, and seductive offer. He is concerned with reality and not fantasy. This may partially explain Muggeridge's drastic challenge to his readers to do what he did with his own set: 'Throw it away!' Behind both Ellul's and Muggeridge's approach lies a belief in the primacy of the written and spoken word. In their eyes a visually dominated culture, represented and formed by television, has the power to undermine the foundations of faith.

This disparaging trio - Postman, Ellul and Muggeridge - numbers but three representatives of a whole group of iconoclastic scholars who are highly critical of television and of the communicative environment it pollutes. Their three critiques can be located within a wider series of critical or iconoclastic texts published in the 1970s and 1980s (Key, 1973; Lewis, 1977; Coakley, 1977; Mander, 1978; Schwartz, 1983; Winn, 1985; Mitroff & Bennis, 1993). Patrick Brantlinger (1983, p.19) draws on several of these books to illustrate how 'television' is perceived 'as the chief culprit in the alleged decline and fall of contemporary culture'. For many of these authors who are highly critical of television, the 'tube' is an 'electronic Trojan horse' (Schultze, 1992, p.11). The American art historian Gregor Goethals (1993) suggests that 'most religious thinkers struggling with media mythologies' have worked more as 'iconoclasts than iconofiers'. From this perspective the media are seen as in direct competition or even in conflict with religious traditions. My point here is that while these criticisms of television may now sound somewhat dated, similar responses manifest themselves in other highly critical accounts of other kinds of new and old media.

The iconoclastic approach towards television, film and the internet, both within and outside the Christian tradition, has a number of weaknesses. It ignores the more positive elements inherent in current communicative environments, and the importance of the visual within the Christian and other religious traditions. It yearns for an imaginary golden age of books and word-based discourse. More recent critical accounts over-simplify the nature of many different distinct communicative settings, and fail to recognise that the convergence of television, film, video, computers and the phone is changing the relationship between senders and receivers, and is thereby creating a more interactive setting. Postman, Muggeridge and Ellul, for example, are more concerned with attacking the 'idol' of television, than with considering how it or other newer media can also provide opportunities for new forms of religious communication. I have outlined some weaknesses in general terms, while acknowledging that there are individual differences between these critical voices. There are more nuanced evaluations to be done. For future studies it is worth turning my opening enquiry in this section around and asking a less commonly posed question: What are the dangers or threats posed to different media by various religions?

Opportunities?

The second common question is almost an antithesis to the first: What are the opportunities for communicating religious faith or teaching about religion to be found in different media? Like my first question, this also has historic resonances, just as some fifteenth century writers embraced printing as a gift of God (Chadwick, 2001, p.2), so some five centuries later many writers celebrate new forms of communication as examples of divine providence. Rather than worrying about the potential dangers of media such as television, film, radio or the internet, many writers or practitioners also emphasise their potential for reaching new audiences. This group of media advocates can be described as iconographers, and are partly made up of those religious leaders who seek not to reject media as a threat, but rather embrace it as enthusiastic users. Ben Armstrong, for example, former Executive Director of National Religious Broadcasters in the USA, sees the 'awesome technology of broadcasting' as one of the 'major miracles of modern times'. For him, television and radio have 'broken through the walls of tradition' and 'restored conditions remarkably similar to the early church' (Armstrong, 1979, pp.7-9). Armstrong may have been writing over thirty years ago, but his belief in the powerful nature of broadcasting is by no means unique. Both the internet and the cinema have also provoked similarly enthusiastic affirmations. These are far from confined to Christian advocates, with many Muslims, Jews, Hindus, Sikhs and Buddhist making extensive use of media technologies for both proselytising and pedagogy.

Such optimistic understandings of the mass media, and of television in particular, are to be seen in one extreme form in the work of many

American electronic evangelists, especially during the 1980s (see Sweet, 1993; O'Brien, 1993; Hoover & Abelman, 1990; Hoover, 1988; Horsfield, 1984). They viewed television and radio as God-given tools which should be used to preach to the 'ends of the earth'. On this basis many of them have accepted the 'values of the world of commercial broadcasting' and concentrated on 'producing slick 'professional' products for precisely targeted audiences' (McDonnell & Trampiets, 1989, p.15). It is often assumed that the fall from grace of many of the leading American TV evangelists, such as Jimmy Baker or Jimmy Swaggart in the 1980s, marked the end of this genre of religious broadcasting. It certainly undermined its popularity, but over the past two decades religious television has evolved into a more fragmented communicative form, sometimes becoming more professional, slicker and even closer in style to its commercial competitors. Fundamentalist, evangelical and Pentecostal Christians with a strong sense of mission appear more naturally drawn towards making use of television and other media, though in order to win audiences they find that they often have to dilute their message. Programmes produced in the USA are still exported all over the globe, but religious leaders in South and Central America, in West Africa and in parts of Europe are increasingly producing their own programmes, embracing television, radio and the internet as vital parts of their ministries (Asamoah-Gyadu, 2005). Similarly, many religious leaders or groups in both Western and Non-Western faith traditions have been equally rapid in taking up the media to promote their interpretations of the world.

TV evangelists, whatever religious tradition they belong to, are but one group within this category of electronic opportunists or iconographers. Another group makes use of television, but also retains a critical stance. As a broadcaster, Colin Morris embraces the television, but as a scholar of religion he also reflects on its role. Over twenty years ago, in *God-in-a-Box*, for example, Morris (1984, p.230) raised the problem of how Christianity, a faith with the symbol of a bloody execution at its centre, can translate into the high-tech and carefully ordered world of the television studio. Whilst Morris (1990) reflects critically on the role of television, his work as head of BBC Television's Religious Broadcasting, as a producer of television documentaries and as a regular religious broadcaster, illustrates how he appears nonetheless to have been happy to work as a producer of religious programmes.

Thomas Boomershine (1990), an American biblical scholar, is another example of an electronic iconographer. Like Morris, he has written thoughtfully and critically about the role of media in communicating the Christian faith. He has also been one of the central figures behind the American Bible Societies' project to translate the Gospels into the audio-visual language of MTV (Arthur, 1993, p.36). Morris and Boomershine are two examples of those who want to go beyond iconoclasm. They refuse to reject wholesale media technology or forms of discourse. In both their writing and practice they recognise different media's potential: not only can it affirm religious insights, it can also communicate them to a wider audience. Their arguments could now easily be expanded to encapsulate newer media technologies, an area of work that Boomershine himself has invested considerable energy. This translation work, moving from written script to audiovisual production, raises significant questions meriting further study: what kinds of transformation take place when sacred texts or traditional religious faith or teaching is translated from one medium into another (see, e.g. Hodgson & Soukup, 1997)?

Resources?

What resources are available for researchers when they seek to go beyond the contrasting 'dangers' and 'opportunities' paradigms? In many scholarly contexts around the world the iconoclastic and iconographic approaches towards media are analysed through critical interpretative lenses. From this perspective different media are primarily perceived as neither being a threat nor providing an opportunity for communication. My argument here is that there is much to be learnt from how interpreters, beyond the media and religion field, have analysed different aspects of media technologies, media production and media consumption. While there is not space here to detail the complex history of media interpretation (Katz et al., 2003), it is useful to consider four of the most influential forms of analysis.

First, several scholars have charted the evolution of different media. Taking a historical perspective, writers such as Harold Innis (1950, 1951), Marshal McLuhan (1962, 1964) or Walter Ong (1982), have developed what are sometimes described as 'grand theories' of media technologies. While several scholars have identified historical continuities and discontinuities in study of religion and media, no-one has yet attempted to follow in their footsteps and outline a grand theory of media and religion. Nonetheless, the histories of media offer rich perspectives for researching aspects of religion and popular culture. This is becoming an increasingly popular area of study, with media histories being used to shed light upon current communicative transformations. For example, several scholars have reflected upon the continuities and discontinuities between the rapid advent of printing in the late fifteenth and early sixteenth centuries and the explosion of the internet over the last two decades (see, e.g. Bawden & Robinson, 2000).

Second, numerous scholars have devoted their professional lives to attempting to understand the precise extent of media effects. While several researchers have investigated the effects of watching religious television (see, e.g., Horsfield, 1984), few have asked how the consumption of popular media make audiences more open or closed to specific religious traditions. This is an interesting kind of question, but it is useful, however, to go beyond the media effects tradition and the concern with direct impact and behaviour changes to consider wider contextual issues (see Gauntlett, 1998).

Third, in the first half of the twentieth century scholars witnessed violence piled upon violence, leading some to conclude that media used as propaganda tools contributed to ideological hatred and nationalistic violence. The bloody turmoil through these decades contributed to the development of a third tradition within media scholarship: critical theory. This phrase is often used synonymously with the Frankfurt School. Researchers operating in this tradition analyse both the content of what they see, read and hear as well as the institutions and structures behind these productions. These are important questions, but critical theory, and many of the leading figures of the Frankfurt school, had a tendency to overlook or even oversimplify the role of the audience (see, e.g., Mitchell, 2007, esp. chap.6).

This leads us to the fourth and perhaps most dynamic current tradition, which concentrates upon the role of the viewer, listener or watcher in the communicative process. Over the last 30 years there has been an important turn towards the audience, and an increased rigour in thinking about the nature and locations of reception. Many different theories have been developed to make sense of both the unpredictable and the varied interactions with various media that is to be found among viewers, listeners and web users. Media analysis has shown how audiences are always changing, always developing. This is a significant phenomenon, which media scholars (e.g. Livingstone, 2003/2006), cultural theorists (Miller, 2006), anthropologists (Askew & Wilk, 2002, esp. pp.237-322; Rothenbuhler & Coleman, 2006), and other social scientists have mapped in detail, and I will consider in greater detail in the following section.

Several essays in this book are grounded in parts of these traditions, which take the complex activity of the audience into account. They demonstrate that audiences are by no means bound to be passive receivers of messages, but have the potential to become dynamic or creative producers of meaning in the face of what they see or hear. These four approaches, centred on histories and technologies; effects and impacts; texts, economies and structures; as well as audiences and reception are by no means water-tight categories. Nor are they comprehensive as the increased interest in aspects of media's role in material religion and ritual studies demonstrate (see, e.g. Couldry, 2003). Many scholars make use of these and other traditions, theories and methodologies to inform their research and writing about media and religion. My own approach also tends to be eclectic, drawing upon different aspects of these research traditions, particularly in relation to religion, media violence and peacemaking. When it comes to peacemaking and media, the role of the audience is an area which is often overlooked. This is a theme that we will reconsider in a moment. Beforehand, it is valuable to indicate another easily overlooked question. Given that the resources I have identified have primarily been academic and textual, what popular cultural and non-textual resources are most useful to study for researchers working in the field of media and religion?

Audiences?

What is significant about the role of the audience? Scholars analysing media from this audience-centred perspective, instead of being concerned with media as mythmakers or media as instruments of communication, investigate how and where audiences construct their own myths, rituals and meanings out of what they see (Hoover & Lundby, 1997; Hoover & Clark, 2002). The viewers themselves become the mythmakers. Where they do this is of interest. Rather than over-emphasising the power of different media and the passivity of audiences, this approach investigates the ways in which audiences interact dynamically with a multiplicity of media.

Viewers often draw on aspects of their religious traditions to define their own identities, but recent research has shown how some teenagers also use television dramas such as *The X Files, Star Trek,* and *Buffy the Vampire Slayer* and films such as those drawn from *The Harry Potter* series or *The Lord of the Rings* trilogy to help them make sense of their own lives. Many teenagers appear to weave together sacred narratives with stories found on television (Clark, 2005). As communication technologies continue to converge, viewers in affluent settings are increasingly able to use computer technologies to connect themselves with other members of the audience thousands of miles away. Web sites, chat rooms, and other digital media facilitate instantaneous conversations across the world around specific television events or popular programmes. So, for example, audiences in Ghana, Korea, Hong Kong, India, Hawaii and Russia can not only watch news about a mosque bombed in Iraq, they can also discuss the implications of this over the Internet. While audiences can be brought together through the web, the sheer diversity of choice now available through satellite and cable has ensured that 'television audience-hood is becoming an ever more multifaceted, fragmented, and diversified repertoire of practices and experiences' (Ang, 1994, p.382)

How audiences actually use a range of media for religious purposes has come under increased scrutiny in recent decades. In much the same way that there has been a turn towards the audience in communication studies in the second half of the twentieth century so there has been a similar shift among scholars analysing how viewers from different religious traditions actually create meaning around media today. This includes considering the ways in which audiences develop practices of viewing that ensures that they can resist, negotiate or play with the meanings of what they see. This is a question which has been under consideration for several decades. For example, some viewers in China during the 1980s appear to have used certain television programmes as 'a cultural reservoir of alternative visions', which allowed them to 'question traditional values and official interpretations' and thereby helped 'them to imagine alternative ways of living' (Lull cited in Thompson, 1995, p.178). The symbolic resources that media offers are often appropriated and recycled as people attempt to define their own identity, narrate their own life stories and understand the traditions and communities of interpretation that they belong to. Media need provoke neither total avoidance nor uncritical opportunistic use. Another news report showing a distraught parent over the body of a child or cityscape devastated by war, may lead to a sense of powerlessness, but it can also lead viewers to question the role of religious institutions or openness to alleviate distant suffering. This observation leads to another question worth sustained study: What are the habits, routines and practices that help audiences to move from apathy to compassionate engagement?

Definitions and Conclusions?

Finally, I would like to ask one further question: what is the significance for research into media and religion of redefining the term 'media'? Elsewhere I have defined the word 'media' as 'a channel that enables communication to occur' (Mitchell, 2002, p.213). On further reflection, this definition needs to be stretched to do justice to how people now interact both with different media and with their communicative environments. Media are far more than simply channels or mere instruments of communication. Consider the word's actual singular form: 'medium'. This older word can be used to refer to 'a channel, method or system of communication, information or entertainment' (Webster Third International Dictionary, 1971). This is a far broader definition and begins to reflect more accurately the different media people embrace, even if it doesn't include the media-scapes that they inhabit. It will be valuable for the development of the field of media and religion to extend the narrow functional usage of the word media which primarily associates it with radio, film, television and the press, also to include more traditional media such as books, paintings and plays as well as newer media such as computers, the internet and mobile phones. By defining media more broadly many new areas of study become pertinent to this field of study.

For instance, in *Democracy and Tradition,* Jeffrey Stout (2004, pp.163,166) suggests that 'more people seek their moral edification from poems, novels, essays, plays and sermons than from moral treatises or philosophical articles', and that 'there is a massive modern democratic literature on character and the virtues awaiting exploration outside of the philosophical canon' (see also Nussbaum, 1986, 1990). How far can Stout's claim be stretched to go beyond the traditional media forms that he identifies? In other words, how far have the popular electronic media, such as films, web sites, television and radio programmes become the places where many people consciously and sub-consciously seek their moral and even religious edification? There is definitely space for further reception studies which investigate whether the family, friendship circles and other formative settings, provide resources for this reflection. The cultural context provides more than simply a backdrop for detailed discussion of specific media it is an environment in which sacred and profane can interact (Sumiala-Seppanen, Lundby & Salokangas, 2006, pp.197-215).

While the cultural context, communicative environment and nature of the audience are important topics to analyse critically, so too is the actual content of what is produced. That is one reason why it remains valuable to analyse specific news broadcasts, news photographs, films, television programmes, web sites and adverts. These narratives, whether realistic, historical or fantasy-based reflect a great deal about the storytellers themselves as well as the worlds from which they emerge. Drawing upon this tradition ensures that critical questions will be asked about why many media texts often ignore, for example, how ethnic minorities and the poorest groups of society are regularly overlooked by powerful multi-national media organizations. What could be described as a third generation of critical theorists (following on from Adorno and more recently Habermas) does not stop with media texts or media audiences, they also ask structural causative questions such as: Why is this the case? Or which structures or lines of ownership contribute to these patterns of production? Certain elements of their approach have proved attractive to a number of more recent scholars (see, e.g., Lynch, 2005, pp.70-77, 193-4). This line of questioning demonstrates how one significant tradition in media studies, content or textual analysis, can lead to another, structural or production analysis which in turn can lead towards another, reception and audience analysis. This is by no means a one way circuit, but illustrates, what I argued earlier, that scholars of media and religion can usefully draw upon more than one tradition within media and communication studies.

In this essay, I have outlined five areas of significance for those studying media and religion. In each case a word has been used to summarise a cluster of approaches and questions (dangers, opportunities, resources, audiences and definitions). In each of the previous four sections I closed with a question which was intended to gesture towards areas worthy of further research. As I made clear in the introduction, this is not intended to be a comprehensive analysis. It is aimed at showing that the recurring divide between those who view media as a threat and those who believe that it provides many opportunities for religious communication can be analysed and interpreted in a creative fashion, allowing researchers to go beyond this over-simplistic dichotomy. This can be done by first, focusing more closely upon how questions of reception and the role of the audience are studied, and second on highlighting the rich range of resources available for scholars that goes beyond the confines of the media and religion research conversation. By bringing these different strands of scholarship together, scholars can ensure that appropriate attention is given to the audience, the producers, the media texts, the cultural context, the wider communicative environment, the political economy, the forces of globalisation and the media technologies and their histories. I am advocating an inclusive approach which also ensures that practitioners are included within the dialogue, exemplified, for example, by Horsfield, Hess and Medrano (2004) and Badaracco (2005). This can be further extended through broadening the definition of media to include not only television, film and the internet in the discussion, but also other more taken for granted media such as printing, writing and painting. This may in turn help to ensure that the apparently insignificant artefacts of popular culture and less spectacular media histories are not overlooked.

4

Reflections on the Past and Future of the Study of Religion and Popular Culture

JEFFREY H. MAHAN

When I began my theological education in the mid-1970s I was interested both in religion and in popular film and literature, but these seemed disconnected matters. In addition, my higher education was largely designed to wean me from my interest in the popular. At the time it was assumed that an educated person might be interested in the films of Bergman, Truffaut and Fellini but Ford, Hitchcock and Capra were guilty pleasures. Thus, I had little sense that exploring the relationships between religion and popular culture would shape my work for the next 30 years or more.

A pioneering seminary course on religion and popular culture with Gerald Forshey invited me to consider how I and others brought these things together in our religious and aesthetic practice. I went on to incorporate work in film theory and history into a Ph.D. program in religion and society. Among my earliest published essays were efforts to think theologically about detective fiction (Mahan, 1980) and the western (Mahan, 1984) as uniquely American explorations of the individual and society. At the time there were relatively few places for this conversation, and those of us involved still had to argue for the significance of studying the interests of everyday people.

Ten years later my colleague Bruce Forbes and I served as the founding co-chairs of what would become the Religion and Popular Culture Group at the American Academy of Religion as a way to expand the opportunities for ongoing discussion. The group provided a place for religious and theological scholars interested in popular culture to test our work and get feedback from colleagues. Many subsequent publications, some cited in this essay, were first tested before the group. For Professor

Forbes and me the conversations with and about the group led to the publication of *Religion and Popular Culture in America*, an edited volume that is now in its second edition.

Arising out of this background, this essay firstly offers one overview of the emergence of the subfield within religious and theological studies of religion and popular culture, then reviews some of the field's key insights and accomplishments, considers the methodological limitations of our work, and finally suggests possibilities for further study.

Emergence

Religion and culture have always been overlapping categories and religion's interactions with the cultural and economic systems of its day have always troubled and intrigued observers. The gospel accounts of Jesus driving the money changers from the temple (see Mark 11:15-17) are but one early expression of concern about the commodification of religious practice and identity. Conversation with Tom Boomershine, one of the originators of the Society of Biblical Literature's Bible in Ancient and Modern Media Group, helped me to see the Reformation as the result of a faith community's struggle with the communication revolution of its day. Cheap printing created widespread literacy, which in turn heightened the authority of the individual reader, and a new religious movement responded to those changes. Similarly, the success of the Wesleyan movement in America, and of the Great Awakening, can be understood in part as the emergence of forms of religion shaped by the situation and sensibilities of frontier working people.

The distinctive work on the relationships and overlaps of religion and popular culture of the last several decades emerged out of several developments in religious and theological studies. Scholars of religion, like those in other fields, were giving greater attention to the lives of everyday people. Gerald Forshey (1984) provides an overview of the emergence of this subfield. He points particularly to the influence of the publication of Paul Tillich's (1959) *Theology of Culture* and of the work on religion and literature of Nathan Scott at the University of Chicago. This germinal work drew our attention to the relationships between religion and art. However, it remained focused on idealized relationships within elite culture. Marshall McLuhan's provocative arguments about the growth of communications media and the way they reshaped individuals and society (McLuhan, 1962, 1963) created a context to think about the importance of popular entertainment media.

Two precursors to the wider scholarly conversation about religion and popular culture can be found in Robert Short's (1967) *The Gospel According to Peanuts*, which used Charles Shultz' Peanuts cartoons to invite a popular audience to reflect theologically, and Robert Jewett's (1973) *Captain America Complex*, which drew on the comic book hero as a way to make theological sense of Americans' support of the Vietnam War.

Others would also explore the interactions of religion and popular culture. In her book *The TV Ritual*, art historian Gregor Goethals (1981) argued that television took on an iconic function and served as a 'substitute for sacraments.' Andrew Greeley's (1988) reflections on popular culture were gathered in *God in Popular Culture*. In these and other works religious and theological studies began to enter into the conversation about a culture increasingly shaped by the mass media.

Recognition of the Subfield

This early work emerged at a time when religious and theological studies, and indeed academic culture in general, were going through a radical shift in focus. Academic culture was still largely wedded to high or elitist culture, and the dominant forms of academic study still assumed their task was to introduce students to the most complex and sophisticated forms of culture. Those of us who wanted to think about popular religious practices, or to reflect theologically on popular film or music, had to overcome a widespread suspicion that our work was trivial. Those within professional associations, such as the American Academy of Religion (AAR), and who were interested in religion and arts tended to focus on the relationships between theology and high art. Yet this was a time of transition. As in virtually every field, scholars of religion had been moving away from the focus on great leaders and ideas and turning their attention to understanding the lives of everyday people. Liberationist approaches questioned the way that higher education alienated students from their communities of origin. It began to be more acceptable to study less elitist culture, or indeed to dismiss the high/low distinction altogether.

These changes in scholarly focus did not happen in a cultural vacuum. Societies themselves were changing. In America, post WWII prosperity and leisure created the 'teenager,' the growth of television and other forms of mass media made culture more accessible and less local, the religious center was beginning to shift from the old Protestant mainstream, and the civil rights, anti-war and feminist movements turned our attention to questions of diversity and difference.

It would be 15 to 20 years before attention to these matters found a regular place and scholarly respectability within the guild. By the 1990's, such study was formalized at the AAR with the development of what are now the Religion, Film and Visual Culture, and the Religion and Popular Culture groups, a development which paralleled the earlier emergence of the Bible in Ancient and Modern Media group at the Society for Biblical Literature (SBL). The variety of approaches to engaging the movies illustrates something of the range of interests that shaped the study of religion and popular culture. On the SBL side, authors like Robert Jewett (1993) and Bernard Brandon Scott (1994) explored the way apparently secular contemporary film illustrated biblical themes. Others, including Lloyd Baugh (1997) and Stern, Jeffords and Demona (1999) examined films which were based on biblical materials asking about the cultural and theological sources of their varied portraits of Jesus. Joel Martin and Conrad Ostwalt (1995) brought together theologians who wanted to think about film. At the same time, work like Colleen McDannell's (1995) pressed us to think beyond popular film and literature and consider the way popular religious sensibilities were embedded in material culture.

Though the definitions and accuracy of these terms remains contested, this emerging work has been deeply shaped by religious studies conversations about 'post-modernity,' 'commercialization' and 'commodification.' Though earlier religious communities were also formed by the culture of their day, the rapid acceleration of ways in which religion and popular culture interact in late modern and post-modern society demands particular attention.

In the late '70s Michael Real (1977) introduced the term 'mass-mediated culture' to describe societies in which the media provide our primary picture of people, places and ideas. Real suggested that, in such a culture, the importance of people and events is confirmed by their appearance in the mass media. A friend, reflecting on Real's argument, recalled a tourist in the cathedral at Siena who looked through the lens of his video camera throughout his visit. The tourist never looked at what he was taping, demonstrating that the image was more important to him than the experience. Real's description seems to have become even more accurate in the intervening three decades.

Understanding religion's interactions with popular culture in the mass mediated world is crucial if we are to understand how religion functions and finds its place in contemporary society. We live in a society where the media draw on themes and symbols from religion and where religion is shaped by its embrace or rejection of the tools and narrative forms of popular media. Real's insight reminds us that religion's presence in the media serves as a cultural marker of religion's importance and expresses questions and concerns about religion at work in society.

Insights and Accomplishments

We seem safely past the point where every book or paper on the topic needs to begin with a defense of the very idea that serious academic attention should be given to seemingly frivolous entertainments. Yet, we can rightly ask, what has this attention to religion and popular culture taught us? How have our understandings of the nature of religion, its place and function in society, and its concerns and expressions changed in light of our attention to the relationships and overlaps of religion and popular culture? What methods and approaches have been most productive in revealing and interpreting the relationships of religion and popular culture? Can understanding these developments allow religious communities to adapt appropriately to the world their members inhabit?

Attention to religion and popular culture provides a location for conversation about religion's nature and function. Finding religion in surprising cultural locations, and seeing where religion is shaped by society, raises questions of definition. What is 'religion?' How is the 'sacred' related to the 'secular?' Our work challenges the assumption of secularization, which suggested that religion occupies an ever shrinking sacred circle in contemporary society. Rather, our studies suggest that the location of religion shifts, that theological and metaphysical questions remain a part of popular discourse, and that religion is practiced in diverse and sometimes surprising ways in contemporary culture.

Definitions of Religion

David Chidester first presented his inventive essay 'The Church of Baseball, the Fetish of Coca-Cola, and the Potlatch of Rock and Roll' (1996) to the Religion and Popular Culture Group at the AAR. Chidester playfully demonstrates how attention to theory and careful definition helps to clarify complex and interesting human phenomena in ways that deepen our understanding of the practice of religion. What is religion? How is religion a part of culture? Are there boundaries between religion and other cultural activities and if so, how are they to be understood? He reminds us that the definitions of religion remain contested and that at the heart of our work are questions central to religious and theological studies – an issue taken up in later chapters in this current volume by Lynch and Pinn.

The Sacred Secular

The attempt to draw clear boundaries between the sacred and the secular (or profane) has an elegant theoretical simplicity. Surely there is some clear marker between mundane activity and that which connects us to the transcendent. Yet the study of the interactions and overlap of religion and popular culture in a Madonna music video in which she uses religious imagery and ends up on a cross reveal that in post-modern communities, religion is multivalent and the wall between sacred and secular is clearly porous. We must attend to what this classical definitional distinction reveals about religion and also to what it conceals. It once seemed that, in contrast with traditional societies, in modern society the sacred existed within an ever shrinking circle. The discovery of the existence of the sacred within the profane world of popular culture challenges that interpretation.

My theological students' assumptions and piety sometimes limit their readiness to think broadly about what constitutes religion and the range of ways people might live out of religious understandings. When challenged to think about the interactions between religion and popular culture in soap operas, hip hop, or detective novels their understandings of their own practice and their readiness to think about the religious lives of people with assumptions quite different from their own are expanded.

Theology in Popular Culture

Theological themes and concerns appear in popular culture, sometimes quite overtly and at other times subtly. Attention to the use of religious imagery and the exploration of theological questions about the nature of human life in popular film like *The Matrix* helps my students consider the way their own religious imagination is shaped both by the beliefs and practices of their faith tradition and by the way that religious questions are explored in the cultural material they engage. Michelle Lelwica's (2005) study of the sacralization of weight loss practices, like Michael Jindra's (2005) examination of the *Star Trek* fandom, demonstrate the way that cultural practice takes on the language and form of sacred practice. Lynn Schofield Clark's *From Angels to Aliens* (2005) explores the way individuals construct their own religious world from a range of sources. Clark examines the way that seemingly secular teenagers draw on and combine images and themes from popular culture to construct a moral and metaphysical frame to interpret the world, often in response to quite theological concerns about God, hope and evil. My own work on the Jesus films (Mahan, 2002) points to the way that the gospels are reshaped by both the narrative and visual forms of popular culture and by political issues of the period as they are transformed in translation to popular film.

Religion Shaped by Media Culture

Both traditionalists and religious reformers move back and forth between the seemingly sacred and the seemingly secular. One example of the effect of mass mediated culture on religion can be seen in the ways that worship has been shaped by media's tools and assumptions. Sanctuaries sprout projection screens, music for worship embraces modern pop forms, sermons get shorter and silence is harder to find. Religious communities need to be more curious about how religious beliefs and practices change when the form of worship changes.

Evangelical Christians, in both North and South America, have been particularly adept at adopting the communication forms of modern mass media both in worship and in addressing the wider society. These evangelical media practitioners have often assumed that form and content were easily separated. But careful observation suggests that the form of their worship and the content of their preaching are changed by their embrace of the tools of mass media. When evangelical television programs like the *700 Club* adopt the talk show format we know from *The Tonight Show*, they also embrace celebrity culture. Too little attention has been given to the way such practices shape the theological assumptions of the community.

What once seemed an increasingly secular world in which religion played an ever shrinking role now looks quite different. While some forms of organized religion have fewer adherents, other religious communities emerge and grow, individuals construct elaborate religious practices, and religious and theological images, themes and concerns appear in surprising places.

Ritual Practices

One intriguing development in the study of the interactions of religion and popular culture is the growing attention to the tools and insights of ritual studies. Attention to the ritual forms of our engagement in popular culture helps to explain the cultural importance of these seemingly secular events and the way the location of religious activity has shifted. Students of ritual attend more carefully to the form of religion than to its essence or its claims about supreme beings. The ritual scholar does not ask what the religious community believes, but what participants do with their hands, bodies and voices. Such an approach reveals the ways that cultural activities we may not usually think of as religious take on the forms of religious practice. In studying religion and popular culture we see this work most often in studies of the ritual gathering of nations around sporting events like the Super Bowl in America or soccer's World Cup in much of the rest of the world. Other studies have looked at the way more specialized communities gather around weight loss or events such as the Burning Man Festival, a counter cultural celebration of music and performance art celebrated over the past two decades in the America desert (see, e.g. Gilmore & Van Proyen, 2005). Studied in this way it seems that such events, like more traditional forms of religion, take people out of the everyday, draw them into something larger that gives meaning and focus to their lives.

Del de Chant's (2002) *The Sacred Santa*, while too speculative to be a true example of ritual studies, thoughtfully appropriates the insights of ritual studies. He disagrees with those who argue that Christmas has been secularized. Rather, de Chant contends that Christians have lost the holiday to a cultural religion in which meaning and value emerges from elaborate practices of commercial acquisition and consumption. He builds a narrative about this 'religion of consumption' that helps us make sense of a complex social phenomenon.

I argued above that too much emphasis on the division between sacred and secular could lead us to miss their interactions. A ritual approach to religion can have the opposite effect, making every ritualized activity seem to be sacred. My theological students are at first surprised by an approach to the study of religion that cares little about belief and much about practice. Yet they are quick to adopt a ritual approach describing everything from mountain climbing to collecting 'American Girl' brand dolls as religion. We can be left with the 'so what' question. If everything can be described as religion, how is the concept of religion helpful? More sophisticated appropriation of the insights and methods of ritual studies are needed to help us understand more clearly the embodied practices through which religion and popular culture interact.

Methodological Problems

Having established some of the achievements of past studies in this field, our attention will now focus on questions and challenges for the future. A key issue for future work in this field relates to the development of greater methodological sophistication in our work. In short, how can we more adequately study the relationships and overlaps of religion and popular culture? There is a truism that if the only tool you have is a hammer, every problem looks like a nail. To advance our work we need to gather the appropriate tools. Here the divide between film and media studies is instructive. Film studies use the tools of textual analysis drawn from literary studies and aesthetics and focuses on the examination of popular texts, while mass communication uses the tools of the social sciences and focus on the practices of audience/consumers.

Faced with moral critique of their work by religious commentators, the producers of popular film and television often respond that their humorless critics do not seem to understand either the economic realities of production or the aesthetic and narrative forms within which they work. Those who spend their lives studying film and television often say something similar about the work of religious scholars who venture into their territory. There is a dangerous and unhelpful dilettantism to too much of our work on popular culture. Theological and religious studies scholars, who decline to be engaged by discussions of religion that lack sophisticated understandings of its forms and history, often feel free to speculate wildly about popular culture without bothering to develop understandings of its forms and the forces that have shaped it. Too much of the work on religion and popular culture reflects little awareness of the narrative, visual and musical forms of popular culture or of its economic and aesthetic norms.

The Assumption of Passivity

One limitation of the metaphor of consumption introduced in the previous section is that it often assumes that the audience is passive. Jindra's (2005) study of the phenomena of *Star Trek* fandom moves us beyond the assumptions of passive consumption by a single undifferentiated mass audience. He invites us to pay attention to the complex and creative ways that particular communities appropriate and manipulate popular culture to articulate and enact ethical and metaphysical systems. We must learn to ask more complex questions about what it means to 'consume' a text and attend to how audience members manipulate, interpret and participate in popular culture. We need to understand how actual individuals and communities relate religion and popular culture in their own lives.

Analyzing Texts

Rooted in the traditions of the humanities, film departments rely on analytical approaches rooted in textual study. Here and elsewhere I use 'text' broadly in order to suggest any aesthetic object/experience which may be subjected to close 'reading.' Thus not only literature, but film, music or other productions may be thought of as texts. Textual approaches are attentive to questions of genre and authorship and to visual and narrative construction. At their best these approaches lead to elegant and insightful interpretations of the text as text. At their worst they can provide intricate readings that show little awareness of how actual viewers make sense of and interact with the material.

In order for our work on popular culture to be taken seriously outside of religious and theological studies, we must spend more time acquiring the tools of those who study popular texts. They will teach us to attend with greater care to the forms, contexts, and audiences of the texts of popular cultures. For example, while much attention has been given to studying films with religious content or from a theological perspective, it is embarrassing to note how little attention is given in most of that work to film as a visual medium, and to the way that the visual presentation shapes the way we read the narrative. Too much of our work reduces film to a summary of its narrative and then analyzes that narrative from the perspective of religious studies.

I remember a panel at the American Academy of Religion on the film *The Crying Game*. One panelist came to theological studies as a gifted photographer trained to think about visual composition. Her paper addressed, in a quite sophisticated manner, the visual construction of gender in the film. Rather than being challenged by the presentation to think more carefully about how awareness of the film as visual experience might enrich their own reading, the rest of the panel attacked her for not taking the same ideological approach to the film that they had.

A more sophisticated visual and narrative analysis will help the theological critic see the popular text more clearly. Viewers sometimes ask whether the Denny Arcand's film *Jesus of Montreal* has a sufficient sense of the idea of resurrection. To respond adequately one must see that both in the narrative and in the placement and movement of the camera, Arcand offers a range of possible resurrections. Following the film's exploration of crucifixion are several scenes and images which portray a variety of understandings of the concept of resurrection. Perhaps resurrection is experienced in the anticipation of the disciples? In one scene Arcand uses light, camera angle, and the direction of the actors' glances to demonstrate their anticipation of the arrival of a Christ figure whose resurrection is not yet confirmed. Arcand then uses the transplanting of organs to suggest a more physical resurrection. With evident skepticism, Arcand also considers the possibility that resurrection is to be found in the founding of a church. The film's closing title sequence continues the speculation with a long complex camera movement that first pans to the left through the catacomb like subway, then turns up, apparently moving through the earth, and out past the now empty cross and into the starry heavens. Only attention to the complexity of the narrative, and to the film's visual presentation, gives access to Arcand's multi-faceted reflection on resurrection.

Just as our work on film has given too little attention to the visual, much of our engagement with popular music is inattentive to musical form, reducing music to the content of the lyric. Can our interpretations of music be taken seriously if we demonstrate no attention to such matters as meter, rhythm, harmony, musical genre and instrumentation? How much richer are works like Anthony Pinn's *Noise and Spirit*, (2003) which takes music seriously as music, attending to the way that both form and lyric inform our experience and interpretations of the piece.

Audiences

In contrast to the work on texts carried out by those trained in the humanities, mass communication scholars focus on social science approaches to understanding audiences. Their work seeks to identify who is reading the text, or watching the video, in order to clarify their assumptions and perspectives, and to understand the way meaning emerges as they read and manipulate the text. These scholars have often been attentive to questions about how popular culture expresses cultural attitudes related to issues race, gender and class. At its best, this approach leads to nuanced examinations of the way the audience interacts with and interprets the text. At its worst, this approach offers un-nuanced readings that miss the subtleties of actual texts.

There is too little productive conversation across this methodological divide. Surely understanding the text more clearly will deepen our understanding of the audience's use of it, and vice versa. The world of religious and theological studies often has a similar divide between scholars who study sacred texts and histories, and those interested in the practices of individuals and communities and the way they adapt and interpret these religious texts and histories.

The study of religion and popular culture seems a likely meeting place where those approaches might inform each other, thus enriching the broader study of religion. Amy Johnson Frykholm's *Rapture Culture* (2004) provides an example of the fruits of reading that takes both text and audience seriously. She examines the phenomena of Tim LaHaye and Jerry Jenkins' popular *Left Behind* novels. Frykholm sees these fictional explorations of the idea of 'end times' both as texts to be read carefully and as part of larger cultural and religious phenomena that includes the way they are promoted, the audience they find, and the use actual women and men makes of the series to express cultural and religious identity.

Some argue that students of religion and theology are not media scholars or musicologists and are entitled to bring their own tools and insights to bear on popular film. It is true that we bring our own unique perspectives, tools and questions to our work on popular culture. If we do not, we will simply do badly what others are better trained to do. But if we serious about studying popular culture, the readings that we offer must be shaped by our unique theological perspectives *and* by a deeper understanding of the forms, structures and cultural histories of the popular material that we study. To do that will require more engagement with colleagues in other fields and their work.

Possibilities for the Future of the Field

We live in a world where religion is both more evident and more contested than in the recent past. Struggles over whether 'intelligent design' has a place in the science curriculum, Christmas decorations are appropriate in the public square, or Muslim women can wear head scarves in the classroom, clog the courthouse. In public debate politicians and citizens are often quick to identify the religious roots of their convictions. Both news and entertainment media give regular attention to religion. *Time* and *Newsweek* sell more copies when religion is on the cover. Mel Gibson's *The Passion of the Christ* filled the theaters and *What the Bleep Do We Know?* found an art house audience for its blend of science and new age religion. Media attention confirms Americans' interest in religion and its place in the public square. The subfield of religion and popular culture has carved a place for itself in the conversation.

Those of us who study religion and popular culture have, however, been accused of being contemporists. We have been so focused on recent phenomena that we fail to put the relationships between religion and popular culture in historical context. Our work on contemporary film, music and television, and on practices like the Burning Man Festival or *Star Trek* fandom, too often suggests that the relationship between religion and culture is a product of late modernity or post-modernity. While there is a compelling case to be made that popular culture, in contrast to folk culture, did not exist until the emergence of mass produced commercialized culture, our work would be enriched if we gave more attention to how contemporary interactions of religion and popular culture are like and different from the practices of popular lay religious life in other times and contexts. A clearer picture of the past helps us understand the ways forms, issues and practices are consistent over time, and helps us see where change is happening. We might ask, for example, how contemporary public rituals are like and different from medieval festivals, the ancient Olympics, or hunting rituals in traditional societies.

Attention to changes in popular culture over time allows religious and theological scholars to 'take the pulse' of society in ways that should inform our analysis and contributions. Changes in the form and focus of popular culture can help us identify changing social attitudes and assumptions.

Films like *Invasion of the Body Snatchers* expressed the anxieties of the cold war era by exploring the threat of annihilation by hidden external forces. In a more hopeful era science fiction films like *Close Encounters of the Third Kind* presented contact with the alien world as a source of hope for the future. Given America's post-9/11 anxieties, scholars will be well advised to look at how recent popular culture locates evil, and expresses anxieties about difference, immigration and contact with the alien today (for example in the recent television re-make of *Battlestar Galactica).*

Day-time drama (soap opera) has always been a form within which changing social understandings are expressed and explored. During the late 1970s and '80s when new attitudes toward homosexuality began to move out of the avant-garde into popular consciousness in the U.S, the soaps were among the earliest television programs to have ongoing gay characters. The typical pattern would be for a homosexual character to be introduced, or an existing character to identify as gay or lesbian. First other characters would express long standing anxieties about homosexuality and awkwardness about relating to gay people. This would be followed by the reestablishment of relationship and affirmations of the gay character's place in the community. In this way the soap operas first expressed the anxiety produced by changes in common attitudes and then integrated the emerging acceptance into the ongoing narrative, thus helping the audience internalize emerging understandings.

The perspectives of religious and theological studies help us to identify how religious themes and images are being used and allow us to see, evaluate, and respond to the way that theological and metaphysical concerns are being worked out within society. Changes in popular religious forms and practices can similarly reveal shifts in assumptions about the nature and place of religion. Like all religious architecture, the medieval cathedral embodied the theological assumptions of its day. Designed to stand a thousand years, the cathedral expresses a confidence that religious truths are unchanging. In contrast, by its architecture and construction, the contemporary church in the strip mall suggests a religious life ready to change in response to shifts in population, style and need. Even if that community's expressed theology assumes fixed religious realities, such worship centers reflect a religious world in flux as it adapts to commercial culture.

Conclusions

I take personal satisfaction in the way that this work on religion and popular culture has become a regular part of our study of religion. I regard it a significant professional contribution to have both participated in the conversation about religion and popular culture and to have been part of creating a space for those conversations at the AAR. We have participated in a broader movement to root the discussion of religion in the practices of everyday people in specific cultural locations.

My frustrations are that we have not gotten further in creating a sustained conversation. Because of the range of interests that bring us to reflect on popular culture, and because we have not developed a clear theoretical base, too much new work seems oblivious to the foundations laid by the scholars described above. Religious and theological scholars are often still unsophisticated in their consideration of aesthetic form. And too much of our work is still focused on the white norms of centrist popular culture. With the exception of attention to African American music (see Dyson 1996 and Pinn 2003) we have given to little attention to the popular culture of minority communities.

I do not mean to suggest that religion is merely an expression of other cultural forces, or that the portrait of religion that we find in the media is accurate or adequate. I do argue that religion is best understood when we take its context seriously. Whether religious communities openly embrace the tools and values of a mass mediated world, or resist participating in that world, they make themselves in response to it. Whether or not they participate in a formal religious community, most people in this complex consumer culture create a symbolic universe by integrating language, practices and symbols from seemingly religious and seemingly secular sources. We must understanding this complex cultural process, and the way that religious communities participate in and respond to it, if we are to accurately describe religion in the midst of mass mediated cultures.

As a student of religion, I want to describe and interpret religion accurately in the context of our mass mediated cultures. I am interested in observing how religion is lived out, both in what we have traditionally called the sacred circle, and in the midst of what we once assumed was a purely secular sphere. Work on the interactions of religion and popular culture helps to create a rich and interesting picture of religion and its implications and practices.

As a theological educator and a practitioner of religion I want to go beyond description. My students and I, and the religious communities and institutions in which we participate, must ourselves embody religion in mass mediated culture and bear witness to the sacred in the midst of a society shaped by the values of consumption. We are not separate from that culture. With everyone else, we participate in it, view our lives through the lens of the media, and participate in the process of creating meaning from the complex of symbols and rituals available to us.

One key function of the religious leader, whether imam, priest, pastor or rabbi, is to interpret a religious tradition. The leader helps a community interpret their tradition and texts for the cultural context in which they find themselves. Both pastoral care of the wounded and prophetic response to culture require an accurate interpretation of cultural forces. If my students are to make a difference in the communities where they will serve, they must understand that people live in a symbolic universe shaped by the values of consumption and celebrity and help people to construct compelling alternatives to those values.

In order to understand religion in the post-modern world we must explore the porous boundary and creative tension between the seemingly secular and the seemingly religious. Accomplishing this requires bringing theological and religious studies perspectives to bear on both traditional sacred texts and the texts of popular culture, on the media through which people view the world, and on the complex practices and rituals through which individuals and communities make meaning of the worlds they inhabit.

5

"What We Make of the World"

The Turn to 'Culture' in Theology and the Study of Religion

ELAINE GRAHAM

At the end of January 2006, a message was posted on a message forum of the British Broadcasting Corporation's (BBC) website. It announced a forthcoming television production and invited readers' responses:

> There's going to be a major production on the streets of Manchester this Easter telling the story of the last days of Christ which will be shown live on BBC3. It's a modern version of the Passion featuring well-known songs by Manchester bands including New Order, Joy Division, The Smiths, Oasis and M People. Some famous Manchester musicians are being lined up to play the parts of Jesus, Mary, Judas and Peter etc. The final crucifixion scene will take place in Albert Square. What Manchester songs do you think should be in there? And who should play the main parts? How would you give the story of the Passion a modern Mancunian twist?' (Manc-host2, 2006)

The programme, Manchester Passion, was staged in Manchester city centre on the evening of Good Friday, 14 April 2006, and broadcast live on a minority TV channel, BBC 3, with an edited version shown later the same night on BBC 2. The reaction to the programme on the same message forum after the screening was lively, articulate and, by and large, enthusiastic. One such contributor was Webstercat71:

I'm watching Manchester Passion just now, it's fantastic!!!! A contemporary version of the story of Jesus accessible to everyone. I want to ask if anyone was offended by the re-telling, was it wrong or blasphemous to use modern music to tell the story of the last days of Jesus? I'm not a Christian but felt that it told the story in an interesting way that kept me hooked. That's got to be a good thing right? I'm also amazed that so many modern songs could be interpreted to tell the story. (Webstercat71, 2006)

Another participant posted this message in response:

I am a Christian and I thought that the Manchester Passion was fantastic too. I thought the use of all the songs was so clever, and just served to show the hunger and soul-search that was already there in all of those songs. If Jesus is going to be accessible to all as I think the play showed was his ultimate intention, then Christians need to be at the cutting edge of engaging with contemporary culture, meeting the culture head on with all of its questions and unresolved pain, rather than retreating into the church out of fear... Good luck with your search. In my opinion Jesus is well worth investigating. (frenchification 2006)

In his/her concern that the play may have caused offence, Webstercat71 may have had in mind the way in which previous attempts by the BBC to present religious subject-matter in the context of light entertainment had ended in controversy. In January 2005 the Corporation's television adaptation of the West End musical hit *Jerry Springer: the Opera* had encountered virulent protests from many Christian groups, in particular the conservative organization *Christian Voice*. The show, which features prolific use of the F-word and depicts God, Jesus and the Virgin Mary as a dysfunctional family appearing on a confessional daytime talk show, was eventually broadcast but in the face – allegedly – of death threats to the programme's producer (Plunkett, 2005; see also Branigan, 2004). Hence the assumption, perhaps, that religious people would inevitably be opposed to any portrayal of sacred characters or theological issues in the performing arts, be that film, TV, popular music, musicals or live theatre. Yet frenchification's positive reaction showed that many other Christians regarded shows such as the *Manchester Passion* to be entirely appropriate opportunities for their faith to be presented in a refreshing and accessible way.

Clearly, there are differences between a production which uses music to punctuate a traditional Passion narrative, and a show which deploys scatalogical and iconoclastic devices to satirise the tendency of daytime TV to sensationalise any human experience, however extreme or profound. Yet these two programmes demonstrate in different ways that the contemporary encounter between religion and popular culture is both delicate and complicated. In the days when Christianity was the predominant world-view in the West, a broad consensus would have existed between the Church and the creative and performing arts; yet this is no longer the case, due to the impact of secularisation and religious pluralism. The chances are that over the next generation societies like Britain will witness a widening gulf in social attitudes between a large and increasingly secular majority, and a small but articulate minority of people of faith. The potential for misunderstanding is therefore great, and representations of religion of all kinds, in news media and popular entertainment, will become increasingly influential either as means of staking out a common ground of religious and spiritual exploration, or as contested territory over which bitter battles over freedom of expression are waged.

My main interest in this chapter lies in the theological dimensions of such engagements between religion and popular culture. What is going on when the traditional canon of Christian practices and doctrines meet the sources and resources of popular culture in all its many manifestations? Are such attempts to be celebrated as an opportunity to make the Christian faith more 'relevant' to an increasingly post-Christian (but not necessarily post-secular) society (Crockett & Voas, 2006; Vulliamy, 2006)? Or are they a risky business in which the integrity of the Gospel will inevitably be undermined by the forces of commercialism and profanity?

I begin with questions of what motivations there might be for those engaging in the study of theology and popular culture, from both church and academy, and some of the chief manifestations of representations of religious and theological issues in popular culture. I will then ask what critical tools are at scholars' disposal in making sense of the encounter between theology and popular culture; and what evaluative frameworks might be deployed to enable researchers to move from 'consumption' to 'critique', and whether the theologian should be expected to advance normative judgements on popular culture.

This is essentially a line of enquiry about the ways in which popular culture might serve as a vehicle for what is sometimes termed 'theological reflection': or how everyday experience prompts engagement with the sources and norms of tradition in order to articulate the principles of faithful living (Graham, Walton and Ward, 2005). Yet there is a second dimension to the 'turn to culture' that represents further potential for an understanding of the very nature of theological enquiry itself. I shall argue that 'culture' may be viewed as the entirety of human creative activity: not just a matter of high culture or the existential search for meaning, but the whole framework of lived human experience. Culture and cultural practices thus figure as essentially both the product of, and the context for, human *being, making and imagining*. This, in turn, engenders new insights into the very nature of theological discourse itself, effecting a shift from theology as <u>doctrine</u> or belief, to theology as *practice*: and thus an opportunity to conceive of theological reflection as one of the activities by which human beings build worlds of meaning and significance, and experience themselves as creative, moral, and purposeful beings.

Signs of the Times: Theological Motivations for Engaging with Popular Culture

At one level, an interest in popular culture may appear to be no more than a somewhat questionable search for 'relevance' on the part of academics and the churches alike. If undergraduates in theology and religious studies seem increasingly less knowledgeable about specific religious traditions, or appear reluctant to engage with written texts, then it is seductive to make use of areas of contemporary culture where they do show astonishing enthusiasm, sophistication and lucidity: visual culture, cyberspace and popular music.

Yet there are perhaps more substantial motivations stemming from a missiological or evangelistic agenda on the part of many Christians. If the churches are failing to connect with 18-24 year-olds through traditional means, then why not harness the resources of popular culture for the purposes of mission and outreach? Writing from a broadly evangelical perspective, Pete Ward has written that 'existing patterns of church fail to connect with the evident spiritual interest and hunger that we see in the UK and the US' (2002, p.3). There is no doubt that such an evangelistic impetus has contributed to a significant proportion of the literature in the field: not simply in a narrow sense of converting souls to Christ, but to establish new patterns of discipleship and church organization that correspond more closely to prevailing cultural trends.

This is part of the agenda of the various debates about 'fresh expressions' of Western Christianity, which is often but not exclusively related to the 'emergent church' movement. Just as society is moving from 'solid' to 'liquid' so too must the Christian churches adopt more flexible structures, greater informality, an emphasis on networking, on 'doing' and 'being' rather than 'believing' and 'belonging' (Ward, 2002; Cray, 2004; Carson, 2005). This includes recognising the extent to which popular culture provides the framework through which many people's search for meaning – and thus the proclamation of the Gospel – is mediated. Yet it goes beyond mere expediency to articulate the theological conviction that God needs to be apprehended not only through tradition but by reading 'the signs of the times'. The following statement by Sanctus1, a 'fresh expression' based in Manchester city centre, is typical of this understanding:

> We are a welcoming Christian community and believe that *God is not defined by theology*. We welcome dialogue between different theological positions but also recognise that *dialogue* involves listening and real listening involves *change* ... We believe that God is already in the world and working in the world. We recognise *God's indefinable presence in music, film, arts and other key areas of contemporary culture*. We wish to affirm and enjoy the parts of our culture that give a voice to *one of the many voices of God* and challenge any areas that deafen the call of God and hence constrain human freedom. (Sanctus1, 2002, my emphasis)

Calls for the re-establishment of a culturally sensitive and renewed Christianity are not restricted to evangelical sections of the Church, however. It resonates with much Roman Catholic theology after Vatican II, in which 'culture' is described both as the sum of human achievement and the milieu in which the Christian faith is necessarily proclaimed and practised (Cobb, 2005, p.8; Gallagher, 2003, p.121). In missiological terms, this is to say the Christian Gospel must be 'inculturated' and expressed in the vernacular of local cultures. In *Virtual Faith* (1998), Tom Beaudoin extends the concept of inculturation from a cross-cultural transmission to one conceived as intergenerational. Beaudoin is especially concerned with the religious values of so-called Generation X, namely those born between about 1960 and 1980, whose outlook is characterised by a mood of disconnection from the idealism and political activism of the 'baby-boomer' generation. The Church must acknowledge the aspirations of young people if Christianity is to make any impression:

> If part of the pastoral task of the Church is to communicate God's mercy and God's freedom in a way that people can understand, then you have to use the language that they're using, you have to use the metaphors and forms of experience that are already familiar to them. You can't ask people to believe in something their own experience forbids them to believe; that's just elitist ministry. We still have that going on in some places, where it's believed people need to be converted from one cultural system to the Church's cultural system. (Tom Beaudoin in Nickel, 2006, pp.18-19).

For many, therefore, the ubiquity of popular culture has made it a primary medium for the construction of self and community and for the on-going human processes of meaning-making. This is particularly apparent in those who have focused on popular culture, as opposed to 'high' culture, such as Gordon Lynch.   He defines popular culture as 'the shared environment, practices and resources of everyday life for *ordinary* people within a particular society' (Lynch, 2005, p.14), thereby privileging the forms of expression or entertainment that are most likely to be at hand for large portions of the population. Craig Detweiler and Barry Taylor (2003) have argued that scholars of religion need to take popular culture seriously as the dominant 'canon' of literacy and information. As the institutions of organized religion recede and the incidence of active religious affiliation amongst the indigenous population declines, so it is argued that people turn to the sources and resources of popular culture as a means of rehearsing and examining questions of belief, meaning and spirituality. This has given rise to the contention that at a time when institutional religion and formal theology are connecting with a dwindling fraction of the population, (popular) culture is one of the few shared 'matrices of meaning' within which discussion can take place and values can be debated. As institutional religion recedes, and its narratives and norms no longer furnish ordinary people with moral or existential bearings, so popular culture moves into the vacated space, offering alternative archetypes, myths, heroic figures or soteriologies to form the stories we live by. To engage with popular culture enables scholars of religion to map the fragments out of which ordinary people are piecing together their own 'vernacular' or commonplace theologies (Lynch, 2005, p.166; Gallagher, 2003, pp.6-8).

Popular culture is conceived theologically not only as a vehicle for converting people to faith, therefore, but a vital medium through which ultimate reality itself is mediated and revealed. Popular culture is believed to constitute a central source and resource for theological understanding. Just as in the past, philosophy or writings of classical writers may have served as a resource for theological understanding, or even a generation ago the insights of modern psychologies and psychotherapies served as windows into the human condition for pastoral theology, maybe now questions about good and evil, life and death, what it means to be human, identity and community are mediated as much through popular cultural expressions as via the voices of 'high culture'. If theology is to respond authentically to its human situation, then it must be ready to respond in kind.

Mapping the Intersection of Theology, Religion and Popular Culture

I want here to map some of the ways in which popular culture is serving to mediate understandings of the nature of religious belief and practice, or to facilitate theological reflection on the world. The following categories are intended to reflect some contemporary trends within Western culture, both in popular experience and academic debate.

Screening the Sacred

This covers the portrayal of traditional religious figures and narratives. It could refer to something as straightforward as the telling or retelling of classic Biblical stories, or the reworking of enduring myths; what Lloyd Baugh (1997) has termed the 'Jesus-Film'. Thus, Biblical epics and films such as *Jesus of Montreal*, *Jesus of Nazareth*, *Last Temptation of Christ* and *The Passion of the Christ* would fall into this category. However, it could also involve the exploration of wider aspects of religious characters or controversies, such as *40 Days and 40 Nights* in which the hero abstains from sex as a wager with his friends, a scenario which parodies evangelical Christianity's campaigns on teenage chastity and virginity such as 'True Love Waits' (DeLashmutt, 2006). Yet it might also embrace more ambivalent portrayals of religious figures such as the flawed heroes in *Elmer Gantry* and *The Apostle* (Grainer, 1999).

Whilst we may consider this genre to be essentially the telling and retelling of classic stories, clearly all these examples are 'representations' of Christ-figures rather than straightforward portrayals. For a start, the original Gospel accounts do not provide historical accounts of Jesus of Nazareth; but when comparing Pasolini's *Gospel According to Matthew*, for example, with Mel Gibson's *The Passion of the Christ*, it is apparent that both reflect very different Christologies.

Seeing Salvation

These may be cultural expressions that are essentially vehicles of encounter with the sacred, transcendent and redemptive. Such forms of popular culture may not deal with explicitly theological themes, but nevertheless may be regarded as instances of 'hierophanies of the sacred' (Eliade, 1959). They may feature a central figure who embodies redemption (Lloyd Baugh's 'Christ-Figure'), such as in *The Matrix* or *Cry Freedom*; or a strong central motif of salvation, such as *The Shawshank Redemption* (Marsh, 2004, pp.45-59), or *Schindler's List*.

You'll Never Walk Alone

This category considers the ways in which popular culture serves as an outlet for or expression of 'spirituality' beyond organized religion. This might furnish evidence for scholarship seeking to assess how far in spite of institutional decline religious belief and affiliation persists, albeit at the level of non-institutional, non-credal forms (Davie, 1994). Manifestations of this in popular culture might include the interest in Gothic and supernatural themes in TV series such as *Buffy the Vampire Slayer* and *Angel*, or the enormous commercial success of the J.K. Rowling's *Harry Potter* series and despite - or because of - their implicit critiques of religion, Philip Pullman's *His Dark Materials* trilogy and Dan Brown's novel, *The da Vinci Code* (Wagner, 2003).

Other scholarship has focused on the way people appropriate familiar forms of popular culture which may not have initially been ascribed a religious association, yet develop them to refer to sacred subjects. For example, Ian Bradley's work on popular hymnody has analysed the growth in the use of popular music such as *You'll Never Walk Alone*, *Bridge over Troubled Water* and *Candle in the Wind* at funerals and weddings (Bradley, 2004).

Meaning of Life

This category indicates forms of popular culture which explore aspects of what it means to be human, especially in terms of ethical and existential themes (Cobb, 2005, pp.177-210). Examples often trace the boundaries between human and almost-human, using alien characters as mirrors against which normative and exemplary humanity is refracted (Graham, 2002). Such examples would be *Bicentennial Man, GATTACA, Frankenstein,* or *Blade Runner* (Aichele, 2005). More broadly, the Home Box Office TV series *Six Feet Under,* set in a family-run funeral business, provided rich resources for explorations of existential issues such as death, bereavement, sexuality, religion and the nature of family relationships (Akass and McCabe, 2005).

Like a Virgin™

This category makes use of sacred themes in post-religious contexts, where many sacred symbols and cultures are available for appropriation and reappropriation. In this area of study, scholars might examine the ways in which displacement of religious imagery or references is taking place, often in ironic or syncretic-eclectic forms. Examples might include any Madonna music video; or Kevin Smith's film *Dogma* (Cobb, 2005, pp.22-24, 137-142).

The question is whether the ironic tone of much of this points us towards, or away from, any affirmation of theological significance. *Dogma,* for example, is hugely irreverent, and yet its purpose is to poke fun at religious bigotry and also at the Church's desperate search for relevance by assimilating to the values of corporate culture. Yet one question prompted by such material is whether its impact is essentially parasitic on a bedrock of shared religious and theological reference-points, and what happens once its audience is no longer capable of 'reading' such references.

The Empire Strikes Back

This is potentially one of the most complex and nuanced areas of religion's engagement with popular culture. It represents a seemingly paradoxical harnessing of sophisticated forms of new media and popular culture to reinforce traditional religious practice, using secular methods or technologies to pursue explicitly religious themes or causes. These may have the function to reach out to non-members as evangelistic devices, or to strengthen the cultural identity of conservative religious groups (Hendershot, 2004; Gormly, 2003). Alternatively, 'mainstream' consumerist culture becomes a means of adopting a radically counter-cultural lifestyle. One such example, from the Muslim world, is the brand *Qibla Cola*, which identifies itself explicitly as practising fair trade, but also offering an alternative to other global brands of Cola and thus possibly a form of resistance to US neo-colonialism (Qibla Cola, 2003). The term 'Qibla' indicates how the faithful Muslim at prayer should locate him/herself in relation to the sacred site of Mecca; thus, by analogy, to consume this fizzy soft drink is a means of orientating oneself correctly: a way of demonstrating one's religious loyalties through the medium of the market.

Theological Discernment: Commendation and Conversation
Whilst it is important to affirm the various ways in which religious and theological themes are mediated via popular culture, questions of discernment or evaluation cannot be ignored. How, then, might the scholar move from description to analysis? How would theologians distinguish legitimate uses of the Christian canon, or set boundaries for acceptable use of theological themes within the plethora of examples surveyed above?

One such analytical tool has been advanced by a number of scholars (Marsh, 1997; Gallagher, 2003; Lynch, 2005), who all adapt H. Richard Niebuhr's classic study, Christ and Culture, 1951, to suggest a range of approaches to theology and culture. Niebuhr set up five different relationships between 'Christ' - the claims of the gospel - and 'culture' - the world - which were opposition, conformity, dualism, syncretism and conversion. In revisions of this, Marsh and Gallagher have both developed similar three-fold schema, broadly tracing the alternatives of opposition, identity and mutual critique.

The first approach thus sets theology *against* culture, articulating the notion that there is nothing to be gained theologically from engaging with (secular) culture. There may be a number of reasons for this, such as a conservative view that Christian lifestyle is to be set apart from anything that might contradict Biblical revelation, through to a more general rejection of humanistic or liberal moral attitudes. Note, however, that 'culture' is assumed to be 'secular' and that no account is taken of either of the way in which Christianity informed Western culture in the first place, or of how conservative Christianity is often highly selective in its rejection or assimilation of mainstream culture.

At another level, however, such an approach may afford some degree of counter-cultural critique to the mores of media, commercialism and consumerism. Popular culture, it is argued, is inherently about triviality, celebrity, diversion; and the values of popular culture reflect constant search for novelty, titillation and sensation rather than any serious engagement with our humanity or ultimate reality (Postman, 1986). Thus, popular culture conforms to hegemonic not Gospel values: what is celebrated is strength, celebrity, individualism, wealth, competition and glamour - the antithesis of any identifiably Christian ethic. This oppositional stance may also choose to stress the transience of much of popular culture, with the resulting danger that any theological engagement will rapidly look anachronistic.

In some respects, such critical perspectives remind theologians of the contingency of any cultural expression of ultimate values. Yet whilst there is a sense in which God's revelation transcends human cultural expression, such a model has a relatively low doctrine of 'secular' culture and creativity as spheres of encounter with the divine.

A second option is often represented as the polar opposite of 'hostility' between Christ and culture (Gallagher, 2003, p.135), and points to an identity of revelation of God through culture and faith. In Niebuhr's terms, Christ is the fulfiller of culture, making the universal meaning of the gospel clear to all, available through the work of reason and cultural membership. We might see it as related to traditions of 'natural' theology and a very 'immanentist' model of God, or even as an affirmation of the entirety of popular culture as a form of 'implicit religion'. Yet as Clive Marsh has commented, to argue that popular culture (in this case, cinema-going) is an alternative to religious practice and affiliation is not the same as saying it is a substitute for religion. The tendency to collapse theology and culture - with their differential histories, contexts and sources - denies either any degree of autonomy, thereby preventing any critical space to emerge. Thus, whilst this model celebrates the presence of faith and spirituality outwith the institution, it may veer too far into what Gallagher terms 'innocent acceptance' (2003, p.137) on the part of theology towards culture, lacking any critical edge towards mainstream cultural values.

Yet as with any kind of heuristic framework of this kind, we need to be wary of erecting typologies which distort rather than clarify empirical evidence. To my mind, these extremes serve more to sketch out critical benchmarks by which a more interactive or synthetic relationship is articulated, rather than being discrete positions in their own right. This can be demonstrated by the way in which whilst some of my earlier examples may appear at first glance to inhabit the extremities, further examination reveals more dynamic factors at work. For example, the genre of 'The Empire Strikes Back' may appear to be about rejection or withdrawal from popular culture – an oppositional stance - but is in reality a complex mix of appropriation of modernity in order to effect a recapitulation of an actively counter-cultural (and in some respects pre-modern) identity.

The third dimension of this typology may therefore be closer to reality of the   relationship between theology and culture, being one of conversation or dialogue in which the processes of interaction are those of mutual challenge, affirmation and critique (Marsh, 1997; Loughlin, 2005, pp.2-5). Theology is understood to be inescapably part of culture and shaped by its cultural contexts, yet claims to transcend the particularity of any one context or expression. At the same time, however, it allows the language of popular culture to speak on its own terms, thereby granting an intrinsic integrity to the secular.

In this respect, the history of Christian theology itself carries an important precedent, in the preaching of the apostle Paul in Athens. The story from the Acts of the Apostles has him speaking publicly at the Areopagus, or public forum, with a concern to become 'all things to all people' and stressing a universal human search for the divine (Graham, Ward and Walton, 2005, pp.140-142; Gallagher, 2003, p.139). Whilst he is seeking to commend the Christian Gospel to his audience (what we might term a stance of 'apologetics'), there is also a strong dialogical element to his proclamation, acknowledging the possibility that pagan culture is capable of theological discernment.

Perhaps this should commend itself to theologians as a strategy of 'responsible engagement' (Gorringe, 2004, p.15). Such an approach upholds a theological conviction that the ultimate purposes of God may be discernible here and now (which grants culture an integrity of its own), yet will require divine action to bring human affairs fully to fruition (which introduces an eschatalogical horizon into theological reflection on culture). Such a model keeps faith with the idea of an enduring 'script' of Christian narratives, symbols and meanings which constructs a normative framework, as well as the potential for popular culture to carry seeds of revelation that do not merely confirm meanings already present within the faith tradition but may offer new or corrective insights (Cobb, 2005, pp.72-75).

Studying 'Ordinary Theologies'

Typologies such as Niebuhr's are useful as heuristic tools, but they have limitations if they reify or over-simplify complex, shifting perspectives. The emphasis on popular culture as 'lived experience' strongly suggests that there needs to be a greater use of empirical and phenomenological approaches in order to trace the contours of 'ordinary theologies' (Astley, 2002) emerging out of the synthesis of tradition and experience. This entails scholars approaching the subject with new critical tools which enable them to take seriously the specificity of the medium they are studying. This is an important but sometimes overlooked distinction, between the study of popular culture as essentially about a critical reading of 'texts', and more ethnographically-oriented methodology, which focuses on the function those 'texts' fulfil for their audiences, and the ways in which consumers of popular culture make use of them.

Examples of attempts to bring audience reception into the study of theology and film might be Clive Marsh's (2004) recent *Cinema and Sentiment*, or John Lyden's (2003) *Film as Religion*, which concentrate on the practices of regular cinema-goers, and the various ways in which actual film-going functions for them as a means of engaging with moral dilemmas and exploring different avenues of significance. Marsh draws analogies between this mode of study in cultural and film studies, and the emergence of 'reader-response' theories in literary and Biblical studies (Marsh, 2004, p.36). It is notable, however, that despite Marsh's emphasis on audience reception and the experience of movie-going as multi-dimensional, there is little primary research data of the kind he commends, and many of his case-studies are conducted without reference to audience response.

Nevertheless, such areas of study should alert scholars to the fact that popular culture exceeds the limits of text or visual image, whilst the consumption of popular culture is revealed as a far from passive pursuit. It is important to locate people's use of media and popular culture in relation to religious traditions in their own context of everyday phenomenology. This serves as a good example of how researchers need to be alert to the multiplicity of methods available. Such research is necessarily interdisciplinary, as it calls on tools of social analysis in order to offer an adequate account of religious practice in its cultural contexts. Without such inter-disciplinarity, scholars risk making superficial and inadequate analyses of their field of study and are unlikely to have their work taken seriously by their academic peers.

I have argued that the focus on popular culture has rendered the lived experience of people of faith a priority for study, often via empirical or ethnographic methods. It offers legitimacy to popular or vernacular expressions of religious praxis over and against institutional, dogmatic theology. Potentially, then, this represents an important shift in our understandings of the nature of religious belief and practice. It presents a resistance to the reduction of religion to propositional belief, or of theology primarily as doctrine. This is a question to which I now return: is 'culture' simply a mode of consumption, or a set of meanings; or is it more appropriate to consider culture as a form of 'practice' or lived experience from which constructive theological reflection can proceed?

If we consider theological reflection as essentially a series of conversations between a contemporary situation and the sources and resources of faith, this 'turn to culture' offers very exciting avenues. We might consider this to be something akin to a 'theological imagination', which characterizes human religious engagement with culture in all its forms. It is because culture is always revealing something of our humanity and potentially of God. If 'talk about God' is to a large extent a human activity, the work of the human imagination, then fruits of our cultural imagination will be arenas within which God will be revealed (Loughlin, 2005, p.5). This casts theology as a process of enquiry and reflection – a practice - rather than body of truth or doctrine. 'Rather than studying theological ideas as a static body of knowledge that is universally applicable, theology is better understood as a process of exploring traditional theological resources in the light of contemporary questions, beliefs, values, practices, and experiences.' (Lynch, 2005, p.96)

'What We Make of the World': Theology as Cultural Practice

So far, I have not offered any definition of 'culture' or 'popular culture' beyond the quotation from Gordon Lynch at the beginning of this chapter. But Tim Gorringe, in his recent book *Furthering Humanity* (Ashgate, 2004), provides a helpful pointer in this respect. At one level, there is an anthropological definition, relating to all aspects of human activity and endeavour; and this is a profoundly materialist understanding, in which we think of the ways in which humanity transforms the raw materials of 'nature' into built environments, artefacts and activities of manufacture and exchange. But 'culture' also has associations with those more artistic, literary, symbolic expressions that constitute human creativity: as Gorringe says, the linguistic link is there between the 'cultivation' not only of fields, animals, even human bodies, but the cultivation of minds and spirits.

Famously, Clifford Geertz has represented culture as fundamentally and primarily a system of meanings: 'an historically transmitted pattern of meanings embodied in symbols, a system of inherited conceptions expressed in symbolic forms by means of which men [sic] communicate, perpetuate, and develop their own knowledge about and attitudes toward life.' (Geertz, 1973, p.89). As he says, human beings are creatures suspended in 'webs of significance' that they themselves have spun. But perhaps we can combine this notion of culture as a 'web of meaning' which human beings create for themselves – the stories, myths and constructions which shape our understanding of the world - with a more materialist understanding of culture as essentially the realm of human fabrication, a systematic outworking of the achievements of *homo faber* – humanity the tool-maker, the builder of worlds. So 'culture' reflects something of our innate abilities for making, building and imagining worlds, both metaphysical and material, as well as our capacity to move adroitly between the two. For Gorringe, therefore, 'culture' denotes not so much the elevated realms of high culture, but any kind of lived experience or practice; it is, as he says, 'what we *make* of the world'.

> Human beings, says Clifford Geertz ... are animals suspended in webs of significance that they themselves have spun. 'Culture' is the name for these webs. It is *what we make of the world*, materially, intellectually and spiritually. These dimensions cannot be separated: the Word is necessarily flesh. In constructing the world materially we interpret it, set values on it. To talk of values is to talk of a culture's self-understanding, its account of its priorities. (Gorringe, 2004, p.3, my emphasis)

'Culture' is therefore more than just a realm of meaning, but is a world of material fabrication as well as one of signs, symbols and ideas. I want to emphasise this dialectic between the anthropological and the aesthetic because it gives us a very useful and theologically resonant definition of 'culture'. All is the result of human making and transforming, but it allows us to think of culture as both the exceptional, the heights of creative excellence, and the everyday, the result of the human labour that forges the material world in which we live.

In terms of theological reflection on popular culture, therefore, it is all very well to focus on ways in which popular culture elicits questions of meaning: of popular culture as a way of articulating questions about what it means to be human, the nature of the sacred, and so on. However, to consider 'what we make of the world' as a working definition of culture introduces further dimensions, which stress much more the ways in which culture as the realm of human practice serves as the environment within which religious belief and behaviour is conducted: culture not only as realm of meaning, but realm of practice.

There are parallels between the 'cultural turn' within the study of religion and theology with that of a renewed focus on 'practice' within the discipline of theology, especially practical theology. In its reinvention from an 'applied' discipline of clergy hints and helps to a primary discipline of the hermeneutics of theological reflection on practice, practical theology exhibits many of the same emphases as emergent trends in the study of religion and/in popular culture. Indeed, 'culture' as a category plays a significant part in contemporary practical theology as the context which generates the practical questions and challenges from which the process of theological reflection and formation stems.

The emphasis on 'orthopraxis' (or right practice) from Latin American liberation theologies, together with a sensitivity to the sociology of knowledge drawn from a range of liberationist theologies such as Black, feminist, LGBT and Third World theologies, have been key influences shaping the reinvention of practical theology as a primary theological discipline. Theology is regarded as a form of practical wisdom, enabling a critical account to be made of the values and truth claims enacted in the world by individuals and communities of faith. In its most postmodern versions, practical theology argues that theology is essentially 'performative', so that theology is not primarily or exclusively expressed in doctrinal statements or academic treatises but enacted and embodied in the liturgical, evangelistic, sacramental and practical/caring actions of faithful communities (Graham, 1996). Methodologically, practical theologians are attuned to the extent to which all theology is necessarily contextual, and how culture, tradition and experience are inextricably interwoven.

Thus, the twin turns to culture and practice have a number of implications for the rejuvenated discipline of practical theology, many of which resemble similar trajectories in the study of religion and popular culture. Firstly, there is a resistance to the reduction of religion to propositional belief, or of theology primarily as doctrine. Instead, the lived experience of people of faith becomes a priority for study, often via empirical or ethnographic methods. Secondly, practical theology is also interdisciplinary, as it calls on tools of social analysis in order to offer an adequate account of religious practice in its cultural contexts.

Thirdly, it offers legitimacy to popular or vernacular expressions of religious praxis over and against institutional, dogmatic theology. Finally, as the institutions of organized religion recede in increasingly secular societies of the West, practical theologians look to the ways in which, in the absence of the infrastructure of formal religious affiliation, people turn to the sources and resources of popular culture as a means of rehearsing and examining questions of belief, meaning and spirituality.

There is also a strongly incarnational thread to this positive theological appraisal of the potential of culture, insofar as people's engagement with the material and aesthetic dimensions of their world provides a ready-made affirmation of the sensual, affective, embodied dimensions of human life and, by extension, the gathering up of these aspects into the life of God. It also affirms the power of the creative arts to reflect and explore aspects of the human condition, including human beings' relationship to transcendence. There is an affinity between the arts and theology because they both open up and gravitate towards, questions of ultimate human concern. So the creative imagination and material culture furnish the raw materials for divine disclosure; they both represent potentially ways in which humanity can apprehend the divine.

This turn to culture also offers us different media through which that 'talk about God' can be made manifest, too: not just in words, or the conventions of systematic theology, but in visual arts, hymns, popular song, story, film, music, even the built environment. To see talk about God take shape in such cultural and aesthetic forms offers a different kind of theological literacy, a different medium of expression from the logic-centred mode, as Pete Ward discusses further in the next chapter in this volume.

So culture is what humans use to inhabit the universe, both in terms of making it physically habitable but also in making sense of things: culture is the sum total of the indivisible activities of being, making and imagining (Heidegger, 1993). Human beings are constantly moving between the material fabrication and transformation of the world, and the processes of interpretation, meaning-making about that very same world. Yet our physical transformation of the world is driven by the narratives, values and goals we have constructed for ourselves; so the objects we build – such as cathedrals, canals and computers – are dialectially connected to the concepts and values we weave around them.

This intertwining of the concrete and the imaginary tells us something about our humanity as made in the image and likeness of God. Philip Hefner's work on technology (2003) has elaborated this theme theologically, arguing that humans' need to project themselves beyond the mundane, the immediate and the concrete to imagine 'new worlds' of meaning and the imagination is an expression, theologically, of humanity's potential for transcendence. Culture, both as world of meanings and world of practices and material artefacts, thus holds the potential to disclose more about ourselves as human beings, and provides the sources and resources whereby we can contemplate fundamental and ultimate realities. Culture (material and metaphysical) like Scripture or any other conventional theological resource, becomes a source or conversation partner in theology's task of 'reading' the divine (Loughlin, 2005, p.9).

Some of this might be illustrated through a piece of testimony by Tom Beaudoin. In a recent interview with Jeremy Nickel, a documentary maker with particular interest in rock music subcultures and religion, Beaudoin reveals that his own academic work in theology and popular culture is indivisible from his own involvement in music-making. He observes that often implicit in research in theology, religion and popular culture, is the researcher's own personal investment in the subject on which they are writing. Rather than seeing such personal investment as an embarrassment to be ignored or to be justified by more 'academic' reasons, it could be profitable instead to recognise the subjective basis of the work as an integral element to it.

Beaudoin provides an example of how such experiential and reflexive analysis can lead into a theological direction. He speaks of how his music assumes a 'sacramental' significance in which cultural practice becomes a vital avenue of self-expression and encounter with the divine: 'an imaginative palette for faith', as Beaudoin puts it:

> Playing in rock bands over the past 20 years has been a huge, huge part of my life. It's given me a mystical vocabulary that is also a religious vocabulary - a set of experiences that I draw upon when I do theology. For me, what gets worked out in every bass line is my own restless and searching eros, or spiritual seeking. That's what gets expressed in every creative expression on bass guitar ... To

know that this practice conducts me into God's mystery is all I need
... I just need the promise. And that's all Christian theology is in a
sense, and especially my own tradition, Catholic theology, we're very
big on looking for those hints and we're very interested in the tastes
of God here in this world. (Beaudoin in Nickel, 2006, p.21).

Beaudoin's reflections on the 'practical theology' of popular culture - as
something consumed and produced - is an articulate and profound
expression of the potential of human making, building and imagining to
'speak of God' and point us towards transcendence in the midst of
everyday life. Viewed this way, participation in culture - as producer,
consumer and interpreter - could be understood as a form of 'theological
reflection on practice': critical evaluation of one's own cultural practices
sharpens one's creative awareness and serves as a glimpse into the spiritual
dimensions of everyday, lived experience. This is not intended to be
solipsistic or self-indulgent, but rather an experiment in self-reflexive
academic enquiry, and an investigation into the ways in which the
theological imagination is sparked through different forms of lived
experience.

It is possible, therefore, that this renewed engagement with 'culture' as
a category can go further than simply offering critiques of *Jerry Springer: the
Opera* or wondering whether football is a surrogate religion, to take us to
the heart of what it means to be human. Our very participation in culture -
be that prosaically everyday or expressed in the creative achievements of
high art, mediated through the narratives of self-acceptance and self-
actualization of modern psychotherapies or in the traditions of
contemplative spirituality - are all many-layered accounts of our human
story which call forth interpretation in the light of *God's* story. It offers, I
think, a way forward for us to conceive of culture as the arena of human
being, making and imagining and for theology to undertake further
reflection on *what we make of the world*, both materially and metaphysically.

6

The Eucharist and the Turn to Culture

PETE WARD

In her book, *Theories of Culture,* Kathryn Tanner (1997) suggests that what she calls an 'anthropological' view of culture offers a significant dialogue partner for theology. In proposing this she accepts that ideas of culture influence a good deal of contemporary theological debate but she points out that:

> this influence on theology often, however, remains implicit and unself-conscious, thereby blunting the capacity of such a notion to establish fruitful avenues for theological study and hiding from the theologian's purview a decisive postmodern shift in the anthropological understanding of culture within the academy. It is this postmodern modification of an anthropological notion of culture that holds the greatest promise as a tool for theological study. (ibid., p.x)

In this paper I want to explore what this 'postmodern' notion of culture might mean, although I might prefer to describe it as a post-structuralist turn to culture rather than as postmodern.

In foregrounding the cultural I am seeking to address two issues in theological studies. The first relates to the on going debate concerning the relationship between revelation and experience, or the 'cognitive-propositional' and the 'experiential-expressivist' as Lindbeck (1984) puts it. In this paper I use the Eucharist as means to examine how the collapse into the cultural might play out. Central to this discussion is the idea that in the Eucharist, doctrine is performed. As performance it is lived in (as culture) at the same time it also mediates divine encounter (and is thus in-dwelt). The Eucharist as it is performed is therefore both lived-in and in-dwelt. In this reading of performance Lindbeck's categories are seen to co-inhere and co-exist. The propositional and the experiential are mutually dependent, as they occupy the same space. Moreover, as they do so, they make present to us the transcendent. The turn to culture facilitates the collapsing of theological categories without diminishing what is at stake in these distinctions.

The second issue follows on from the first. Practical theology has been shaped by the wider debates within modern theology. It has evolved as a discourse of mediation or correlation between the doctrinal and the social scientific, the experiential and the propositional. With its methodological concern for the analysis of practice and context, its utilisation of social scientific methodologies and its focus on the interpretation of religious expression, practical theology has often struggled to engage with more traditional theological sources. If the turn to culture collapses the propositional and the experiential into one another then practical theology as a discourse of mediation and correlation is also reframed. One of the consequences of this reframing is that the perceived dichotomy between the theological expression of the canon and the expression of communities and practitioners is significantly blurred or intermingled.

The Performance of Doctrine

My starting point for this exploration is a biblical text:

> For I received from the Lord what I also handed on to you, that the Lord Jesus on the night when he was betrayed took a loaf of bread and when he had given thanks, he broke it and said. "This is my body that is for you. Do this in remembrance of me" In the same way he took the cup also after supper, saying, "This cup is the new covenant in my blood. Do this as often as you drink it, in remembrance of me." For as often as you eat this bread and drink the cup, you proclaim the Lord's death until he comes. (1 Corinthians 11: 23-26, New Revised Standard translation).

Clearly this text has a place within a biblical and Pauline context and at the same time it also has a place in the worship of the church. A consideration of meaning in relation to this text may consider the use that has been made of it within the Christian community. Meaning therefore can be seen as being in some way linked to the place that these words have found in Christian identity, expression, worship and so on. Framed as the narrative of institution, this biblical text has a central place in Eucharistic liturgy. In the liturgy the text is enacted, re-enacted or performed. It is worth noting that performance is inherent in the text itself. Since here the Christian community is commanded, 'Do this is remembrance of me.' To speak of performance is to run with the grain of the biblical text.

The performance of the text in the Eucharist can be seen as an embodied theology. When a Christian community performs the liturgy these words become 'lived in'. At the same time the performance of the liturgy is also 'in dwelt' i.e. it becomes a place of divine revelation and encounter. To be lived in and in dwelt this biblical text needs to be performed. Moreover to speak of the 'lived-inness' of the Eucharist does not preclude talk of 'in-dweltness', since in performance these two are interdependent. Performance as embodied theology is situated in particular communities, liturgical rites, and historical contexts. The question of meaning in relation to this biblical text is thus articulated by performance. This means that if we want to explore the question of meaning in relation to the performance of this text in the Eucharist we need to find ways of seeing which take account of the cultural complexities of community life, social context and liturgical formulation and expression. To do this I want to draw upon a pattern of cultural analysis, which has become common place in cultural and media studies. Such an enterprise, it should be stressed, does not necessarily reduce the theological to the cultural since it is the nature of the Eucharist that it is a text in performance, i.e. it is both lived in and in dwelt. To speak of one therefore is to also speak of the other.

Patterns of Enquiry in Cultural and Media Studies
In media studies analysis is often divided between the consideration of media texts, how those texts are produced through the action of media institutions, and how texts are received by audiences (Taylor & Willis, 1999). This threefold pattern of institution, text and audience is used to shape the discussion of most kinds of media (see, e.g., Johnson et al., 2004). Within cultural studies Stuart Hall has proposed a similar pattern for the study of contemporary culture as representation, production, and consumption (see, e.g du Gay, 1997). Representation relates to how a cultural product is encoded with meaning, production is a discussion of how the culture industries act to shape meaning within products and consumption relates to the way that people make use of products and use them in developing identities. These categories in cultural and media studies are largely interchangeable.

Production	Representation	Consumption
Institution	Text	Audience

To illustrate how cultural analysis works through the use of these categories we can briefly consider ways in which the music of the Beatles can be discussed as representation/text, production/institution and consumption/audience. A consideration of representation or text might include a discussion of Beatles' songs and meaning e.g. is *Lucy in the Sky with Diamonds* a reference to drug use, or to what extent is the guitar solo on *While my Guitar Gently Weeps* entirely successful, or what is the relationship between John's early sexual encounters and the song *Norwegian Wood*? Exploring institutional contexts and production might include a discussion of the significance of George Martin as a producer for the Beatles, or an account of the role that ineffectual amplification equipment played in the bands decision to stop touring, or a discussion about the role that Yoko Ono did or did not play in the final years of the band. Consumption or audience might include discussion of the behaviour of the fans in what was termed 'Beatlemania' or perhaps an assessment of the way that particular songs become a 'sound track' for our lives e.g. being used at funerals and weddings, or perhaps a discussion of the different ways that individuals have interpreted a song such as John Lennon's *Imagine*. Within media/cultural studies it is recognised that while individual studies may focus on either production, text or audience, questions of meaning generally require a consideration of each of these areas. If we want to ask what is the meaning of the Beatles for instance we will need to some extent to make a journey through each of these kinds of enquiry and the methods of analysis and interpretation which are related to them. I want to follow this kind of journey of interpretation in relation to my chosen text 1 Corinthians 11: 23-26 and its performance in relation to the Eucharist.

The Production of the Eucharist

The performance of the text as the Eucharist can be read as production. The Eucharist is 'produced' in the way that it has been shaped by the history of liturgical development. In this production there is an interaction between liturgical scholars, ecclesial bodies and the production of particular liturgies. An account of production might therefore include the key role of individuals such as Dom Gregory Dix or Gabriel Herbert in liturgical reform during the twentieth century or a discussion of the role of the Anglican liturgical Commission and its revision of the Prayer book culminating in Common Worship. Alongside this kind of production we could place the various theological debates concerning the meaning of the Eucharist. This kind of debate would include an account of the on-going debate about the presence of Christ in the Eucharistic elements and the various doctrinal formulations adopted by different denominations. Production therefore relates to the way that individuals and institutions have acted try to shape meaning around Eucharistic performance. The text is produced because it has been 'inscribed' or encoded in the various liturgical texts. The liturgical texts are therefore produced within ecclesial and theological traditions. These traditions can be explored to reveal layers of inscribed meaning. Traditions however are not solely textual, therefore, but they are also social. An example of this is the way that individuals may be shaped an ecclesial tradition such as Anglo-Catholicism. The culture of priesthood is passed on within this tradition not simply through theological text but also through formation. Formation within Anglo-Catholicism is a social process whereby individuals are shaped in their sense of self and their understanding of the meaning of the Eucharist. Formation therefore can be seen as a kind of production in that it not only trains and shapes individuals as priests, it also produces a particular understanding of the Eucharistic performance.

If we are to discuss how a text like 1 Corinthians 11:23-26 is produced we will need to adopt a variety of methods of enquiry. These may be largely familiar to the theologian. Clearly these methods will involve the examination of theological texts, ecclesial formulations, and historical records, and so on. The discussion of particular liturgies and liturgical theolgies will be required to demonstrate changes in liturgical practice. Production however might also involve a consideration of more sociological data. An examination of how priestly formation shapes Eucharistic performance for instance would involve the use of more social scientific methods of enquiry.

Representation and the Eucharist

A discussion of production does not of itself yield a full account of the Eucharist. One of the reasons for this is that while production inscribes meaning, this meaning is not necessarily fixed through productive processes. Inscribed or produced meaning shifts in performance through representation. One way of illustrating how the performance of the

Eucharist shifts through representation can seen in the recent Anglican experience of ordaining women to the priesthood. A woman priest robed and celebrating at the altar is a particular representation. In contrast perhaps we can think of the symbolism of a circle of robed male priests around the altar concelebrating. While the liturgy and large elements of the ritual may be exactly the same the difference in celebrants and style of celebration allows for a complex and perhaps contrasting range of connotations. Performance therefore implies a particular enactment. Each enactment involves representation. Representation articulates inscribed meaning by linking it to a range of complex signifiers. Complexity or intertextuality is a characteristic of every Eucharistic performance. For while there may be a consistency in many of the elements of the liturgy, it is also usual for individual Eucharistic celebrations to involve a changing mix of hymns, prayers, a sermon, and so on. Church practice thereby habitually creates a rich cocktail of interactions and interconnections. An interesting example of this is the way that contemporary forms of alternative worship have used visual imagery and a range of popular styles of music to create inter-textual interactions between traditional liturgy and popular culture. An example of this would be when the track *Firestarter* by the Prodigy is played at ear bursting volume as the backing to a Eucharistic prayer from the Anglican Common Worship which is yelled over the top of the music, or when a video loop of one of the fight scenes from *The Matrix* is projected behind the altar as the Eucharist is celebrated. These kinds of practices are contemporary, and perhaps extreme, forms of Eucharistic performance but they demonstrate how representation re-works inscribed meanings through performance.

Once again it is worth repeating that a consideration of representation does not necessarily entail the reduction of the theological to the cultural. The performance of doctrine means that it is lived in as it is also, at the same time, indwelt. The point is that a consideration of representation is required if we are to be able to explore the way that doctrine is performed (i.e. how it is both lived in and also indwelt). The performance of the Eucharist therefore needs to be interpreted in a way that accounts for the complexity and multilayered nature of representation as well as the inscribed meanings familiar from the tradition. This means that in order to read the complex ways that representation articulates meaning we need to adopt methods of enquiry which can take account of the inter-textual and symbolic play of performance. This means that we will need to develop appropriate ways of reading the semiotics of worship. It will entail the theological engagement with methodologies from musicology, ritual studies and discourse and content analysis. These will not replace the more traditional forms of theological enquiry associated with production, rather they are utilised to develop a more complex reading of performance.

Consuming the Eucharist

The study of cultural consumption or audience-reception concerns the way that individuals and groups make use of cultural products. It focuses upon the way that identities are shaped in relation to representation and the inscribed meanings of cultural production. For our purposes consumption recognises that questions of meaning are not limited to an investigation of theological debates or liturgical formulation and revision. When we consider the Eucharist as performance there is also the question of how the congregation shapes, and are shaped by, the performance of the Eucharist. There is a dynamic interaction between the produced meaning of the Eucharist, the performance of the Eucharist as representation, and how individuals and groups interact with these meanings and make use of them. Here again any account of individual and communal agency in relation to the Eucharist will be complex and multi-layered. There is no straight path between what is produced or what is represented and the way that these are received and made sense of by those in the congregation. An illustration of this is my own experience of preaching in church. On more than one occasion after I have preached, I have been encouraged by an enthusiastic parishioner who says how much they agreed with, or were moved by, the sermon. Unfortunately when they go into more detail I have been more than a little embarassed to find out that they are talking about something I haven't said or even worse they are congratulating me because they have misheard and are agreeing with the opposite of what I said.

Meaning is not fixed by representation, despite the best efforts of the preacher. Meaning in the Eucharist through performance finds a place in the lived world of individuals and groups. This means that if we want to explore fully questions of meaning and significance in relation to the Eucharist we need to find ways to examine the way that meaning shifts as it transforms and is transformed by those in the congregation. Such an exploration needs to open up the way that meaning is circulated through representation indirectly. For instance the indirect nature of consumption is revealed by the way that congregations 'make do.' Making do refers to the way individuals use hymns, liturgies, or sermons which may not be the best or the most contextually appropriate. But despite this people are still able to 'find a way' through these resources to encounter God and shape a Christian identity. To draw on my own experience again, as a teenager I was first introduced to the Christian faith in a very formal and traditional Anglican Church. Although my musical tastes were for bands like Led Zeppelin, at Church I encountered the English choral tradition. I must confess I hated it, mainly for its pretence, but somehow I made do. I found a way to develop my faith. This kind of making do is replicated in churches around the world. Parishioners know that the vicar is not the greatest preacher in the world or the organist is not as dexterous or adventurous as she once was, but somehow we find a way.

In relation to the Eucharist a consideration of audience will serve to complicate questions of meaning. A good example of this is experience of many Anglican young people who find getting out of the pew and walking to the altar to receive the Eucharistic elements to be something of an embarrassment. At the level of representation and production receiving the communion at the altar is often related to sharing of the 'one cup.' So the inscribed meaning speaks of unity. In performance, however, this notion 'unity' may be contradicted. Rather than sharing in this ecclesial unity, the experience of many young people, especially those in early adolescence, is that the Eucharist makes them feel uncomfortable and ill at ease. The main reason for this is that they perceive that they are on display as they stand up and walk to the altar. An enquiry into what individuals make of the performance of doctrine may reveal a further level of complexity. Individual, and indeed congregational, belief and practice may be more intuitive and responsive than 'produced' theology. An example of this is seen in the way that individuals may hold contradictory or inconsistent theological positions on a range of themes. For example, when asked about their view of biblical authority evangelical Christians will probably respond with some form of theory of biblical inerrancy and be very clear that their faith is fundamentally based on a biblical framework. When their spiritual practice is examined however it may well be the case that they rarely if ever read the Bible. Similarly evangelical students may be very insistent on the importance of doctrinal on the authority of the Bible, yet their actual knowledge of the Bible may be very limited. These anomalies indicate the extent to which questions of meaning in production and representation are complicated as they are articulated through congregational and individual agency.

Again it needs to be emphasised that a consideration of meaning as it is constructed by congregations does not necessarily mean a reduction of the theological to the cultural. There is a symbiotic relationship between the produced meanings of theological discussion and liturgical formulation, the way that these are articulated through processes of representation, and the re-working of these meanings by participants in the Eucharist. Exploring lived engagements with these institutionally produced and represented meanings, and understanding the nature of these engagements as performed theologies, is necessary to a full description of the Eucharist as performance. A range of research methodologies are required to analyse and explore meaning as it it lived in. These would include ethnographic methodologies, participant observation, structured and semi-structured interviews, reflexive methodologies such as auto-ethnography, narrative congregational studies, and so on.

Production, Text, Audience: General Approaches

In media/cultural studies the pattern of institution, text and audience is used to develop a complex and multifaceted approach to cultural analysis. Each area of analysis is seen as being complementary to the other. It is accepted that studies may focus on aspects of production and the culture industry or representation or audience reception, but it is also recognised that a full account of any aspect of popular culture requires some consideration of all of these areas. This means, for instance, that a discussion of how individuals and congregations shape identities around the performance of the Eucharist needs to take account of the interplay between communal reality and the specifics of representation. Thus Baptist Eucharistic identity may be shaped by the way that the ritual is performed and the way that the tradition has developed through theological debate. Baptist congregations however also produce and represent. They produce as they participate in the performance of the Eucharist. Production therefore relates to the way that they identify themselves with the Eucharistic act in performance. Participation in performance however can also be read as a form of representation. Congregations mediate Baptist Eucharistic identity. Individuals are socialised into Baptist practice not simply through the words and actions of the liturgy (and the tradition out of which these are formed) but also through worshipping within the congregation. In this way congregations can be seen to both produce and represent as they are actively participating in the Eucharistic event.

A consideration of the interrelationship between production, representation and consumption is particularly important when it comes to questions of evaluation and critique in relation to cultural practice. Failure to take account of the range of issues at stake when dealing with cultural expression can lead to problematic conclusions. An interesting example can be seen in the way that some conservative Christian commentators condemned heavy metal music and artists such as Ozzy Osbourne and his original band Black Sabbath because of the satanic references in their songs. When Osbourne's music, and particularly the early Black Sabbath recordings, are examined, there clearly is an emphasis upon the occult. Research into audiences however seems to imply that the occult lyrics in Heavy Metal music is more likely to resonate with issues of rebellion and masculinity rather than any specifically religious inclinations among teenage boys (Walser, 1993). A further moderating factor relates to Ozzy Osbourne's repeated denial that he or the band had any interest in the occult. What this means is that the occult aspects of this music operate almost entirely at the level of representation. They form a part of the act rather than a part of the lived reality of the band or their audience. So the symbolic function of the occult in heavy metal operates in a way that is possibly more akin to the use of the occult by Shakespeare in a play such as The Tempest. In other words, the occult forms part of the artistic context in which audiences and artists are working symbolically with a range of issues and concerns. When theological commentators focus on representation to the exclusion of production and consumption they often fail to understand fully what is actually happening when bands perform or audiences listen to this kind of music. Moreover in concentrating on the occult elements in the songs they miss the important theological issues, which are at play in questions of masculinity, sexuality and rebellion among some young people. A similar observation could be made concerning the evaluation of Eucharistic practice. For instance a theological evaluation of the construction of meaning through representation in the Eucharist might focus on the significance of certain ritual movements and actions utilised by a priest at the altar, and miss the fact that most people in the congregation have never noticed these actions for the simple reason that they usually have their eyes closed at this point in the service.

Conclusion

I have focused on the Eucharist because it offers what is perhaps a relatively uncontentious test case. Most Christians would accept that there is a natural and probably a necessary relationship between doctrine and its performance in the Eucharist. My purpose however has been to chart a course which has implications beyond liturgical studies. I want to argue the much more general point that doctrine should be seen as performative. The social and embodied character of lived faith, as discussed here in relation to the Eucharist, entails a performance of doctrine. This is to suggest that questions of meaning (and therefore also of theological reflection and evaluation) need to take account of the complex and multi-layered inter-play between the way that theological and ecclesial traditions are produced, the various ways that these produced meanings are then situated through representation, and the way that meaning is transforms and is transformed by congregations.

This kind of practical theology is recognisably theological. What I mean by this is that it does not bracket out the propositional or the doctrinal. Rather it recognises that there is a necessary relationship between the lived culture of faith and what might be termed the theological canon. At the same time it deals with the social and the semiotic without necessarily reducing the theological to the cultural. Instead it proceeds by assuming that there is a necessary relationship between these two. In other words it attempts to collapse the dualism between the social scientific and the theological. This has a wider significance for practical theology because it realigns the structure upon which much of its methodological framework has been based. If it is the case that the turn to culture collapses the experiential and the propositional then theological discourses of mediation and correlation will obviously need to adjust.

The collapsing of categories into the cultural I would suggest is of particular significance for the practitioner. The experience of ministry is that the social and the theological co-exist, the doctrinal is prayed and preached, and the theological is embodied as identity. The dislocation between experience and doctrine is counter-intuitive for the practitioner because it presents the social scientific and the theological as two distinct worlds that must be in some way reconciled. The turn to culture suggests that these disciplinary fragmentations are not entirely necessary. The turn to culture means that experience and doctrine are not read 'against the grain' through alienating disciplinary frameworks. Yet that the same time these disciplines are not discarded - rather they are reframed by the cultural. If the experiential and the doctrinal are to be read in relation to one another it will be necessary to make use of social scientific and theological methodologies. The interpretative scheme drawn from cultural and media studies in terms of production, representation, and consumption, shows how the social scientific and theological methodologies might be related through notions of performance. What is at stake in the theological debates concerning doctrine and experience is not simply the primacy of a discipline. It is much more significant to consider this debate as a struggle concerning the revelation of God. How and where is God present and how can we speak of his presence? The approach set out in this chapter moves beyond cognitive-propositional and experiential-expressivist perspectives to offer an alternative understanding of the encounter with God in the midst of cultural performance. As I have argued here, performance is not just lived in (by its human participants), it is also indwelt (by God). This again I would suggest is a recognizably theological approach to practical theology. The collapse of the experiential into the doctrinal in the cultural turn does not mean that the divine is at the same time reduced to the cultural. If the performance of doctrine is in-dwelt then the divine presence is mediated in the midst of cultural complexity.

7

Popular Culture Scholarship as a Spiritual Exercise
Thinking Ethically with(out) Christianity

TOM BEAUDOIN

Is there any way of going on that is not a turning back?
(Teresa of Avila 1957, p.123)

As this volume testifies, there has been a tremendous interest in relating theology and religion to 'popular culture' in the last few decades.[1] There has been a surge of publications in the last decade alone. While the reasons for this deserve their own research, the developments presented by these studies afford an opportunity to stand back and look at some of the larger questions raised by this turn to the popular and media culture in religious and theological studies.

I have had the opportunity to review many manuscripts in this burgeoning field. While I have learned something from each new exploration, I would like to recall one specific moment that provoked a question that drives the queries of this chapter. I was studying one of the many recent edited collections of essays about religion and popular culture. In this manuscript, movies, television, and music were made to interact with analyses drawn from sociology of religion, psychology of religion, and Christian theology, usually grounded conceptually through borrowings from cultural studies. Such collections have become one influential shape for theological and religious research in popular culture today (see, e.g., Mazur & McCarthy, 2001; Mitchell & Marriage, 2003; Gilmour, 2005; Marsh & Ortiz, 1997; May, 1997; Flory & Miller, 2000). Their form and content provoked fundamental questions in my reading that I shall submit as questions for the field. What is the value of our work? And whence do we draw a critical appreciation of such value? The emerging field has not been able to sufficiently raise or answer these questions.

In the collection before me—as in the field more generally—it was not clear why certain studies were grouped together and made to represent a field called 'religion and popular culture.' One minimally unifying element was that these particular essays dealt in some way with popular culture. Using Simon Frith's (1996) broad definition of popular culture—as the production of cultural objects 'of,' 'by' or 'for' 'the people'—these essays, and most all approaches in the field today, qualified. Another minimally unifying feature could be found in the use of religious or theological frameworks to situate popular culture, showing its overtly or covertly religious or theological character, or making it the site of critique—either from or toward religious or theological positions. Frequently, such research also celebrates popular culture's religious or theological character.

In asking about the value of our 'diversity' for a relatively young field, I do not mean to suggest that there needs to be one point of all such work, nor that such a 'point' or 'purpose' ought to be final, transparent, or available to a normative assessment. I raise the question not for the purpose of forcing a 'field' called 'religion and popular culture' out of a productive heterogeneity of scholarly advances. My interest, in other words, is not to attempt yet another theological disqualification of academic heterogeneity in method, commitment, or theme. It is, rather, to find a way both of understanding the significance of this heterogeneity, on the one hand, and thematizing this critical appreciation into a task for the future of the field, on the other.

What might theology have to contribute to the question of how a reader might receive a collection—or a field—that manifests a strong plurality, if not polycentricity, of topics, methods, and ethical, religious or theological commitments? Perhaps due to the 'blessed rage for order' (Tracy 1975) so characteristic of the contemporary theological mind, Gordon Lynch (2005) and Kelton Cobb (2005) have recently advanced research that attempts to name the ambiguities about the theological significance of popular culture, and its research, and to find a way of making clearer spiritual distinctions about the value of popular culture. Both seek to go beyond mere religious studies commentary, on the one hand, or a poorly theorized spiritual celebration or condemnation, on the other. Lynch portrays what is at stake in the field as a matter of judgment, and in particular, of 'normativity'. That is, how is one interpretation of popular culture authoritatively to be judged better or worse than another?

Cobb discerns what popular culture has to say about classic theological topics in ways that may lead postmoderns toward or away from devotion to God. The question becomes how one can spiritually 'sort out what is going on in the depths of popular culture' (Cobb 2005, p.294). I shall render the chief problem before us slightly differently: what is at stake for readers and writers of religious or theological engagement with popular culture? What I share with Lynch and Cobb is a curiosity whether an indifference to judgment adequately fulfills the ethical task of the one who attempts to think and teach theology or religion in the academy.

I would like to frame this problem as a question about the production of meaningful claims in the theological or religious scholarly engagement with popular culture. In so doing, I mean to locate such questions about our work in popular culture in relation to broader queries regarding the ethics and politics of academic theological production. In other words, how do we come to think that something significant occurs when we read or write of relating popular culture to theology or religion? To state this as a problem of ethical formation, how do you and I learn to read each other's pop culture analyses? Or to state it as a more personal and rarely raised problem: how do we learn to read our own analyses of pop culture? Approaching a way of thinking about these questions requires a brief consideration of two commonalities of work in the field: its self-involving character, and the economies of analysis generating such work.

Self-Involvement in the Field

In this field, scholars of religion or theologians are typically personally invested in their research topic, in a particular way. They seem to have some experience, usually not without pleasure, of the popular culture they are analyzing, or on rarer occasions, pleasure and personal investment in the religious renunciation of pop culture's relationship to religion. In other words, despite many of the topics dealt with in this 'field' being bound up with consumer capitalist culture, the academic engagement with them seems the occasion for, and the fruit of, the subjectivity of the scholar being thrown open. Indeed, one defense sometimes given for writing about pop culture and religion is that the topic allows for the pleasures of the scholar to be explored. 'To enter into reflection on the meanings and influences of popular culture [...] because "it's fun" is an effective starting point that requires no apology' (Forbes 2000, p.17).

Sometimes the personal relationship of the scholar to their topic is evident, sometimes only indirect; sometimes unabashedly foregrounded, and sometimes all but occluded by recourse to a sophisticated theoretical scaffolding (as if to signal, yes, this is fun, but it is also quite serious, and even if I didn't like movies, rap music, comic books, or *Sex and the City*, please understand that I am treating universal human themes, delimited qualities of a particular community, the construction or reception of meaning, or a critical issue of concern to contemporary religio-theological discourse). The participation of the subjectivity of the scholar in the analysis of culture is conceptually striated, worked up, organized, made clear or obscure, but made nonetheless. Religious and theological studies of popular culture seem to draw the sort of scholar who is involved emotionally, intellectually, and existentially, with popular culture. 'We' tend to be scholars who are aware of that our sense of ourselves has been governed by popular productions, whose are 'subject' in some way to, in, and through popular culture.

Such observations have become a clue about how to begin learning to read works in this field, allowing me to acknowledge that such an existential involvement was also true of my own writing about popular culture. My published theologizing began a decade ago with a rhapsodic essay on theological themes related to the musical *Rent*, continuing through essays on media, suffering, and the Iraq war, music video, the *What Would Jesus Do?* phenomenon, and corporate branding. I have been more or less aware from the beginning that in doing this sort of theology, I have been attempting to justify, appreciate, question, or expunge certain formative influences on who I have become in my dealings with pop culture, the theological life I have or have not been able to lead through my relationship with pop cultures, and also, who I see my students, friends, co-religionists, and fellow North Americans becoming in their relation to popular culture.

Such placements of the popular culture scholar are both signaled and withdrawn by many instances of autobiographical glimpses into scholars' vital investments in popular culture. These are rarely considered of significance, however, for the basic argument itself. For example, when Margaret Miles (1996, pp.xi-xii) writes about the freedom that movies offered from her restrictive and confusing religious upbringing, or Randall Holm (2005, p.160) writes about being 'strangely drawn' to the singer Jon Anderson through the 'undeniable spiritual import' he experienced in the rock music of Yes, or Robin Sylvan alludes to a 'long strange trip' (2002, pp.214-5) taken spiritually through profound musical experiences in Africa and California, such comments play the rhetorical role of 'prefatory' personal introduction to the more serious scholarly work to be done, although they presuppose an invite an analogous sympathetic identification from the reader, and more or less acknowledge that the relation of author to reader is that of fan to fan. It is at least as likely that the formative experiences hinted at by such modest disclosures play a silent structuring role in the work itself. As Bruce Forbes (2000, p.17) allows, 'Many of us come to the analysis of popular culture with a particular special interest, related to our own private enthusiasms (comic books, the Beatles, soap operas, or whatever).' It also seems significant that so many such 'peeks' allowed in scholarly work reference experiences with media culture during deeply impressionable stages in life, from childhood through young adulthood.

It seems, then, that scholars of religion or theology think about pop culture because we have felt the significance of being involved in it, or more, because in doing so we are also writing about ourselves, or further, because in and through this exercise we are aiming, with irremediably crooked arrows, to hit a target not yet in view—or already too much in view: ourselves. It makes sense, in other words, to read our intellectual engagements with popular culture in religion and theology not only as scholarly productions, in the accepted academic sense, but as a form of work on, or 'therapy' (properly understood) for, those who write and read them—in other words, as what I would like to call 'spiritual exercises.' These spiritual exercises are at varying degrees of awareness of themselves as such, whether conscious, inchoate, or potential, or most likely, a humid admixture.

Economies of Analysis

While Frith's three categories (and the schematizations of others – e.g. Strinati, 2004) provide a way of giving the field some coordinates by which to locate what it means by popular culture, the question of the economies of the production of meaningful works in our field can be productively examined, and can be related to the constitutive role of self-involvement outlined above. Indeed, the cultural formation of the scholar in their personal and academic life, which 'peeks through' our field with perhaps more frequency and legitimacy than many other areas of the academic study of religion and theology today, suggests a development of Frith's tripartite definition. As noted earlier, he defines popular culture as those cultural 'products' constructed 'by', 'for' and 'of' the people. However, the present consideration of the unacknowledged and pleasurable involvement of the scholar in their work in this field calls for attention to a fourth and perhaps counter-intuitive aspect, the popular culture of popular culture studies itself: that is, the question of how and why we are incited to write about popular culture and religion. In other words, the culture of the popular that facilitates the constitution of our field can be understood as that which scholars are permitted and encouraged to think about their own basic categories by their own religious and secular understandings of religious experience.

Why draw attention to the popular culture of our field itself? Kathryn Tanner (1997) has made a thoughtful and creative argument that academic theological production is its own form of 'popular culture,' analogous to everyday popular culture in its provision of cultural materials for authorized use (from materials like books and conferences, to ideas like *physis* and *psyche*) that are re-used by scholars to gain political advantage in the field by rhetorical strategies that fabricate weaknesses in others' texts as the site on which to take things in a different direction, and to 'trope' prevailing readings so as to be appropriately within and without acceptable boundaries—in order to be considered fresh research. This is analogous, Tanner shows, to how people in everyday life make do with the products and notions they are given, turning them to their own purposes based on the political and personal needs at hand. From such a perspective, it becomes possible to see how research in 'religion and popular culture' is not (only) the furtherance of a well-defined field of study, but a way of operating in and constituting objects for that field itself.

It is not Tanner's project, however, to define a way of thinking about what might be at stake for those who operate in these 'popular' fields. I therefore wish to complement Tanner's locating of the academic study of theology in postmodern cultural theories, with Michel Foucault's journey through his development of theories of social practice.

In particular, I refer to the research of Foucault on the fashioning of historically particular understandings of the popular, and the creation of the experience of the existence of a popular culture, through the governance of peoples by way of cultural practices that conduct them into a certain 'population'. This focus has been highlighted by several of Foucault's recently published Collège de France lecture courses from the 1970s (Foucault 2003a, 2003b, 2004; see also Burchell et al., 1991). This period of Foucault's work is the time of 'discipline' in his research, as famously schematized in *Discipline and Punish* (Foucault 1978). It is this period that is of particular preparatory importance for his later turn to an understanding of philosophical research into culture as a spiritual exercise. In short, a comprehension of the history of the Western disciplining of subjectivity was the clearing away that helped prepare for his so-called 'ethical stage,' the exploration of a more 'positive' sense of discipline: spiritual disciplines and experiments with *askesis* in his late work. But before I get to the more 'positive' meaning of exercise, I would like to indicate something of the exercises of social control from one of his works of this period.

We can take the recently published *Abnormal* (Foucault 2003b) as exemplary of this period of his work. In seeking to find out how Western culture came to be a site of continual incitements to declare one's sexuality and other 'deep truths', allowing one to be fitted into modern regimes that govern everyday life, he returned to the middle ages to ask: how did Catholicism create a population that thought that in order to be Christian one had to confess, and to confess in a certain way? In other words, how did a culture of confessing people come to be created and rendered normal in Western culture? In short, he answers, through the technology of the confessional. That is, through the creation of the experience of being part of a human society with unruly desires, and an ecclesial society with the cathartic redemptions of confession, so long as one can learn the practices that allow the passage through speech of one to the other.

Foucault comes to discuss the confessional as a way of explaining what happened to penance in the Western Catholic tradition. He describes how penance became bound up with practices of confession, and those practices were then situated in the official ecclesial language of 'sacrament,' and as a result, penance became a way that the power of the church was exercised over the faithful. In other words, the ancient Christian practice of penance becomes, with the Council of Trent, the site for an extension of 'ecclesiastical power' over the faithful, over their souls, desires, and bodies. Such an extension and concentration of power needs not only juridical declarations, such as Trent propounded, requiring yearly reception of the Eucharist and, in preparation for that, yearly confession. It required more than a juridical interlocking of these two sacraments. It required also a material space in which to symbolize this power and practically to allow it its reach. The confessional became such a space. As Foucault argues, the confessional was 'the material crystallization of all the rules that characterize both the qualification and the power of the confessor... There were no confessionals before the sixteenth century.' (Foucault 2003b, 181)

Confession becomes a technology that operates in society under the jurisdiction of the church. As the church manages confession through the sacramental system and ties it to the Eucharist, then that ecclesiastical power tightens by an elaboration of erotic investigation. Borromeo is an exemplar of this power, in its ability to open a relationship between people and themselves, on the one hand, and their confessor, on the other. To teach people to manage themselves according to this detailed and rigorous investigation of desires, temptations, excitements, curiosities. In a word, the flesh. This what Foucault names the 'Catholic technology' that is one of the major contributions of Christianity to Western culture. This governance of the Christian conscience becomes a way of teaching clergy and faithful a certain way of relating to themselves: through exercises of self-examination, they learn to suspect interior movements, feelings, desires. The existential value of the sacrament becomes its ability to effect surveillance over the body, or more specifically, that aspect of the body that threatens: the flesh.

What we learn from this movement in his thought, for present purposes, is that an ethics of religion and popular culture research can emerge from genealogizing the problem of the study of religion and popular culture itself. This would mean an examination of the cultural constitution of the disciplining of the popular and of popular religion, which—as Foucault's trajectory shows—raises both the question of the *askesis* not only of popular religion in culture but also of the researcher, insofar as to be concerned with the popular is, given Western history, to risk being an accomplice to social control (see Beaudoin 2004, 2005). Foucault speaks directly to our discipline:

> For a long time ordinary individuality—the everyday individuality of everybody—remained below the threshold of description. To be looked at, observed, described in detail, followed from day to day by an uninterrupted writing was a privilege. The chronicle of a man, the account of his life, his historiography, written as he lived out his life formed part of the rituals of his power. The disciplinary methods reversed this relation, lowered the threshold of describable individuality and made of this description a mean of control and a method of domination. It is no longer a monument for future memory, but a document for possible use. (Foucault 1978, p.191)

In other words, what we are doing in this field when we attempt to render clear the religious or theological plane of popular culture should be considered an ethical problem analogous to inviting people into a box to speak of their unruly desires. How does one imagine one's place as an ethical subject in a field such as ours?

For assistance, and as a theologian writing for an extra-theological audience, I shall turn to conceptions of spiritual exercises as I have learned them through Foucault and Pierre Hadot. From them, we can begin to comprehend that intellectual work on cultural problems can be a way of changing one's relationship to oneself in accord with a desire to live a certain sort of life, that making religious or theological sense of popular culture can be a spiritual exercise.

Spiritual Exercises Introduced - Foucault

In the last several years of his life, Foucault began to suggest that his researches were a way of working on his relationship to himself, of changing his relationship to himself and others (see Bernauer, 1994). Although such a clarification was perhaps never fully spelled out, the last years of his work are marked by this reframing of intellectual work as a spiritual exercise.[2] The question of how one evades entrapment to a presystematized relation to self was already built into Foucault's philosophy of practices of subjectivity, knowledge and power (Bernauer 1990). Foucault worked on his own attempt at greater freedom through careful intellectual work; practicing philosophy, he saw, could affect one's very mode of perceiving the world, one's existential orientation.

One of the clearest expressions of this new appreciation for his philosophy as a spiritual exercise occurs in his book *The Use of Pleasure*, published the year of his death, 1984. In this work, Foucault named his motivation for his research the 'only kind of curiosity...that is worth acting upon with a degree of obstinacy: not the curiosity that seeks to assimilate what it is proper for one to know, but that which enables one to get free of oneself.' He contrasts a mere 'knowledgeableness' with the importance of 'the knower's straying afield of himself' (Foucault 1990, p.8).

> There are times in life when the question of knowing if one can think differently than one thinks, and perceive differently than one sees, is absolutely necessary if one is to go on looking and reflecting at all...What is philosophy today—philosophical activity, I mean—if

it is not the critical work that thought brings to bear on itself? In what does it consist, if not in the endeavor to know how and to what extent it might be possible to think differently, instead of legitimating what is already known? The 'essay' — which should be understood as the assay or test by which, in the game of truth, one undergoes changes, and not as the simplistic appropriation of others for the purpose of communication—is the living substance of philosophy, at least if we assume that philosophy is still what it was in times past, i.e., an 'ascesis,'...an exercise of oneself in the activity of thought. (ibid., p.9)

The path to dealing with, and exchanging, one's self is indirect; a game of doubles. James Miller argued that Foucault tried on many occasions 'to unriddle a part of himself by writing about someone else entirely.' (Miller 1993, p.331) Miller argues that Foucault's different interpretations of Kant, Saint Anthony, and Diogenes were windows on Foucault's own struggles to comprehend and change himself. (ibid., pp.332, 342-4, 360) For Miller, Foucault struggled profoundly with a preoccupation with death that expressed itself in dangerous gay sexual practices. 'All of Foucault's books,' argues Miller, 'comprise a kind of involuntary memoir, an implicit confession,' all witnessing to his struggle to deal with 'the truth about himself.' (ibid., pp.372-3) 'I take all of Foucault's work to be an effort to issue a license for exploring [the] daimonic possibility—and also as a vehicle for expressing, 'fictively,' his own Nietzschean understanding of [his] harrowing vision of a gnosis beyond good and evil, glimpsed at the limits of experience.' (ibid., p.459 n.73)

But one need not agree with the Miller's judgment about Foucault's psyche in order to acknowledge Miller's insight about the exercise-styled forms of Foucault's spiritual and intellectual explorations. David Halperin (1995) disagrees strongly with Miller's deep psychological claims about Foucault, while agreeing that Foucault's life and work can be understood as askesis.

Halperin has read exercises in the context of Foucault's life as a gay philosopher. 'Foucault ultimately came to understand both philosophy and homosexuality as technologies of self-transformation.' (ibid., p.77) Gay sexual experience was parallel to, and intertwined with, other strategies and practices of truth in Foucault's books. Agreeing in a sense with Miller that the erotic is a central reference point with respect to which he changed his relation to himself, but finding Miller almost violently voyeuristic and 'knowing' about gay sexuality, Halperin shows how Foucault's philosophical writings and understanding/living of a gay sexual identity was a spiritual exercise insofar as it allowed him to get free of himself, to gain a critical distance from forces of social control that would organize, even 'humanely,' his relation to himself and others. Halperin (ibid., p.105) comprehends Foucault's commitment to the study of culture, especially to 'historical inquiry...as a kind of spiritual exercise.' To enact new possible relations to ourselves by understanding the historical contingency of who we have been is the spiritual work of Foucault's historico-philosophical scholarship. Halperin suggests that for Foucault, something about the self escapes the self and this 'alterity' of the self to how it has been constituted is that to which Foucault's politics and intellectual work appeal. Foucault's political work and scholarship show us experiments 'we [can] perform on ourselves so as to discover our otherness to ourselves in the experience of our own futurity.' (ibid., p.106) Gay sexual practices and the recent history of American gay life, for Halperin and Foucault, have helped 'cultivate in ourselves the ability to surpass ourselves, to enter into our own futurity.' (ibid., p.106)

Recently, philosopher Todd May has summarized helpfully how Foucault should be read as a 'philosopher engaged in spiritual exercises,' (2000, p.225) working on his relationship to himself through his intellectual exertion in thinking through the complexities of the European history of subjectivity. This happened through three forms of inquiry: showing the historical contingency of the knowledge of ourselves; showing that 'who we are is not so much the product of disinterested inquiry into our nature but instead of the result of social practices that have their own power arrangements'; and through offering other possibilities in history of relating to oneself and others as subject (ibid., p.225). It was this sensitivity to the imperative to change our relationship to ourselves that allowed Foucault to write of the 'fascism in us all,' in 'our speech and our acts, our hearts and our pleasures,' 'in our heads and in our everyday behavior, [a] fascism that causes us to love power, to desire the very thing that dominates and exploits us' (Foucault 1983, p.xiii). Foucault's comment about the imperative of Deleuze and Guattari's work is also a reference to the spiritual exercise performed by his own philosophy: 'Do not become enamored of power' (Foucault 1983, p.xiv; May 2000, pp.226-7). The philosophical-historical study of 'the popular' and of cultural practices necessitated a form of ethical attention to oneself, with exercises that come through and beyond one's intellectual work.

A Defense of Foucauldian Exercises for the Future of Theological Studies of Popular Culture

Many who have had some initial exposure to Foucault, especially through the power-knowledge texts that have become so influential in the study of religion, may be surprised at both this focus in his work and its being termed a spiritual exercise. Foucault seems to have adopted for his own work the notion of spiritual exercise from, among other places, the historian of ancient philosophy Pierre Hadot, who argued that ancient philosophy understood itself not as a mere rationalistic, speculative or theoretical sparring, nor as a mere 'intellectual' or 'academic' discipline, a potential 'major' or even 'profession,' much less 'career,' in the various senses that we think of the study of philosophy. Indeed, limiting philosophy to 'study' is our modern error—or at least impoverishment. Ancient philosophy, he argues (Hadot 1995a; Hadot 2002a), was a lived experience, a 'way of life.' Philosophical schools were not for the purpose of making a philosophical argument, but for training in the living of a philosophical life. Schools did this by forming philosophers to become a certain sort of person in the world through their unique spiritual exercises, practices that would help them to think and live according to wisdom.

In these works, there is an important link to the Christian theological tradition. Hadot shows how many early Christian theologians conceived of their work as a philosophy precisely in relation to the ancient sense, by which they meant both a way of thinking and a form of work on themselves, ways of changing one's modes of being in the world in quest of the divine life, which is the supreme life of reason: the *Logos*. Self-control and meditation thus make their appearance in Christian philosophy as spiritual exercises leading to life with God, manifest in a variety of ancient philosophical—now become Christian—practices of theology: exegesis, denomination of revelatory texts, arguments about the proper order of their study, examination of conscience, transcription of misdeeds, cultivation of a peaceful mind, a mindfulness of death, and in all, an attention to oneself. Hadot's exemplars of this trajectory of theology as therapy, that is, as Christian philosophy, are representatives of mystical, monastic and patristic theological traditions. He discusses theology as attention to oneself in Justin Martyr, Clement of Alexandria, Origen, Augustine of Hippo, Basil of Caesarea, Gregory Nazianzen,

Gregory of Nyssa, Evagrius of Pontus, Athanasius of Alexandria, and Dorotheus of Gaza (Hadot 1995b, pp.355-78; 2002b, pp.237-52).

At the same time, the future for which I am arguing in popular culture studies makes the new research on spiritual exercises an occasion and space for unseating the advantage frequently given to the Christian theological character of spiritual exercises (see, e.g., Blythe & Wolpert, 2004; Pungente & Williams, 2004; McNulty, 2001; Gallagher, 1997). This advantage has been so taken for granted that it has not been seen as an advantage in theological culture. Spiritual exercises have been, in theology and spirituality, more or less generally taken to be Christian provenance, property, or propensity. But if I can restrict myself to my own Catholic tradition for the moment: what if Christian exercises are full of holes that have already let in an ancient philosophical air that Christians have been inhaling and renaming in the same breath? Foucault (1990) argues that it may not be so much a matter of continuity of themes and topics between ancient philosophical exercises and Christian exercises, so much as the form of the exercises themselves, that migrated from 'pagan' to 'Christian' practice, like a Rubiks Cube that is at once quite limited in the ways it can shift in relation to itself, but at the same time within that narrow morphology can allow itself thousands of possible recombinations of colors. What cubes traversed (what we often too confidently think of as) 'the divide' between the 'pagan' and 'Christian'? Examination of conscience; rehearsal of aphorism; meditation on text; slow maturing progression through authorized writ; recollection of the master; memorization of useful and essential verses; remembering and rehearsing death; remembering and rehearsing birth; envisioning life from on high; serious conversation; teaching to influence the soul: through one's classes and through one's writing... and even (with Plotinus, says Hadot) through one's writing as a reflection of the dynamics of the classroom itself.

In our present moment, acceding to the depth of the 'technologies of self' that Christianity took over should occasion a radical sobriety on the part of Christian theology. It means that some of the most valued, respected and trusted forms of 'Christian' experience are strongly 'pagan', however much the contents may have shifted during transit. When Christians engage in exercises, they give themselves over to pre-Christian experiments in relationship, claiming their own version of Iamblichus' ancient neoplatonic conviction: we shall be saved by rituals of incomprehension.

But this also means that theology, if it can bear this askesis in and of its thinking, can help point the way toward a clarification of the ethical dimension of engagement with culture. After all, all of these exercises were 'moral' in the senses Foucault outlined: they were ways of taking up a relationship to culture, of making one's way through crises of action by means not of a 'code' to serve as constant yardstick for every situation, but by means of a way of experiencing oneself, others, and the world (and the cosmos, as Hadot's (1992) posthumous dialogue with Foucault reminds us) through practices that habituated oneself to be in a certain way, to, as Foucault tells it so well, have one's conduct emerge from the sort of learning that transcends moral codes.

Christian theology has its own duty to divest itself, through interrogation of its own history and practices, of—in principle—all claims to ahistoricity, first, and to uniqueness, second. The study of Christian spirituality, as exercises, should begin with a genealogical divestment for the sake of understanding what we have done, are doing, and might do to ourselves and others because of our exercises. And further, part of theology's therapy, or its penance, can be to help the theological, and religious, study of culture to understand itself as a self-involving and potentially self- and other-governing (in a word, subjectifying) pursuit, whether on the part of the scholar or of anyone willing to risk the demand to be (in the famous formulation of Bernard Lonergan (1990)) attentive, intelligent, reasonable, responsible, and loving.

In other words, on the one hand, Christianity (especially its sacramental tradition that prides itself on exercises) was wrong to think that how one interprets, studies and teaches—that is, how one learns to read what they themselves are writing about culture—the most basic, say of scholarly exercises—derive from an inner-ecclesial history and can be practiced in ways that are *sui generis* Christian. On the contrary: every Christian exercise of making defensible sense of culture—interpretation, study, and teaching—is a releasement to 'paganism,' a reliance on ways of being and registering the world that represents a profound otherness already within (and which will take much more careful research to appreciate its complexity). On the other hand, Christianity (especially the sacramental tradition that prides itself on exercises) was right when it has held that how a person interprets, studies, and teaches—that is, how they learn to read what they themselves are writing about culture—has an unavoidable importance for how that person relates to themself, to others, to culture, even to the cosmos. Writing about the religious or spiritual significance of culture is in our day, especially in regard to pop culture, an obvious, and frequently quite openly, self-involving task. It is also necessarily social and political, raising the question of the exercises that form the scholar to make religious or spiritual sense of culture, and (another way of saying the same thing) of the exercise that religious or theological writing about culture *is*.

For the Future of the Field

If popular culture changes the mind, soul, or perceptions of the individual scholars that are making the field, and if scholarship on popular culture can have that effect on people interested in the field, a turn to the ethics of learning to read one's own work and that of others in our discipline seems imperative. Thinking through exercises can be one way of beginning to approach that problem. Indeed, this chapter is intended as a contribution toward an ethics of theological and religious studies of popular culture. In taking the perspective of exercises, we may reconsider the very form of intellectual inquiry in the field, that is, beyond the problematization of theology 'of', 'or', 'and' popular culture, to emerge into the ethical problem of theological and religious *writing* about popular culture.

This perspective can be joined to the larger conversation about the self-involving character of the study of religion. Such work has criticized the study of religion as the covert advocacy of religiousness, lacking a sufficient criticality (see, e.g., McCutcheon, 1997, 2003). From the vantage of the present chapter, this concern can be interpreted as an involvement in religious questions as a form of spiritual exercise for the academic researcher, hence the quality of 'advocacy,' which may be a displaced, indirect way of working on oneself, and an elliptical testament to such work on oneself.

One important anxiety about the self-involving character of our field is that it is susceptible to dilettantism. One reason that dilettantism becomes a dirty word in pop culture studies is that it raises the specter that our inquiries are not entirely professional, academic, objective, or critical— generally accepted hallmarks of the modern study of religion. The objection to dilettantism is often a way of criticizing overly personalized interpretations published as scholarship. So Lynch (2005, p.41) criticizes analyses that 'may be of personal interest to the author but have little impact on wider cultural analysis or criticism', and Miles (1996, p.xi) self-effacingly writes of her 'relation to 'the movies' [as] one that may not be shared by many readers.' While Lynch's point about the threat to sophistication in scholarship due to retreat into private analysis is apt, and Miles allows some access to her own personal history of investment in the power of film, these distinctions can be read as trading on a dichotomy between an individual scholar's desires and the level of the cultural in intellectual work that a turn to spiritual exercises would read as a problematic bifurcation. There is still room for developing a conviction like that of Karl Rahner (1990, p.19) in the field of popular culture studies: 'I want to be a deeply thinking dilettante—and one who at the same time thinks deeply about his dilettantism and factors it into his thinking—but all with reference to theology's ultimately foundational questions.'

Dilettantes or not, theological or religious studies of culture are enactments of our relation to ourselves and others that re(in)habit the forms of experience that make us who we are. Letting through this politics of production of theological meaning can work as therapy—that is, thinking through the theological-religious government of self involved in the constitution of theological-religious interpretations of culture can bring the spiritual exercise that theology of culture already is into more critical, personal, and cultural perspective, an experience of the truth of theological interpretation of culture more efficacious for healing and insight because more available to conduction into the incomprehensible through which Christian faith thinks life practices.

This way of understanding the interpretation of culture is thus not finally selfish, or about 'getting in touch with ourselves,' nor about rehearsing a romantic autobiography, but about a critical releasement to who we have become and what we do to ourselves and other people. It is neither self-affirmation nor utopic social plan. Such analysis is a call to readiness for justice: 'Many are those who are entirely absorbed in militant politics, in the preparation for the social revolution. Rare, very rare, are those who, in order to prepare for the revolution, wish to become worthy of it' (Friedmann cited in Hadot, 1995a, p.70). A different perspective on our interpretations of popular culture is given, through an ethics and politics of theological production.

For the 'future of the field,' I would like to see this problem explored, which of course does not mean an uncritical repetition of the Hadotian or Foucauldian lines on these issues. In part, then, such exploration suggests an enrichment of our vocabulary, a defamiliarizing of our passions. But it is an enrichment about what is already going on, a matter of appropriating what is already happening in much of our writing: theological or religious analysis of culture as conscious, inchoate, or potentially indirect and retrospective figuration, refiguration, or—at the limit—transfiguration of the subjectivity of the author.

Learning how to read our works will be the first step into the future of the field. This, 'one of the most difficult' spiritual exercises, according to Hadot, is the one Goethe himself recommended at the end of a life lived much longer and more richly than the brief history of our field: 'Ordinary people don't know how much time and effort it takes to learn how to read. I've spent eighty years at it, and I still can't say that I've reached my goal' (von Goethe, cited in Hadot, 1995a, p.109).

---

[1] I am grateful to Jessica Coblentz for her research assistance and critical commentary.
[2] Foucault's lecture courses at the Collège de France, from 1971-1984, are now being formally published, and the last several years of courses promise to yield rich material on the topic of Foucault's understanding of spiritual exercises. The 1982 course has recently been published (Foucault 2005). See also on this theme McGushin (2007), Moss (1998), Taylor and Vintges (2004), Bernauer and Rasmussen (1987).

8

House Negro with a Field Negro Mentality

New Positions in Theology and Culture

ROBERT BECKFORD

I want to testify, that is share the themes that shape my standpoint, the place from which I gaze on the world as a theologian and documentary filmmaker. This is not a completely new task, as reflexivity has been the starting point for making connections between my story and the 'generalised other' in my work. In my published books, an auto/ethnography moves beyond the stilted subjectivity vs. objectivity debate and affirms inter-subjectivity as a means of determining knowledge (Beckford, 1998, 2000, 2001, 2004, 2005; Roth, 2005, pp.5-7). In my documentary filmmaking the boundaries between, art, life and ethics is dissolved by personal narrative.

These theoretical perspectives have emerged not merely from reading academic theory but also through participating and learning black Pentecostal liturgy, in particular the traditions of 'testifying,' 'signifying;' and 'prophesying.' The technique of *testifying* - sharing of personal (salvific) experience features in the worship of black churches where the African survival of 'call and response' is still practiced. Testifying is not merely concerned with sharing faith it also *signifies*: a focal point for passing on survival information. For instance, in my home church testimonies referring to 'defeating the work of the devil' is simultaneously an account of how to survive hardship and outwit racism in a hostile climate. Testifying has *prophetic* potential through dialectic of thought and action. When the saints of God think about the testimony they expect their words to result in action and ultimately change the way things are done. So for me, foregrounding my personal position is antiphonal: a call seeking a response and hoping for positive change.

Testifying has become an important strategy as a theologian and documentary filmmaker – two fields where the 'personal as political' cannot be escaped. I have never set out to be a theologian or filmmaker who happens to black but a certain type of black theologian working with film from particular contexts. Engaging with theology and the media from this standpoint requires continual reflection and renegotiation so as to ensure that my work retains a counter politics. There is a constant danger of complicity as according to Marxist critic, Louis Althusser (1971), education and the media systems are part of an elaborate system of domination, serving to reinforce dominant ideas through a process of interpellation. The fear of my own interpellation, that is, thinking I have a choice when really I do not, compels me constantly analyse the reconfiguration of systems or chart the dominant ideas in educational practice and the image-making machinery of documentary film. I realise that I am part of the dominant order and therefore require at least an oppositional practice grounded in the reality of my relative privilege. I must therefore constantly ask myself whether my work serves to challenge or merely reinforce dominant ideas. Or whether the opportunities I am granted is merely a licensed affair - permitted dissent.

So, I want to continue this testimony by firstly, identifying my gaze on the world. The gaze is the politicisation of looking and influenced by the double consciousness motif of diasporan cultures. My gaze is informed by three distinct standpoints. These are black theology, black British film theory and post reggae aesthetics. After examining these three positions, my main concern is to distil them into a new perspective on doing theology and culture from the privileged location of the 'ebony tower,' that is, the black theological academy.

The Gaze

My introduction to the socio-political dynamics of the gaze came from watching my parents. There were times in public when they confronting authority figures in an office situation or on the street when at a key point in the discussion they would *look* at their adversary in a particular way. I remember one occasion when my father was stopped in his new car by a police officer. I was only four years old at the time. My father had a way of looking people with a mix of inspection and distain, with his head slightly cocked to one side. He performed this ritual as the police officer checked his driving licence. What made this particular look distinctive was that he would turn immediately afterwards to look at me so as to invite me into the experience and learn the syntax. In *Black Looks: Race and Representation* bell hooks (1992) examines the ways in which diasporan folks 'looking' is politicised. In a context dominated by white supremacy, where there was retribution from whites for blacks that dared to verbalise their opposition to the status quo, it was necessary to signify. To look, stare or peep was one way to gain direction through indirection. In response, blacks developed an 'oppositional gaze', a transforming way of looking:

> By courageously looking, we defiantly declared: "not only will I stare. I want my look to change reality." Even in the worse circumstances of domination, the ability to manipulate one's gaze in the face of structures of domination that would contain it, opens up the possibility of agency. (ibid., p.116)

In this sense, the gaze creates a space where subjugated people can through looking at the 'Other,' look back and name what is seen. It is the naming that completes the construction of a language of recognition. hook's consciousness of looking has diasporan identification with my father's Jamaican tradition. So when my father looked at the police officer that had stopped him in his new car his looking at me was to teach me practices of resistance. I became aware that these 'dutty looks' (dirty looks) expressed a deeper level of meaning and required me to be inside and outside of a situation, a sort of double take on life. In fact, the politics of looking are grounded in the political culture of double-consciousness. Let me explain.

The double take on life, or double-ness, has a distinctive history in diaspora cultures. Double-ness as an existential condition was first given meaningful expression by the great African American intellectual W.E.B. Du Bois. Writing out of the segregated world of early twentieth century America where the post-slave world was still in the making, Du Bois presents double-ness as a conflict. In *The Souls of Black Folk* he states:

> the Negro is a sort of seventh-son, born with a veil, and gifted with second sight in this American world - a world which yields him no true self-consciousness, but only lets him see himself through the revelations of the other world. It is a peculiar sensation, this double-

consciousness, this sense of always looking at one's self through the eyes of others, of measuring one's soul by the tape of a world that looks on in amused contempt and pity. One ever feels his twoness - an American, a Negro; two souls, two thoughts, two unrecognized strivings; two warring ideals in one dark body, whose dogged strength alone keeps it from being torn asunder. (DuBois, 1903, pp.1-2)

For Du Bois, double consciousness was characterised by the struggle over social identity (American/Negro) and the fracturing of the Self (two-souls). But this affliction is contested, preventing a splitting the psyche, and it is this willingness to overturn the limitations of double consciousness that concerns me here. The problematic side of double-consciousness has been explored in a variety of scholarly works and none more forceful that the psychological studies of post-colonial intellectual Frantz Fanon (1967/1991). But there is another side to double-consciousness – the ways that diasporan blacks have made a potential affliction into a resource for example, double-consciousness as a hermeneutic.

Black British cultural critic Paul Gilroy describes double consciousness as a hermeneutic of marginality providing diaspora blacks with a unique (learned and taught) objectivity. It facilitates a decoding of modernity's complicity with racial terror; the ways that reason has served to brutalise and barbarise black bodies in Western histories and cultures. For Gilroy, being 'inside and outside' of the West has resulted in innovative responses. He identifies two: the politics of fulfilment and transfiguration (Gilroy, 1994, p.37). The former concerns black cultures' fascination with the hope for a better world or the notion that a future society will realise what is unaccomplished. The latter is rooted in a complex articulation of culture and exists 'on a lower frequency' where transfiguration is 'played, danced and acted' (ibid.). Here diasporan music, art, language and other forms of expressive cultures are inscribed with particular intellectual and moral genealogy that distinguishes them from many Western modes: for example, the ways that black popular cultures conflate art and life so as to 'refuse the modern occidental separation of ethics and aesthetics, culture and politics' (ibid., p.39).

Within the frame of double consciousness, the gaze has a dual role. Looking is not only a physiological but also a cultural function where looking is coded. In other words, looking is a 'language' shaped by history, culture and politics, and to decode the look one has to be able to understand it in the first place.

Looking is also related to place. I always look from a particular location and look back at myself in order to make sense of where I am. So on another level, my gaze is always personal and historically specific, and is open to being reconfigured and refocused. As Euro-American feminist Adrienne Rich (1987) noted in her reflections on location politics - race, class, gender, sexual orientation and geography all influence the way that the subject negotiates their position. So, I now turn to the second concern, to name the standpoints that influence my gaze. These are black theology, black British film studies and a post-reggae aesthetic.

Theology

The question of situating oneself is integral to theologies of liberation. Liberation theologians take seriously existence as a starting point, believing that all theologies are a quest to make sense of the universals of faith in particular social locations. This is not a new thought in Caribbean history, where the idea of making the subjective 'racial' position a point of departure can be traced back to the ethnic rationale behind the Baptist leadership of the Morant Bay Rebellion in Jamaica in 1865. It is a theme that resurfaces with the religious teachings of the early twentieth century pan African movement of Marcus Garvey. In recent years the notion of context has been developed in black liberation theologies in South Africa, the USA and the UK. There are two themes at work, first social location in scripture and second, the social location of the theologian.

Black Nationalist preacher Albert Cleage and Black theologian James Cone were some of the first diasporan thinkers to explore the social location of divine revelation. For Cleage (1968), the New Testament world is divided into two levels of operation: those of the oppressors (Romans) and oppressed (Jews). Naturally, the social location of first century Jews was resonant with the social realities of blacks in the 1960s. Within Cleage's ethnography first century Jews were black men and women - further solidifying the relationship between blacks in the text and the American context. For Cone, the relationship was more theological than biological. Within Cone's (1974) Christology, Jesus suffering as a Jew under Roman oppression is a sign of God's preferential option for the oppressed past and present. In addition, the resurrection is a signal of God's universal liberation action on behalf of the oppressed in the world today (ibid., p.134). But this view is contested. For some time, womanist theologians such as Delores Williams (1992) have suggested that God's preferential option does not always secure full, holistic 'liberation.' Through an analysis of Hagar, Williams exposes fissures in the liberation leitmotiv in scripture and contemporary life. So God may elect the oppressed but the nature and content of their deliverance is not so straight forward.

Turning to the second feature of context - the location of the theologian - biblical scholar Itumeleng Mosala (1988) was one of the first to interrogate location politics in the lives of black theologians in late 1980s. Writing out of the incendiary context of Apartheid South Africa, and using a vulgar Marxist approach to ideology, he warned black liberation theologians of the danger of inadvertently rearticulating ruling class values with a 'black face' (ibid., p.21). As an example of good practice, Mosala's hermeneutics calls for a materialist exegetical starting point grounded in the 'crucible of historical struggles' in order to effectively grapple with the black poor at home and abroad. Black Atlantic biblical scholar, Randall Bailey (2000) has reformulated Mosala's critique into an exploration of power relationships in biblical hermeneutics. For Bailey, issues of power including, gender, sexual orientation, race and class must be made explicit as 'biases' to develop hermeneutics with intellectual integrity. It is fair to say that since Mosala's critique serious attention has been paid to 'race,' gender and sexuality, but the niggling question of class location has been neglected, particularly in North Atlantic black theology. Let me explain.

While it is true that James Cone acknowledged the *potential* of Marxist analysis in broadening the critique of race to include class, this encouragement has only produced limited reflections. Amongst second-generation black theologians, African American scholar, Dwight Hopkins has done most to engage with the question of the black poor. In *Introducing Black Theology of Liberation* Hopkins (1999) calls for a social analysis that will help poor black people make connections between global monopoly capitalism and its control of the American economy. This theme is further developed in *Heart and Head* (Hopkins, 2003), where he reaffirms liberation theology's preferential option for the poor in the post-modern world. Drawing from the multiple analysis of poverty in the work of Gustavo Gutierrez, Hopkins outlines a new strategy for the redistribution of wealth.   So, whilst there has been some progress, there is still some way to go to make class location a serious feature of black theological reflection.

In my gaze on the world and looking back at Black Theology, I have prioritised ideological criticism. Viewing ideology as an attempt by a particular group to fix meanings, I have sought to make clear my own class location and how it influences my approach to interpretation. In *God and the Gangs* (Beckford, 2004), I contour a 'reader response' hermeneutic to merge the socio-economic horizons of the biblical text and material poverty and economic disadvantage in the present. In terms of the results of 'looking' from this location, in *Jesus Dub* (Beckford, 2005), I began the tasks of developing a new pneumatology for sharing resources and modelling a new praxis, that is, commonwealth – an inversion of prosperity doctrine. In documentary film I have always located myself as a privileged western black male. This class location receives special attention in my film *Undersize Me* (Channel 4, 2007). In this project, I identify the ways that the World Bank, International Monetary Fund (IMF) and multinationals corporations 'conspire' to keep West African States undersized or 'impoverished. I pay special attention to how diasporan blacks, like myself may inadvertently collude with oppressive global economics.

In sum, my theological standpoint is informed by the location politics of black theology, a position that recognises a tension between material condition and divine activity.

Documentary

The struggle for freedom for black Britain is multilateral and wrestled with at the level of culture. In recognition of the strategic importance of culture as a source for theology, for the last eight years I have been involved in doing theology and culture through documentary film. This expansion of my craft began initially as an attempt to demonstrate to television commissioning editors   that black people were able to do more than sports and music on British television! My early work won critical acclaim and resulted in me becoming a contracted presenter with Channel 4 (one of the main terrestrial TV channels in Britain) in 2005. On average I present three films a year exploring issues of 'race,' religion, politics and culture. Hence, the second standpoint informing my gaze is the politics of visual culture explored in documentary film.

Black British filmmaking foregrounds the subjectivities of filmmakers. While not a crude reflection of the world in which we live, film, including documentary film, is not independent of economic and political processes and material conditions. Every film signifies. I am interested in two things, the politics of hegemony within television output and the politics of difference.

Regarding hegemony, growing up in a highly racialised society, I quickly learned not to identify with and also to question the positioning of black subjects. I can illustrate this with reference to two examples from my watching of a television as a child in the 1970s. At the beginning of *Top of the Pops*, the weekly music programme, I would count the number of black artists in the charts and then compare how many featured in the coveted live appearance on the show. I soon discovered that the numerical dominance of black artists in the top 30 failed to translate into a live TV appearance. Asking more critical questions emerged from viewing the actor Ron Eli playing Tarzan on Saturday mornings children's TV. I attempted to identify with the main character as the filmic codes demanded, but failed. So, instead I sat confused and contemplated the racial hierarchy at work: white Tarzan = Good, Africans = bad. To quote Frantz Fanon (1967/1991, p.153), my 'white' mask was removed and I became cognizant of the fact of blackness. Fortunately, I found alternative spaces for constructing a healthy sense of self particularly through the church. On Sunday mornings through the expressive physicality of worship, the fixed identity of Saturday morning television was overturned and replaced it with the complex subjectivity (Pinn, 2003a) of black Pentecostal faith.

Regarding the politics of difference, the content of television and film attracted sustained discussion in the 1980s. Spurred on by the theoretical support of the fledgling black British cultural studies, black film collectives such as 'Sankofa' and the Black Audio Film Collective began a sustained criticism of the representational politics at work in British television and film. The question of context or the 'politics of location' emerged as a way of identifying the problems encountered when reading cinema theory and literature in the context of ethnicity/sexuality. Put simply, these 'cultural creatives' identified the ways that visual imagery is bound up with socialising processes and is therefore an important space of critical debate and social engagement. In response to what they perceived to be demeaning and stereotyping they developed oppositional practices that set about constructing more complex and dynamic images and themes to explain as well as contest marginality.

Faced with fixed negative imagery they responded in many cases with fixed positive imagery and inadvertently created a limited range of images of black life - silencing minority constituencies within the black community. There was therefore a need to find new tools to examine oppositional practices and move beyond a celebration of black presence to a critical assessment of it. For black British cultural critic, Kobena Mercer (1994), a solution to this postmodern crisis lay within a critical dialogism:

> Critical dialogism has the potential to overturn the binaristic relations of hegemonic boundary maintenance by multiplying critical dialogue within particular communities and between various constituencies that make up the "imagined community" of the nation. At once articulating the personal and the political, such dialogism shows that our "other" is already inside each of us, that black identities are plural and heterogeneous and that political divisions of gender and sexual identities are to be transformed as much as those of race and class. (ibid., p.131)

Critical dialogue reveals a multiple-situationality within us all. It repeals the fear of the Other by identifying the Other within the Self. We occupy a variety of positions simultaneously. In theory a dialogic approach to difference should unite both those who prioritise sameness in pursuit of racial justice and the pluralists affirming diversity. That is, a focus on identity politics that identifies similarities and differences should not fragment of the collective struggle for racial justice. But this has not always been the case as the study of film in the black Atlantic is contested space where essentialists and pluralists battle for the souls of black viewers (see Alexander, 2000, p.110).

In response to these issues, my filmic standpoint, that is, my perspective as a documentary filmmaker, acknowledges the importance of film as a cultural site in the struggle for meaning. Film provides a counter discourse that may, if only momentarily, challenge the dominant ideas. In this sense film provides a more far reaching resource for raising critical questions than written academic texts in theology. In a post-literate culture where visual imagery has displaced the West's fascination with logocentrism, documentary film represents a new frontier in the communication of theological ideas. As a theological text, the religious documentary facilitates theological-aesthetics, that is, visual and aural satisfaction and meaning derived from the digital representation of the faith matters. The strengths and weaknesses of this new approach are too numerous to countenance in detail here, but for now what is important is that my looking involved a theological practice that seeks to capture the existential 'real' to the film 'reel.'. Second, I agree with Mercer's organising principal as a way of forging alliances across class and gender in black communities. That is to say, 'when looking back and naming' as part of the gaze it is crucial to find ways to unite and forge commonality without marginalising that which is different. Finally, I acknowledge in my looking the importance of affirming the politics of 'difference' but agree with Mike Dyson (1997, p.71) that difference and sameness should be held in tension in diasporan cultures because black people were oppressed as a group not because of individual identity.

Post-Reggae

The final framework for my gaze is history. Where we situate ourselves historically plays an important role in structuring the gaze. Historical positioning is another way of identifying how and why I am interested in particular things. I want to identify myself as someone who has lived between the interstice of two radically different paradigms; those who were born in the early to mid sixties and grew up in the 70s with 'old Labour' socialism, but who came to adulthood under Margaret Thatcher in the 1980s and experienced the move from manufacturing to service industries. In Britain, the shift from heavy to service industries, from stockpiling to 'just in time' manufacturing, and from a fixed labour force to part-time workers with few rights or pension provisions, revolutionised trading, working conditions and consumption. This shift in social and economic history played a significant role in shaping cultural identities. The shift is also characterised by movement from a nostalgic notion of a fixed and stable black community to black experience as heterogeneous. Changes in cultural identity also led to a reworking of identity and cultural politics in popular cultural forms and I want to illustrate the impact of socio-economic history though a brief description of the emergence of new territory occupied in reggae music, that is a post-reggae aesthetic. The reason for exploring the changing historical terrain is because the re-positioning of politically motivated reggae music within this new world provides new paradigms for negotiating historical fissures.

A *post-reggae aesthetic* denotes the shifting terrain of popular culture since 1981. While there is some dispute when this new moment arrives, I want to mark the beginning of this new experience with the death of Bob Marley. Robert Nesta Marley embodied the totalising impulse in black cultural identity in the 1970s. He almost single-handedly maintained the dominance of 'conscious' reggae music with its fixed notions of blackness, gender roles and global political positions. Theologically, he promoted Rastafarian sensibilities in reggae music. Rastafari was an exorcism of the sorcery of European Christianity - its collusion with racial terror and black dehumanisation. Reggae's central antidote was to reconstruct the categories of divinity, humanity and soteriology through a theological reflection on Haile Sellassie, the emperor of Ethiopia. Marley's death signalled the decline of a conscious popular reggae and the rise of more complex, fluid and contradictory negotiations of culture, politics and identity in Jamaican music at home and abroad.

But there were other factors that influenced this shift, including the global shifts in the means of production associated with the consolidation of Edward Seaga in Jamaica in the early 1980's. In the Caribbean the more robust global economic climate meant a decline in the prices for raw bauxite, a refocusing on tourism and a tougher trading environment for agricultural produce. The decline in income and increased reliance on International Monetary Fund for economic policing of the economy reduced the capacity of the Jamaican government to intervene and promote good standards of health, education and work programmes. The restructuring of global economies coincided with the weakening of black power movements in the black Atlantic and continental Africa. Rastafari, black power and black socialism failed to produce black-utopia in Jamaican and a new a generation of youth looked to new themes in music to engage with the new social and economic climate:

> [T]hose who rose to prominence in the dancehall in the 1980s exhibited no clear attachment to the ideas and Ideology of Rastafari and African pride, because the ideology of capitalism encapsulated into its own ideas - individualism, materialism and its attendant moral values. (Hope, 2006, pp.13-4)

Set free from the domination of conscious music reggae dancehall appeared to retreat into bio-politics, making the focus of concern physical control, local concerns, and hyper-real sexuality or 'slackness'. However, not everyone agrees with this assessment. Jamaican academic Carolyn Cooper argues that this re-territorialisation represents a new contestation of power relations, particularly in gender relations. She suggests that beneath the references to elicit sexual practice and prowess, lies a subtle critiquing the moral hypocrisy of the Jamaican middle-classes. For Cooper (1995, p.141), the DJ potentially represents 'a politics of subversion, a metaphorical revolt against law and order; an undermining of consensual standards of decency.' It is nothing short of 'a radical, underground confrontation with the patriarchal gender ideology and the pious morality of fundamentalist Jamaican society' (ibid., p.41). Despite this carnivalesque revision of dancehall's cultural politics, the current shift still remains primarily a retreat from the public sphere. The bedroom, 'bashment' and the Benz have replaced the public square, democratic participation and the pursuit of public freedom.

The changing terrain has its own specific and peculiar manifestations in different locales. What is helpful for me is the rise of Rasta-Dancehall DJs such as Damien Marley. As one of the sons of the legendary Bob Marley, Damien chose the craft of the DJ rather than the singer to explore Rastafarian beliefs and sensibilities in the new world order of reggae dancehall. This 'Junior Gong' demonstrated in *Welcome to Jamrock* (Island Records 2005) that it is possible to bridge the old and new orders. Through a clever deployment of a range of subjects to both entertain and educate his listeners he revealed that it is possible to engage in a double subversion – challenging the social world and also re-politicising dancehall culture. Living in two camps provides an opportunity to re-position consciousness within dancehall space as a lived tension (both/and) than an opposing force (either/or) (see Henry, 2006, p.174).

Returning to the gaze, when I look and then look back, I am faced with the tension of living between two historical paradigms. I am particularly motivated by its negotiation by Rasta DJ's navigation of the changing historical and cultural landscape by re-visioning life based on new lived contradictions and strategies. The new vision represents a both/and proposition, that is, conscious DJ's position themselves simultaneously within and outside of dancehall, accepting its genres but subverting their meaning. In the past, I have made use of this new position to rethink the relationship between the disparate traditions of Rastafari and Pentecostalism and also to live in the liminal space of the public theologian (Beckford, 2000).

To restate the testimony so far, my gaze is informed by theology, film studies and a post-reggae aesthetic. The look is interpretive, making sense of what is seen. It is also proactive in that it creates a sense of agency and initiative. The outstanding question is how this gaze is distilled into a critical perspective within the theological academy. I want to suggest that the double consciousness, being inside and outside of a situation that informs the look also structures my critical perspective on the business of doing theology and culture. To address this final concern, I want to revisit Malcolm X's notion of the house and field slaves.

Inside and Outside of the Master's House

Malcolm X tells us of two types of slaves, the house Negro and the field Negro, in order to explain the lack of radicalism amongst the black middle class in the 1960s. The house Negro lived in the master's house, ate his food, loved the master more than he/she loved himself, identified with the master and could not envisage no better place. In contrast, on the same plantations were the majority field Negroes. Field Negroes hated the master and believed that any place was better than where they were. Naturally Malcolm sided with those in the field. In my appropriation of the theory (Beckford, 1998), I was critical of Malcolm's omission of resistance from the location of the 'house'. There were many Caribbean rebellions planned and executed with assistance of house slaves. I want to continue to revise this position, to reveal my academic location. I believe the house and field slave can be conceived as form of double consciousness as I can identify both experiences of being in the house and also the field.

I've never been called a 'house negro' or a sell out - well not directly to my face! I'd like to think that I have not been confronted in this way because I have always worked hard to keep my academic work in the grassroots of African Caribbean life in Britain. My scholarship is inspired by bell hooks' affirmation of an engaged pedagogy or teaching method, and aims towards liberation. Even so, the privilege I am afforded as a lecturer and broadcaster clearly places me in a more central social and economic position. In other words I live and work in the Master's House. However, I was born raised in a poor immigrant family. My parents were part of a wave of post-war immigration from Jamaica in the early 1950s that travelled to Britain in search of a better life. They settled in a working class neighbourhood and set about building a life and raising children. They were colonial subjects and believed that education provided the best opportunity for advancement. I went to a multi-cultural inner-city comprehensive school where education was a fight than a human right. I was one of the few, in fact the only African Caribbean male of my class to go onto higher education. In short, the formative years of my life were spent overcoming social deprivation and what African American educationalist Carter Woodhouse terms state sponsored 'mis-education'.

Like the majority of my generation and in the words of Malcolm X, I was raised 'in the field'.

So if one can be simultaneously in the field and in the house, my academic location can be conceived as a double consciousness of class – 'two souls' of the black privileged in Britain. I want to call my reading of this space as being *in the Master's house with a field mentality*.

This critical position from within the academy has two central modalities for operation. First, recognising that being a theological educator provides access to resources both intellectual and material. However, having a 'field mentality' is to embody the resistance traditions that were evident in my upbringing. In this location I seek to gain cultural influence by aligning myself with the concerns of those outside of the house. It places me in a dialogic, organic catalytic role: what Cornel West (1991, pp.19-20) terms the 'new politics of difference' where one seeks to align oneself with 'demobilised, depoliticised and disorganised people in order to empower and enable social action and if possible, to enlist collective insurgency for the expansion of freedom, democracy and individuality.'

Second, it seeks to engage with the battles in visual culture recognising that discourse influences action. As one of a few African Caribbean documentary filmmakers in the UK, I am uniquely placed to develop a discursive practice geared towards engaging with questions of identity, politics and socio-economic empowerment, what I have termed in *Jesus Dub* as a *praxis* approach to cultural criticism. Finally, and to return to the introduction to this paper, this position is rooted in a black church episteme, that is to say the trickster like practices of testifying, signifying and prophesying inform 'House Negro/Field Negro discourse'.

In closing, I remind you that at the end of the personal testimony in black Pentecostal churches, the congregation have the opportunity to respond to what they will affirm the one testifying with shouts of 'Amen,' 'praise God' and 'hallelujah' or with rounds of applause. But affirmation or identification is never guaranteed. What is guaranteed is the value of deciding to record 'what God has done,' or 'what God is doing.' I submit this testimony in full knowledge that I have at least located myself in time, space and faith. Can I get a witness?

9

What is this 'Religion' in the Study of Religion and Popular Culture?

GORDON LYNCH

As this current volume demonstrates, the study of religion and popular culture has been a flourishing sub-field within the academic study of religion in recent years. New insights have emerged from this literature about the role that media and cultures of everyday life are playing in shaping and transforming contemporary religion, the ways in which various media function as a space for the negotiation of religious identities, debates and conflicts, and the possible religious functions that media and popular culture serve beyond the boundaries of traditional religious institutions. One of the strengths of this literature is that it has typically operated on the basis of the analysis of lived examples, working 'bottom-up' from empirical data, rather than imposing pre-determined 'top-down' theories on cultural resources and practices. There is still more to do in encouraging greater methodological sophistication and rigour in this literature, and scope for developing wider theorising about religion and contemporary culture based on these smaller-scale case studies. But in general this growing literature has the potential to offer a rich seam of insights into the evolving forms of religion in a rapidly-changing globalized and mediatized world.

One significant gap in this literature, however, is the lack of critical attention to the very category of 'religion'. Much of the literature in the study of religion, media and popular culture proceeds on the basis of the assumption that the meaning of religion is relatively straightforward. This assumption is problematic, however, for two main reasons. Firstly, by simply adopting existing definitions or categories of 'religion', the study of religion, media and popular culture cuts off the possibility of making a significant contribution to our understanding of how we can define and understand religion. The study of religion and popular culture should have higher aspirations than simply borrowing concepts of religion taken from other sources, and should rather see itself as having the potential to add to theoretical debates about the nature and structure of religion in the contemporary world. Secondly, the concept of religion has found itself the focus for fresh contestation in religious studies literature in recent years. Influenced by Foucauldian and post-structuralist analysis, writers such as Jonathan Z. Smith (1988), Russell McCutcheon (1997, 2003), Talal Asad (1993, 2003), Timothy Fitzgerald (2003) and Richard King (1999) have sought to demonstrate that categories such as 'religion', 'mysticism' and the 'secular' have particular geneaologies in Western cultural history, and are bound up with different political and cultural projects from Western colonialism to a modern liberal Christian theology which sought religious universals in all human societies. For reasons that I will discuss later in this chapter, I regard these critiques of the concept of religion as valuable, but reject Fitzgerald's claim that the study of religion should be deconstructed and simply dissolved into the wider study of human cultures. As I will argue here, there is something distinctive about religion and the sacred where it appears within fields of human culture, and the study of religion, media and popular culture has the potential to shed more light on its nature and significance. Understanding the nature of 'religion' in the study of religion, media and popular culture is therefore an important step in the process of making connections between this field and the wider academic study of religion and the contemporary world.

Before going on to offer my own analysis of how we might define 'religion' in the study of religion and popular culture, it will be helpful to analyse the strengths and limitations of other approaches commonly used in this field.

Substantive, Phenomenological and Functionalist Assumptions in the Study of Religion and Popular Culture

Literature in the study of religion and popular culture has tended to borrow concepts of religion from three well-established approaches to the definition and categorization of religion used in the disciplines of religious studies, and the sociology and anthropology of religion. The first of these, substantive models of religion, operate on the basis of identifying certain core elements that are present in socio-cultural systems that can be defined as 'religions'. In other words, substantive definitions of religion focus on what religion is. A commonly-cited basic example of a substantive definition of religion is Edward Tylor's statement that religions are fundamentally constituted on a 'belief in spiritual beings' (see Bowie, 2005, pp.18-22). Subsequent substantive definitions (particularly of 'world' rather than 'primitive' religions) have elaborated on this belief in gods by citing common elements such as religious institutions, sacred texts, sacred spaces, rituals, universal religious truth claims, and distinctive religious personnel as constitutive of religions. Whilst this approach runs into certain difficulties around the categorization of non-theistic systems such as Thervada Buddhism – 'can something be a religion when it is not based on a belief in a god or gods?' – it has become a widely assumed approach to the definition of religion in both academic and wider public contexts. Indeed substantive definitions underpin the idea of a canon of institutionalized religions (e.g. Islam, Christianity, Judaism, Hinduism, Sikhism, Zoroastrianism, etc.) which can shape not only academic and public consciousness, but assumptions about what constitutes religion for various legal purposes. The category of 'new age' religion can be understood in this context as an attempt to extend the boundaries of the canon of religion to take in new forms of spirituality, and at the same time to provide a clear label within which a rather amorphous range of spiritual beliefs and activities can be contained. The category of 'new age' does not then fundamentally challenge the idea of a canon of religions, but merely revises it by providing a remainder category into which spiritual initiatives that do not fit into existing canonical religions can be tidied up (see Lynch, 2007, pp.1-6).

Substantive definitions of religion are implicit in large sections of the literature on religion, media and popular culture. Studies which focus on the production, consumption and use of media and popular culture by religious groups, interventions by religious groups in response to media texts and popular cultural practices, and the representation of religion in media and popular culture, all typically assume substantive definitions of what constitutes religion. 'Religion', from this perspective, is defined by the substantive canon of institutionalized religions, and any form of intersections between the structures, symbols and traditions of these religions with media and popular culture are fair game for research.

A second approach to the definition and categorization of religion in the study of religion and popular culture draws on phenomenological understandings of religion. In some respects, phenomenological accounts of religion share similarities with substantive definitions, in that both are interested in trying to identify common features of religion that recur across different historical and social contexts. A significant difference, however, relates to the method by which these common features are identified. Substantive definitions typically proceed on the basis of identifying externally-observable social structures, constructions of time and space, symbols and behaviours (i.e. the institutions, spaces, symbols and practices that people create in relation to a belief in God or gods). Phenomenological approaches to the study of religion place much greater emphasis on understanding universal features of religion through empathic engagement with the lived experience and perceptions of people in relation to religion and the sacred. Phenomenological studies of religion have yielded their own classifications of key elements of a 'religion' (see, e.g., Smart, 1998). Some scholars working within this approach have also argued for the significance of culturally universal phenomena which have religious significance, such as myth, ritual and an experience of the numinous, which may not necessarily be contained within the boundaries of religious traditions and institutions. This opens up the possibility, as Mircea Eliade (1957, pp.204-5) suggested, that influential contemporary myths may be as likely to be found in the cinema as in the church, synagogue or temple. It is not difficult to see why the notion of religious categories that transcend formal religious traditions and institutions would be of interest to scholars studying religious patterns in media and popular culture, and the influence of this phenomenological approach is evident, for example, in Martin & Ostwalt's (1995) study of contemporary myth in Hollywood cinema as well as DeChant's (2002) study of the ritual of Christmas in modern consumer culture.

This phenomenological approach occupies a middle space between substantive definitions of religion, and the third approach to the definition and categorization to be discussed here, namely the functionalist approach. Like substantive definitions of religion, phenomenological approaches seek definitions and categories that establish key features of religion or (to use Eliade's more inclusive term) the sacred. However, phenomenological approaches share the openness of functionalist definitions to seeing forms of religion outside the boundaries of the traditional canon of religions. Where as substantive definitions of religion focus on trying to establish what religion is, functionalist definitions focus primarily on what religion does. Functionalist definitions have been developed particularly in the context of the sociology and anthropology of religion. The two most influential such definitions have emerged from the work of Emile Durkheim (1912/2001), who understood religion in terms of a socio-cultural system which binds people into a particular set of social identifications, values and beliefs, and Clifford Geertz (1973), who defined religion as a framework of symbols which provide a grounding source of meaning for human cognitions, moods and motivations. Functionalist definitions open up the possibility that any socio-cultural system which serves these basic 'religious' needs for community, identity and meaning could be defined as religious, even though it may fall far outside the conventional canon of religions. Thus nationalism, cinema-going, sports fandom, retail therapy in the marketplace of branded consumer goods and the production and consumption of popular music could all be understood as religious insofar as they serve these basic religious needs. Functionalist understandings of religion thus underpin Bruce Forbes' (2000) category of 'popular culture as religion'.

Each of these approaches has both its strengths and limitations as a source of definitions and categories for the study of religion and popular culture. Substantive definitions have the value of delineating a relatively clear field of study. We know what falls within the study of religion and popular culture within this approach, because it will involve structures, symbols or practices relating to one or more of the substantive religions (e.g. the use of Hindu symbolism in Bollywood cinema, Islamic responses to the Danish cartoons of the Prophet Mohammed, or the development of kosher mobile phone products for ultra-Orthodox Jews). As one scholar commented to me, it can make sense to restrict the study of religion and popular culture to this field because it avoids the conceptual and methodological confusions that can emerge when one attempts to look for religion outside of the boundary of the canon of religious traditions and institutions. Even within this clearly delimited boundary of study, research into religion and popular culture still has a great deal to tell us about the ways in which established religious traditions and communities adapt and evolve in late modernity, and what their significance might be in the complex field of modern, pluralist societies. Studying lived cultural practices in relation to religious institutions and symbols can also provide an essential basis for theorising about how religious life-worlds are constructed and maintained. In this respect, the study of religion, media and popular culture based on substantive definitions of religion can form an important part of the current turn to the academic study of religion and everyday life (Ammerman, 2007). At the same time, however, approaches to the study of religion, media and popular culture informed by substantive definitions of religion have significant limitations. As Thomas Luckmann (1967) proposed in his seminal book, *The Invisible Religion*, there can be an inherent conservatism in approaches to the study of religion which focus simply on the fate and evolution of institutionlized religions. Indeed, Luckmann argued, focusing on the decreasing sphere of influence of institutionalized religion risks missing the bigger story about the sources of operative values and beliefs for most people in increasingly secularized, modern societies. Limiting the study of religion, media and popular culture to issues related to institutionalized religions could therefore blind us to some of the most pressing questions about the stories, values and meanings that shape many people's lives today.

A further problem, faced not only by substantive but also phenomenological approaches to the definition of religion, concerns the post-structuralist critiques of the concept of religion noted earlier. In seeking to offer generalized definitions of the substance of religion, substantive and phenomenological definitions of religion have typically failed to provide reflexive accounts of the social, cultural and political contexts which have shaped these definitions. As writers such as Asad, McCutcheon and Fitzgerald have argued, the concept of 'religion' is the product of a particular trajectory of Western intellectual thought, shaped by the Enlightenment, Western imperialism and more recently the Western push for global legal, political and economic frameworks. Rather than offering a framework for understanding universal religious categories within human societies and individual experience, concepts of 'religion' emerge out of a particular phase of the social imaginary shaped by Western culture and may distort as much as clarify our understanding of human cultures. Timothy Fitzgerald has, for example, argued how substantive and phenomenological definitions of religion perform very poorly as analytical lenses through which we might understand Japanese culture and society. Whilst the study of religion and popular culture based on substantive and phenomenological models of religion represents a viable approach within a particular tradition of the academic study of religion, this is still arguably a tradition that needs to be more reflexive and self-critical of its basic categories and concepts, and indeed of the very notion of a canon of institutional religions.

In some respects, a functionalist approach to the study of religion and popular culture avoids difficulties associated with a substantive approach. If we are indeed living through a significant time of religious transition in which significant identities, meanings, values and beliefs are shaped by forms of popular culture rather than institutional religion, then functionalist definitions of religion can provide a more flexible framework for taking the religious pulse of contemporary culture. As Luckmann argued, understanding religion in terms of its functions in bringing meaning to the raw physical data of human experience can raise important questions about how and from where people draw such meanings in the contemporary world. At the same time, however, a functionalist approach also has significant shortcomings. Like substantive and phenomenological approaches, functionalist definitions have shown little reflexivity about the conditions in which they have been produced. As Daniele Hervieu-Leger (2000, p.50) argues, for example, Durkheim's definition of religion can be read as a generalized projection of a model of religion derived from Catholic Christianity in late nineteenth-century France. There is also a need for greater reflexivity about the way in which power is constructed between the academic researcher and lived phenomenon of religion in functionalist approaches. Whereas substantive and phenomenological approaches tend to take seriously the lived meanings that religious affiliation and practice has for its adherents, functionalist approaches claim to discern the true meaning of religious activity beyond the false consciousness of the religious practitioner. Thus, in Durkheimian terms, behind the lived sense of devotion and worship of God, lies the real cultural work of encountering and sacralizing the one and only true source of power, namely human society. Functionalist approaches therefore give the academic researcher the power to claim they understood the real meaning and purpose of religious practices over and against any explanations offered by those involved in them. Whilst the outsider analysis of lived forms of religion can doubtless provide useful insights and balances to insider accounts, there is a danger that the kind of outsider account of religion offered by functionalist approaches can be reductionist to a degree that we fail to understand the significance that lived religion actually has in people's lives. Functionalist approaches to the definition of religion also make possible a form of disciplinary imperialism, in which religious scholars claim new parts of the territory of human cultures to be their valid sphere of interest. This may be useful in refreshing ideas about what it means to study religion, but runs a significant danger of imposing religious concepts and categories onto forms of cultural practice for which they do little useful analytical work and obscure more than they clarify.

Yet a further problem for functionalist definitions concerns the issue of what is distinctive about religion. Is it reasonable to suggest that any socio-cultural system that creates identity, meaning, community and a shared moral order for its participants is 'religious'? As Paul Heelas (2000) observes, Thomas Luckmann's definition of religion as frameworks which make sense of the raw data of our experience, is more or less indistinguishable from the concept of 'culture'. Where does the study of religion end, and the sociological study of cultural values begin? And is there any difference between these two fields anyway? If we answer no to this question, then perhaps Timothy Fitzgerald is right, and we should admit that the study of religion should really be dissolved into the field of cultural studies. At this point, though, I still want to argue that there is something different about religion and the sacred compared to other aspects of socio-cultural systems – a point we will return to in the final part of the chapter. For now, though, it is worth noting that to assume that whatever serves to construct identity, community, meaning and moral order can be defined as serving religious functions (and therefore, in effect, as religious), represents a basic categorical error. I can get to my local train station by bicycle or by car. Both my bicycle and car serve the function of transporting me there. But that does not mean that my bicycle or car share anything in common beyond them being both means of transport. The emotional, aesthetic and practical aspects of using either is quite different, as are their cultural connotations, and the social and environmental effects of their use. To lump the car and bicycle together simply because they serve the same function is to miss fundamental differences in the nature and significance of their use. Similarly, to assume that sports fandom is analogous to being a Charismatic Christian because both provide means of experiencing membership in an ecstatic community that binds its members into particular forms of identity, is to miss the fundamental differences between these two experiences and practices. Experiencing the touch of the Holy Spirit in a Charismatic meeting has neither the same quality, significance or implications as watching one's soccer team score a goal – and blurring these two different experiences under functionalist concepts of the 'religious' obscures more than it reveals.

On further examination, then, there are significant problems with the various conceptualizations of 'religion' that underpin much of the existing literature in the study of religion, media and popular culture. Studies that draw on substantive definitions and categories may have the advantage of a certain clarity about their subject area, but fail to address the potentially religious significance of how issues of identity, meaning and value are being negotiated by the majority of people outside the context of institutional religion in the West. On the other hand functionalist definitions, which seem to offer greater freedom to the researcher wanting to pursue the vein of ultimate concern in particular societies, suffer from theoretical reductionism and the dangers of imposing religious categories onto cultural phenomena in ways that obscure rather than illuminate their subject. All of these approaches also typically suffer from a lack of reflexivity about the cultural and political conditions from which their definitions and categories are produced. Is it possible to have a theoretical concept of religion and the sacred which can inform the study of religion and popular culture in a way that addresses these difficulties? In the final part of this chapter, I will now attempt to set forward such a concept as a thought-experiment for further discussion and refinement.

The Rehabilitation of the Sacred for the Study of Religion, Media and Popular Culture

'[Modern] nonreligious man (sic) descends from homo religious, and whether he likes it or not, he is also the work of religious man; his formation begins with the situations assumed by his ancestors... Profane man cannot help preserving some of the vestiges of the behaviour of religious man, though they are emptied of religious meaning. Do what he will, he is an inheritor. He cannot utterly abolish his past... that behaviour is still emotionally present to him, in one form or another, ready to be reactualized in his deepest being. For as we said before, nonreligious man in the pure state is a comparatively rare phenomenon, even in the most desacralized of modern societies... [T]he modern man who feels and claims that he is nonreligious still retains a large stock of camouflaged myths and degenerated rituals.' (Eliade, 1957, pp.203-5).

The approach to understanding the 'religion' in the study of religion and popular culture that I will propose here involves a return to the concept of the sacred. This quotation from Mircea Eliade illustrates some basic assumptions that have been attached to the notion of the sacred in the study of religion. According to Eliade an orientation to the sacred is a basic element of the human condition – we are all part of homo religiosus – and this grounding awareness of the sacred is only something that has been lost relatively recently through the process of modernization. Yet even now, Eliade suggests, an inarticulate need for the sacred still works itself out in secularized societies through the turn to 'camouflaged myths and degenerated rituals', amongst which he and subsequent writers have included the media, entertainment industries and sport. In this quotation we also see reference to the sacred's 'other', the profane. The profane, in Eliade's terms, can be defined in one sense as everything that the sacred is not (ibid., p.10). Thus if the sacred refers to the way in which the ultimate and transcendent touches spaces, objects and human experience, the profane refers to spaces, objects, practices and experiences which do not bear the mark of the sacred and which are everyday or quotidian. In addition to this Eliade (ibid., p.14ff) comments that the terms sacred and profane refer to two different 'modes of being', or two different ways of experiencing and being in the world. To live in a sacred world means having particular sensitivity to places, objects and practices which provide a focal point of encounter with the ultimate source of reality and power of the cosmos. To live in a profane world means having a flattened sensitivity in which all places, objects and practices have fundamentally the same tone, quality and significance, other than the meanings that are given to them by an individual's personal biography (e.g. 'this place is special because it was where I first fell in love') (ibid., p.24). Similar uses of the concept of the sacred are evident in Emile Durkheim's (1912/2001) sociology of religion – in which the sacred becomes the focal point of the socially-binding cult – and in Rudolf Otto's (1917/1968) phenomenology of religious experience – in which it functions as the focus and source for universal patterns of experience of the numinous.

It is important to say at the outset that I do not think that these concepts of the sacred are in themselves a promising basis for the study of religion and popular culture – or at least not without considerable revision and rehabilitation. The use of the concept of the sacred by writers such as Eliade, Durkheim, and Otto has been subject to such sustained critique in recent years that one might wonder whether Daniele Hervieu-Leger (2000, pp.42ff.) is indeed correct to refer to the sacred as an 'impossible concept'. One of the most telling criticisms of the notion of the sacred as it appears in the work of these theorists is that it despite purporting to offer an objective social scientific tool for the study of religion, it actually represents an implicit liberal (Christian) theological project of maintaining a sense of the transcendent in secular and pluralist societies. By retaining a notion of the sacred as an ultimate other, which may find expression in different forms of cultural representation, it becomes possible to reconcile absolute transcendence with cultural pluralism and to maintain some kind of belief in a universal religion. The concept of the sacred therefore becomes a means for re-branding of God for a modern age. But whilst this project may be laudable in theological terms for those wishing to find a universal religious dimension to human life, it means that the sacred becomes more questionable in sociological terms as an analytical concept through which we can interpret various forms of social and cultural practice.

Whilst there are significant difficulties in how the concept of the sacred has been used in this tradition within religious studies and the sociology of religion, it can still be an important concept for grounding the study of religion and popular culture. To make the concept of the sacred usable for the study of religion means, however, jettisoning some of the scholarly baggage that has become attached to this term over the past century.

Firstly, it is important to reject the assumption made by Eliade, Durkheim and Otto that the sacred is a universal feature of all human cultures (even in its 'degenerated' modern forms). There is a certain circularity to these theorists' argument in this respect. They assume that all societies have some form of the sacred – and therefore whatever binds people into a community, or structures identities, time and space within a given society is interpreted as evidence of the sacred. The concept of the sacred is not so much tested through their work, but functions as an interpretative template into which all social and cultural data are fitted. Their analysis is also based on the highly questionable assumption that what is true of 'primitive' societies necessarily serves as a model on which subsequent societies build, and that broad generalizations can be made about human cultures across a range of historical and social contexts. Assuming that the sacred is a cultural universal may also be theologically attractive for some people, but it is an unnecessary assumption to make in terms of the social scientific study of religion. There is no need to make this assumption ahead of any empirical evidence that concept of sacred is actually useful for making sense of particular societies, and this is a point on which a degree of agnosticism may be preferable.

Secondly, it is important to reject the binary opposition constructed by writers such as Eliade and Durkheim between the sacred and the profane.

This binary is unhelpful because it creates a false distinction between mundane everyday life, and the realm of the transcendent mediated through specific spaces, rituals and personnel. For example, in his account of Durkheim's sociology of religion, Anthony Giddens (1978, p.93) makes the distinction between the sacred time and space created through religious rituals and the 'profane, utilitarian world of economic production'. But one of the achievements of research on religion and popular culture has been to show that such a distinction is false, particularly so in the context of late modern consumer societies. The production of commodities by the contemporary Christian music industry, for example, is both an act of 'mundane' economic and cultural production, yet at the same time functions as an important resource for identity-construction and religious experience (see, e.g. Ward, 2005). Making clear distinctions between the sacred and the mundane is therefore unhelpful because it fails to recognise the role of the mundane in the construction of the sacred. To be fair to Eliade, he did recognise the possibility of the sacralization of everyday life activities when lived in relation to the sacred, writing about the 'sacrality with which man's (sic) vital functions (food, sex, work and so on) can be charged' (Eliade, 1957, p.14). But even this notion still retains too close an association between the sacred and transcendence for it to be useful for the analysis of the sacred in contemporary culture. As Paul Heelas (1996; see also Heelas & Woodhead, 2004) has argued, one of the defining features of contemporary societies has been the sacralization of the self, in which the struggles, growth and interior life of the individual have developed a sacred quality without any necessary reference to a transcendent sacred or external religious authority. Such a sacralization of the self cannot be reconciled with Eliade's association of the sacred with transcendence or Otto's description of the sacred as that which is 'wholly other', and the way in which Eliade negotiates this problem is to see such signs of the sacralization of the self as 'degenerated' forms of the sacred. In sociological terms, however, there is no need to make this kind of value-judgement, which in fact seems to reflect an implicit theological judgement about what constitutes the 'authentic' sacred rather than a social-scientific analysis. It is true to say that concepts and practices of the sacred do create boundaries, and separate insiders from outsiders. But to understand these differences and boundaries in terms of the binary between the sacred and the profane means buying into an unhelpful set of assumptions about the sacred as transcendent and the profane as quotidian, which are simply unsustainable in the analysis of contemporary religion, media and popular culture.

Another reason why the binary of sacred-profane is unhelpful, in terms of Eliade's construction of it, is that it tends to create historically naïve accounts of a golden age of religiosity in the past, and also neglect the ways in which notions of the sacred remain extremely powerful in pluralist, late modern society. Understanding pre-modern societies as lived through a sacred 'mode of being' is to neglect the ways in which pre-moderns may have conducted their lives with little or no reference to the sacred. Equally, the challenges of the resurgence of religious activism in late modern, pluralist societies points to the fact that contemporary culture contains several vigorously competing notions of the sacred. Even if Eliade were right in the mid twentieth-century to point to the desacralization of certain modern societies, the progress of globalization means that competing signs and practices of the sacred flow across national borders, creating an ever more complex field of global human culture. After 9/11, it is very hard to claim that the world of late modernity is one in which concepts and practices of the sacred lack power and significance (see Lincoln, 2006).

A third aspect of the concept of the sacred to be rejected from its previous scholarly use relates to the issue of the sacred and religious experience. The work of William James (1902/2002) and Rudolf Otto (1917/1968) has been important in constructing the idea of religious experience as an internalized, privatized encounter with the sacred or the numinous which may only later take externalised forms of the social and cultural practices of institutional religion. But again, one of the achievements of the literature on religion, media and popular culture has been precisely to demonstrate that religious experience is not something that takes place prior to cultural practices and expressions, but that religious experience is constructed precisely through engagement with particular cultural practices and resources – whether through popular religious iconography, music, dance or other media. The sacred is encountered in and through culture, not in some privatized, mystical space that is separate from it.

If we strip all of these unhelpful accretions away from the concept of the sacred, then what are we left with? I would like to propose the following definition:

The sacred is an object defined by a particular quality of human thought, feeling and behaviour in which it is regarded as a grounding or ultimate source of power, identity, meaning and truth. This quality of human attention to the sacred object is constructed and mediated through particular social relations, and cultural practices and resources. Religions are social and cultural systems which are oriented towards sacred objects.

This definition points to important aspects of the sacred. Firstly, an object can be understood as sacred because of the particular kinds of human thoughts, feelings and actions that it motivates and which are directed towards it. It is an 'object', then in the sense of psychoanalytic object relations theory, in which the object exists in the individual psyche as an externally-perceived reality whose meaning and significance derives from its place in the individual's or group's mental object relations field (see, e.g, Rizzuto, 1981; Greenberg & Mitchell, 1983). In principle any object can be regarded and experienced as sacred – whether G-d, the Buddha, the self or Elvis. There is no need for the sacred object to be associated with transcendence in theological terms. What makes it sacred are the particular thoughts, feelings and actions that are experienced by individuals and groups in relation to it. Secondly, it is possible to identify a particular quality of human response to sacred objects which is constitutive of the human-sacred relationship. This is characterised by a sense of the binding nature of the sacred object, which exerts a gravitational pull on the feelings, motivations and behaviour of individuals and groups that goes beyond their sense of their own free, individual agency (for a rich discussion of forms of engagement with sacred objects, see Orsi, 2005). There is, if you like, a kind of stickiness associated with the sacred. It binds people into particular kinds of identities, communities and ways of living which are experienced as not simply of their own free choice, but as compelled or inspired by the sacred object. Even those for whom the self exerts a sacred quality may feel that their choices are compelled by the sacred pull of personal authenticity. This stickiness may be experienced as loving, empowering and compelling – but equally for others with more ambivalent feelings towards a sacred object, this stickiness can be repellent, a potential trap for being caught into ways of thinking and being that are inauthentic or oppressive. The sacred object may therefore be experienced positively as a binding agent that holds together the lives of individuals and communities, or more negatively like existential fly paper that seeks to trap people and limit their freedom of thought and action.

Such a definition of the sacred avoids many of the difficulties noted above. It does not assume that the sacred is a universal feature of all human cultures, but denotes a particular phenomenon which it may be possible to identify in relation to specific individuals, groups and cultural systems. It does not require the use of the unhelpful binary of sacred-profane, and indeed simply abandons the term profane in favour of raising questions about the kind of social boundaries and cultural practices and resources that emerge in relation to sacred objects. It does not project the sacred as a universal numinous experienced through privatized mystical experience, but recognises the role that specific social and cultural structures and resources play in the construction and mediation of particular sacred objects. Indeed, in terms of Giddens' (1986) structuration theory, the sacred object retains its sacralized quality only through the recursive reproduction of the sacred object through specific practices.

What, then, would the value of this understanding of the sacred be as a basis for the study of religion, media and popular culture? Firstly, it provides a conceptual framework that allows for the possibility of different competing and complementary sacred objects to function at the same time within a given cultural system. This is essential for making sense of the nature and significance of diverse forms of the sacred in the context of the cultural and religious pluralism, mediatization and globalization that provides the background for the study of contemporary religion, media and popular culture. Secondly, unlike substantive definitions of religion discussed earlier, this concept allows for the possibility that culturally significant forms of the sacred may occur beyond the canon of traditional, institutional religions.

Thirdly, it avoids some of the significant problems associated with functionalist definitions of religion. It takes seriously the cognitive, emotional and motivational associations that insiders ascribe to their sacred object as evidence of the particular kind of relationship that they have with that object. Insider accounts of the sacred are therefore taken seriously as data, rather than treated to the reductionist gaze of functionalist analysis. Even more importantly, this notion of the sacred makes it possible to distinguish between sacred and non-sacred sources of identity, meaning and community. The sticky, binding, compelling qualities which are constitutive of sacred objects are significantly different from other sources of identity, meaning and community which are not experienced as binding with the same intensity. Someone might therefore find community, identity and meaning in their participation in a fan group for the band, *Arcade Fire*, but it is unlikely that they will experience *Arcade Fire* as sacred in the same way or to the same degree as a committed Muslim would regard the figure of the Prophet. Indeed there is some evidence that young adults in various contemporary popular cultural scenes can actually be quite critical of their unusual peers who ascribe sacred significance to their activities, seeing them as lacking a proper sense of perspective (see, e.g., Lynch, 2002, pp.78ff.). This point is further illustrated by a recent review of data from the latest British Social Attitudes survey which argues that religious communities are more effective at binding their members into particular identities and (usually conservative) moral values than other cultural sources of identity (Heath, Martin & Elgenius, 2007). Understanding the difference between sacred objects and other cultural sources of community, meaning and identity which are not experienced as sacred is therefore important in clarifying the nature, extent and significance of sacred objects in contemporary cultural life. Through understanding more about the nature and significance of such sacred objects, we may learn more about what are arguably some of the strongest motive forces in contemporary fields of human culture. A fourth advantage is that this concept of the sacred opens up the possibility for greater attention to psychological aspects of the relationship with sacred objects. The literature on religion, media and popular culture is characterised by an almost complete lack of attention to what psychological theories and concepts might have to contribute to this field, and the particular model of the sacred proposed here opens up the possibility for a much greater use, in this instance, of object relations theory as a resource for researchers in this field.

What kind of research agenda would be set if the study of religion and popular culture were grounded in the concept of the sacred that has been set out here? If sacred objects are an important source of cohesion and motivations for individuals and groups, then understanding more about the sacred objects which are operative in contemporary cultures becomes a pressing task. The study of religion, media and popular culture can play a valuable role in clarifying the nature of significant sacred objects, particularly as they are recursively reproduced through various media and popular cultural practices. More specifically, though, this field of research can clarify *how* sacred objects are reproduced through such resources and practices. What role do different forms of media production and consumption play in nurturing (or indeed undermining) the human experience of being bound to sacred objects? How are different human senses engaged through media and popular culture to serve as means of contact with sacred objects? And what role does aesthetics or emotion play in reproducing a sense of relation to the sacred through media and popular culture? These questions focus on trying to identify where the sacred is to be found in contemporary culture, and to understand more about how sacred objects engage with their adherents through media and popular culture. But we might equally ask about the significance of sacred symbols which circulate in media and popular culture in ways that are far-removed from conventional meanings for their adherents. The example of the figure of Jesus in the South Park cartoon series comes to mind here, with Jesus reduced to a failing chat-show host for a local cable TV station in small-town Colorado: a case of a sacred symbol which, in this instance, has lost its stickiness in terms of binding people into an experience of Christian devotion. Contemporary forms of media and popular culture thus not only serve to deepen relations with sacred objects for some people, but at the same time provide a mechanism through which sacred objects can be rid of their compelling nature and treated in playful and ironic ways. What can we learn from these instances of the playful and ironic use of sacred symbols in contemporary media and popular culture? What might this tell us about the ways in which the sacred may not only compel and bind people, but also become a focus for various forms of resistance against the lure of the sacred in the contemporary world?

There is much still to be resolved with these ideas. I have presented this argument with a strong focus on contemporary culture, but as Jeffrey Mahan reminds us in his earlier chapter, the study of religion, media and popular culture should not be confined to the present. If the concept of the sacred explored here is utilised as a basis for research in this field, this raises complex issues for comparative historical work. Is the nature, extent and significance of sacred objects in late modern society comparable to that of pre-modern societies? What is the significance, for example, of pre-modern and late modern understandings of the self for the ways in which individuals and groups engage with sacred objects? Attention to issues of historical difference can only help to nuance our understanding of the nature and significance of sacred objects. Finally, as I noted earlier, other attempts at the definition of religion have been criticised for failing to reflect on the cultural and political conditions of their production. This is something that I have not fared much better with myself here, and is an issue to which I will need to return again in more depth. For now, though, it might suffice to say that I recognise that the project I am proposing here is a product of pluralist, late modern society in which understanding more about competing sacred objects might help us to minimise cultural misunderstandings and conflicts that might otherwise threaten to destroy the fabric of our societies. I do not necessarily claim any universal significance for the definition of the sacred that I have proposed here, but merely suggest that the kind of insights it could help us to gain about our contemporary situation might help us manage the complexities of our cultural situation more wisely.

10

On a Mission from God
African American Music and the Nature/Meaning of Conversion and Religious Life

Anthony B. Pinn

Rap music in particular and hip hop culture in general offer for African American Religious Studies a paradigm shift, a conceptual alteration of African American theological reflection, one that promotes a turn toward a fuller arrangement of organic source material – with theoretical ramifications. By examining the religious rhetoric and practices of rappers Tupac Shakur and Snoop Dogg, this essay exposes the troubled relationship between religious language, and perceived religiously motivated activity. In the process, it offers an alternate means by which to access the nature and meaning, the accompanying framework of religious experience. Rap music is used as a problematic by which to encourage attention to prevailing theories of religious experience promoted as normative within African American Religious (assumed to be Christian) Studies. In this way, theoretical and methodological challenges are posed to the normative manner in which the authenticity of African American religious commitment and experience are gauged and verified.

Black Christianity and the Saved Life
In all cases, one might think of African American religion as the quest for complex subjectivity, the urge toward a fuller sense of one's meaning and importance within the context of community (Pinn, 2003a, pp.157-200). This theory of religion assumes that religiosity involves in part a response to dehumanizing forces (e.g., racism, race-based discrimination) faced by African Americans across centuries of life in the Unites States. Over against what I suggest here, most theories of conversion and African American religious experience tend to highlight and privilege such

experience as explicitly marking a transformation, suggesting a new posture toward existential commitments. They also tend to see such a posture as contributing to a refined sense of one's ontological connections and resulting obligations. This, I would argue, for example, is the basic meaning of African American Christian proclamation of religious experience, particularly conversion, as a 'new' person, one whose thought and practice are guided by a surrender to Christ augmenting certain moral and ethical arrangements. Religious experience and life so understood involves the affirmation of and attempt to perpetuate the substance of conversion as marked by: (1) confrontation with one's spiritual (and related mundane – such as moral missteps) shortcomings; (2) wrestling with old postures and perceptions over against possibilities of a new consciousness; (3) new consciousness and related ways of being in the world (ibid., pp.157-79). Taking place within this context of conversion is a disassociation from the secular, an epistemological tenderness resulting in an attempt to step 'lightly' through the world and in this way avoid its contaminates, and provide a proper example of moral and ethical correctness.

One's newly recognized and accepted ontological significance and merit (i.e., revitalized image of God) is matched by a new posture toward the world in line with a community of the like-minded. In the words of the spiritual:

> You say the Lord has set you free. You must be loving at God's command.

Through this posture, African American Christian workings of religious experience, again with particular attention to conversion, suggest that the weight of transformation revolves around both a new posture toward the world – e.g., an altered perspective on the manner in which bodies occupy time and space – and, more importantly, a set of rather reified ethical and moral norms drawn in large part of a rather traditional reading of the Hebrew Bible and the Christian Testament:

> Therefore, if anyone is in Christ, he is a new creation. The old has passed away; behold, the new has come. (2 Corinthians 5:17, King James Version).

In significant ways, religious experience involves the placement of certain bodies in new contexts, a new matrix of interactions, recognition, and exchange whereby bodies are both 'in the world' but 'not of the world.' Thick relationship with Christ, surrender to the plan and will of God as African American Christians might name it, involves a new experience of the body – one through which the body becomes an interactive vessel promoting and contributing to the will of God. The body continues to change over time, yet such mundane and existential alterations are now viewed as holding secondary significance to the transcendent connection to God through Christ. In this respect, religious experience involves a re-envisioning of the body through an appreciation, tenuous as it may be, of the body while also seeking to place the physical in proper context. Never able to jettison fully the dualism of body vs. soul, African American religious experience of the Christian variety involves a contestation won: the mundane, the physical body and its environ, monitored and controlled to some extent by the mechanics of the soul force (i.e., the Divine and Its will). Albeit a marriage of practices never perfected, there is a continual sensitivity to spiritual failure and its historically arranged ramifications, as well as a push toward 'perfection' in one's behavior.

African American Christian denominations differ with respect to the emphasis placed on the ability of humans to live out 'perfection' in one's commitment to Christ. Some, such as the Church of God in Christ, argue doctrinally for the possibility of a 'clean' life through sanctification and the presence of the Holy Spirit as the internal guiding force or compass for life decisions. However, African American Methodist and Baptist churches tend toward more doctrinal flexibility concerning the manner in which conversion results in rigidly transformed life arrangements. Nonetheless, all seem to agree on a basic assumption that conversion involves at the very least a new epistemological posture toward and sensitivity to how one 'moves' through the world. This is because religious experience, again conversion as a prime example, involves a perpetuated arrangement – a continual maneuvering – marking a tension between the draw of 'this world' and the promise of better possibilities. It is, in a word, a thick and multi-dimensional evolution.

Rap and the Religious Life

Much in popular culture bears out this African American Christian sense of religious experience as extension of conversion; yet, there are ways in which this notion of religious experience qua conversion is challenged by other modalities of popular culture. That is to say, many understand African American religious experience as related to the thinking and living out of conversion in ways that shape the perception of the body and how it occupies time and space – shifting both thought and action along rather rigid ethical and moral standards and frameworks. However, rap artists such as Tupac Shakur and Snoop Dogg, for instance, suggest another way of marking and arranging religious experience. For such figures, conversion involves a more committed and uncompromising posture toward the world. It connotes a shift in one's approach to the world that signals sensitivity to and embrace of one's presence. In this way, for such figures, conversion does not require a change in behavior or interest, but rather a deeper awareness of self, of one's value, and one's 'weight' within the world – not the world as one imagines it, but as it is with all its warts. Such thinking renders useless a typical black Christian pronouncement: 'We are in the world, but not of it.' Such a shift acknowledges the manner in which Tupac Shakur frames his work: 'my music is spiritual, if you listen to it…It's all about emotion; it's all about life' (Dyson, 2001, pp.138-9).

Tupac frames the exposing and unpacking of the spiritual dimension of his existence in ways, like African American Christians, that recognize the absurd nature of historical realities. He notes the difficulties of life, the ways in which socio-economic and political arrangements – the real and raw nature of life – impinge upon efforts to survival, if not thrive: 'You know they got me trapped in this prison of seclusion. Happiness, living on tha streets is a delusion.' ('Trapped,' *2Pacalypse Now*, Jive Records, 1998) Again, in both instances, for the Christian and for Tupac, the world represents a troubled and troubling location – an arrangement of tense relationships. However, the response to such a predicament differs in these two cases. Whereas, for Christians, transformation of such circumstances involves a conversion – a reconstruction of self – that resolves the world by problematizing engagement with the world, Tupac's response involves transformation of self into the 'thug.' In this way, conversion does not mean disengagement from the world, or an effort to purge the si(g)ns of worldly involvements, but rather a more energetic engagement with the world (Pinn, 2006).

The 'thug' does not reject the world. Instead, the mark of transformation entails an epistemological shift resulting in clearer vision concerning the possibilities embedded in the complexities of life. For Tupac, it appears, conversion need not point beyond the world, but to a greater recognition of the beauty within the grotesque. Such a stance, as cultural critic Michael Eric Dyson remarks, has theological and moral consequences. Images of life and visions of existence promoted in rap that run contrary to the dominant Christian ethos 'produce competing views of black selfhood and the moral visions they support.' Furthermore, 'if such visions of black selfhood imply a spiritual foundation, then a conception of God is not far away. It is easy enough to detect the divine in hip-hop communities that value traditional expressions of religious sentiment. But what of thug culture' (Dyson, 2001, pp.210-11). The epistemological posture, existential entanglements, and ontological assumptions that guide traditional African American Christian notions of conversion are not embraced by Tupac. Rather, conversion does not involve a rejection of worldly arrangements and mechanisms of life, but rather recognition of the divine in even the despised – or thug – modalities and aesthetic of life.

For the Christian, conversion amounts to a sustained push toward a Christ-like existence. This is also the case for Tupac, but it is the 'Black Jesus' who shapes life transformation vis-à-vis conversion. Such a religious move does not entail surrender to absurdity, a morphing into an unrecognizable connection to the absurd. Rather, the convert's posture toward the world involves the movement of the trickster, not the traditional Christ. The trickster recognizes and signifies life arrangements that trouble most – pushing for a more vibrant existence that does not fear the world. Tupac, like the African American cultural figure of folktales, Brer Rabbit, or the thug as convert, calls the roughness of the briar patch 'home'. The story goes this way: Brer Rabbit is in trouble for taking an item that did not belong to him. And as punishment he is given the option of being thrown into the briar patch or in fire:

> Some say to th'ow him in de fiah, and some say th'ow him in de brierpatch. Br'er Rabbit, he don't say nothin'. Den, Br'er Fox say, 'Br'er Rabbirt, which one you ruther us do?' Br'er Rabbit, he say, 'Th'ow me in de fiah, please, Br'er Fox; dem old briers jest tear my eyes out, if you th'ow me in de brierpatch.' So dey tuk him and th'owed him in de brierpatch. And Br'erRabbit, he shook he'se'f and jump 'way up on de hill and laugh and say, 'Thank you, Br'er Fox. I was bred and born in a brierpatch.' (Reed, 1989, p.31).

Like Br'er Rabbit, some rap artists like Tupac signify and improvise in such a way as to make the difficulties of life, existential challenges, a place of relative comfort.

It is true that Tupac denounced 'thug life' when interviewed in 1995 by *Vibe Magazine*, but isn't it possible that what he moves against is a certain formation of the thug, one that gives little attention to the deeper shades of existence (Powell, 1995)? Perhaps this is similar to preacher and theologian Howard Thurman's (1979, pp.101-136, esp. pp.113-15) rejection of the form and fashion of Christianity while committing himself to the religion of Jesus? It might, then, be the case that Tupac rejects a modality of the 'thug' that does not reflect authentic embrace of the ways of Black Jesus. In his words,

> All I can say is I always try to be a real nigga in my heart. Sometimes it's good, sometimes it's bad; but it's still us. It's never to hurt nobody. I'm not gonna take advantage of you or bully you. I'm on some underdog shit. And I truly believe I've been blessed by God, and God walks with me. Me and my niggas are on some Black Jesus shit. Not a new religion or anything, but the saint for thugs and gangstas – not killers and rapists, but thugs. When I say thugs, I mean niggas who don't have anything. (Marriott, 1996, p.17)

Such a perspective is not void of moral and ethical sensibilities; rather, Tupac offers an alternative narrative or paradigmatic structure for conversion – one that embraces the world as the arena proper existence. 'I feel like Black Jesus is controlling me,' say Tupac. 'He's our saint that we pray to; that we look up to. Drug dealers, they sinning, right? But they'll be millionaires. How I got shot five times – only a saint, only Black Jesus, only a nigga that know where I'm coming from, could be, like, "You know what? He's gonna end up doing some good."' (ibid.) Such a resolution mirrors the workings of the Black Jesus, rendering Tupac and those like him – thugs – followers of Jesus who, through their actions in the world, live out the precepts of their faith. As the lyrics to the aptly titled track 'Blasphemy' attest: 'They say Jesus is a kind man, well he should understand times in this crime land, my Thug nation.' ('Blasphemy,' *The Don Killuminati, The 7 Day Theory*, Interscope Records, 1996)

It is this Black Jesus, this icon of life in absurdity who provides the parameters of life, who monitors and informs life transformed:

In times of war we need somebody raw, rally the troops
Like a Saint that we can trust to help to carry us through
Black Jesus, hahahahaha
He's like a Saint that we can trust to help to carry us through
Black Jesus. ('Black Jesus,' *Still I Rise*, Interscope Records, 1999).

There is no ontological revolution brought about through conversion. No, it involves a fuller sense of one's presence in the world, a realization of the complexities of one's movement through the world. In this respect it does not entail a new set of moral and ethical guidelines – no metaphysical realities revealed. No special status secured. To the contrary, conversion and religious life for Tupac involve a greater worldliness, and with this comes a certain modality of accountability: 'I play the cards I was given,' Tupac writes, 'thank God I'm still livin'.' ('Definition of a Thug,' *R U Still Down? (Remember Me)*, Jive Records, 1997)

When interviewed in prison in April 1995, Tupac spoke to this worldly accountability: 'The excuse maker in Tupac is dead. The vengeful Tupac is dead. The Tupac that would stand by and let dishonorable things happen is dead. God let me live [after being shot 5 times] for me to do something extremely extraordinary, and that's what I have to do.' (Powell, 1995, p.52). This is not to say, however, that Tupac gives no attention to notions of heaven.

I shall not fear no man but God
Thought I walk through the valley of death
I shed so many tears (if I should die before I wake)
Please God walk with me (grab a nigga and take me to Heaven).
('So Many Tears,' *Me Against the World*, Jive Records, 1995)

Yet, reflection on heaven does not replace, for Tupac, a deep sensitivity and commitment to full encounters with the world, an emersion into the 'stuff' of the world. What is more, heaven does not entail of necessity a radical shift from the mechanisms of life on earth. In Tupac's words, 'if I die, I wonder if Heaven got a ghetto.' ('I Wonder if Heaven Got a Ghetto,' *R U Still Down? (Remember Me)*, Jive Records, 1997) The answer appears to be 'yes,' in that the geography of heaven involves 'no shortage on G's.' ('Only Fear of Death,' *R U Still Down? (Remember Me)*, Jive Records, 1997)

Conversion, hence, involves a turn inward, an embrace of one's connections to both pleasant and repulsive dimensions of our existential reality. This is certainly one way to interpret the illusions to the Black Jesus in 'Hail Mary.' Conversion, a push toward the center of meaning and existence does not require a suspicion concerning life's joys and pains. There, consequently, is no need epistemologically to arrange one's existence in ways that problematize the body's continued longing for the mundane. Connection to the divine through the transformative tone of conversion and religious life means a more refined integration of one's self to the world: 'And God said,' remarks Tupac, 'he should send his one begotten son to lead the wild into the ways of the man.' ('Hail Mary,' *The Don Killuminati, The 7 Day Theory* (Interscope Records, 1996)

Over against religious life *qua* Black Jesus, Snoop Dogg (aka Calvin Broadus) provides a more traditional conception of the Divine and human connection to the Divine. There is no explicitly stated 'thug' orientation in his theology, simply a proclaimed devotion to the Christian God. 'I'm a child of God.' Snoop Dogg (1999, p.1) remarks, 'doing God's work.' Growing up within Trinity Baptist Church (Long Beach, California), Snoop Dogg argues his mother offered an epistemology of life deeply connected to Christian commitment; and he embraced it. Put more forcefully, she 'planted a seed that took deep root in my life' he assures the readers of his autobiography (ibid., p.13). He does not recount the traditional surrender to Christ, the outcome of great struggle of self against the Divine, suggesting instead conversion as a sharpened perspective on the world – clear vision concerning the world's offerings. Yet, he speaks of life guidance as stemming from relationship with the Divine, and in this way he eludes to an orientation framed by metaphysical considerations. When questioned concerning the manner in which he secures life orientation, Snoop Dogg remarks 'I ask for God's help and let him guide me and give me the strength' (Christian, 2000).

In his self-description, there is sensitivity to the workings of Divine influence, to Providence, and the manner in which transcendent realities impinge on human existence. Hence, 'I've got a responsibility to God,' Snoop Dogg, recounts. 'He put me here. He'll take me down in a heartbeat the minute I start tripping on myself and how great I must be because of all the people telling me all the time.' (Dogg, 1999, p.2) When reflecting on his youth, he speaks in muted tones of church involvement, sermons and youth groups; yet, such insular activities do not define for him the life proper lived – the core sentiments of the life devoted (converted?) to God. There is a direct relationship between allegiances to the Divine and 'quality' of life. However, whereas it is typically the case in Christian conversion and consequent life arrangements that such a recognition places restrictions on one's engagement of the world, for Snoop Dogg such devotion is best represented through a mature and focused gaze on mundane pursuits in the manner of representing through word and action the realities of the streets: 'I tried to keep it real, never to sell the truth, but always to tell the truth. And if there's one reason why you know the name Snoop Dogg and I don't know yours, it's because telling the truth has given me the props I need to carry out God's purpose and plan.' (ibid., p.3)

It appears that for Snoop Dogg, history is teleological in nature, unfolding the inner workings of Divine intentions. Large and small events alike suggest this arrangement: 'God used football to teach me about life, and not even so much the game's strategy and discipline and teamwork – that shit any brother can use to improve himself. What I'm talking about is the faith to believe in yourself, to know that God is on your side and that He cares about you trying the best you can, no matter who you are.' (ibid., p.32) He, like Tupac, never offers a defining moment during which the allegiance to the Divine is initiated. There are clear moments of struggle that suggest the need for Divine intervention; but there is no clear and abiding alteration of behavior marking a turn. Rather, there appears a hermeneutically arranged shift, a new perspective on the workings of life through which the presence of Divine intention marks all life activities, regardless of whether or not they fit traditional frameworks of 'proper' moral and ethical outlook.

Framing an Alternate Theory

Traditional African American Christians with their focused sense of conversion are, in comparison, religious savants. That is to say, they are gifted within a small range of religious activities – prayer, church practice, and so on. Engagement with the world in other ways is more troubling, showing a rather limited flexibility and an awkwardly demonstrated ability to engage life existentially. Epistemology by way of traditional conversion, again in comparison, is limited in scope and poorly combined with 'worldly' activities. Put yet another way, discussion of traditional African American Christian conversion suggest an effort (while not always successful) to create 'flat' realities, two dimensional persons who see conflict between transcendence and the world, and attempt to embrace the former while denouncing the latter. A clear sign of the traditional Christian convert as religious savant might be the troubled relationship between soul and body that marks the conversation and workings of the erotic within African American Christian communions – an inability to foster synergy between the nurturing of the soul (or metaphysical concerns) and addressing mundane wants and desires.

In spite of how the above might be read, this essay is not concerned with judging the 'quality' of religious experience in traditional Christian modes over against what is presented by these two rappers. On that score, there are various ways in which both sides would be found wanting. Rather, the concern here is with the manner in which attention to rap music urges attention to the theoretical assumptions that tend to guide African American religious studies in general, and notions of conversion and religious life in particular. The examples of Tupac Shakur and Snoop Dogg pose a challenge to traditional conceptualization of conversion and religious experience. And, we are left to make a decision. One can embrace the grammar and vocabulary of religious conversion/experience that privileges certain formations of Christian frameworks. Or, one can see these examples as useful ways to think through the complex nature of religious engagement. I chose the latter.

Mindful of this, I suggest Tupac and Snoop Dogg offer a corrective to religio-theological discussion of conversion and religious experience. That is to say, more traditional formulations in African American Religious Studies assume conversion entails exposure to resources enabling a push beyond the troubling frameworks of life – a God over against the 'world' paradigm. In this way, the convert is expected to think and live in ways that model this over against the world posture. However, for Tupac and Snoop Dogg, religious conversion involves an embrace of the world, and thereby a signifying of dehumanization through an embrace of the very things despised. This move resembles, I believe, what cultural critic Albert Murray means by 'ritualistic counterstatement.' That is to say, like the blues – a forbearer of rap – rap music as represented by figures such as Tupac Shakur and Snoop Dogg involves not so much commiseration, but rather affirmation. In Murray's (2001, pp.194-5) words: 'You discover that it [the blues] is a music of affirmation; it is not a music of commiseration. It's out of that affirmation that you get all of that elegance....That kind of musical statement is a basic existential affirmation. And the musicians counterstate their problems; they counterstate the depression, despair, despondency, melancholia, and so forth. Blues music is a ritualistic counterstatement.'

The religious narratives offered by Tupac and Snoop Dogg, however, call this into question and instead suggest that conversion and religious experience involve a certain posture toward life whereby the quest for greater life meaning and being is harvested not over against the world but through thick engagement with the world. In this respect, conversion involves a hermeneutical shift, an alternate way of viewing the world whereby proper morality and ethics is premised on the 'realness' or 'authenticity' of one's actions and not the manner in which they fit neatly into doctrinal structures.

This alternate hermeneutical posture problematizes a rigid determinism and focused range of 'accepted' signs of religiosity as lived. Rebuffed are efforts to define religious engagement in terms of formal commitments to an array of relationships that seek to jettison life lived within the world as it is. Embraced is a commitment to a religious posture that accepts and works through mundane wants and needs, and views life not through a hermeneutic of escape. Rather, life is arranged through a hermeneutic of style, whereby the movement of bodies in time and space as a matter of creative impulse and sensibilities has vital value and allows for a full range of life pursuits (e.g. being a thug). And, as is the case with the traditional Christian conversion, some rap artists express the tone and texture of their religious experience, and articulate the dimensions of their new life, using a specialized language. One need only think in terms of the vocabulary of rap in order to understand this point.

At stake through conversion is a marked shift in orientation – a matter of difference. This, however, does not assume the certainty of particular moral arrangements of difference – just an altered perspective, new insight into the arrangements of life involving simple resistance to irrelevance – or ontological and existential destruction. Granted, my inclination, as a liberation theologian, is to assume such a stance. Yet, the work of rap artists like Tupac and Snoop Dogg challenges such an assured perspective (Pinn, 2003, p.159). Of further note, however, I am not suggesting that accountability be discarded. Hence, rap artists remain, even within a discussion of this type, accountable for the more troubling dimensions of their artistic production. Misogyny, unabated materialism, and so on, remain problematic. But, the presence of such problematic attitudes and behaviors do not offer final judgment, the last best criteria, for assessing the nature and meaning of conversion in that conversion and religious life involve change in posture that may not be fully realized in terms of output. In a word, '…this elemental feeling and new consciousness can be interpreted and acted on in a variety of ways, some less progressive than others. In all cases, converts in community understand themselves to be working toward liberation, but the outcomes of this effort do not always manifest this attitude.' (ibid., pp.175-6).

Yes, I would continue to hold that conversion as religious experience involves a push against reified and dwarfed life meaning. Nonetheless, the outcomes of this push are not so easily judged. What it means to have a proper sense of self, of one's 'fullness' is not reified through talk of conversion, but remains open to debate and framed by the particular existential-cultural context of the convert and the community of converts. This communal dimension is vital, yet it does not suggest a certain ethical stance in that conservative African American Christians constitute such a community pushing for more life meaning, as do the 'thugs' Tupac speaks for, or the 'homies' of vital importance to Snoop Dogg. In each case there are recognized and constitutive aesthetics, practices and beliefs. As Snoop Dogg (1999, p.5) notes, 'the truth I tell comes from the streets, where every day is a matter of life and death, where what matters is family loyalty and honor in the 'hood' and a code of survival that can't be betrayed.' The convert's efforts to live a proper life may involve simply signification of dehumanization in ways that do limited damage to the mechanics of oppression. Nonetheless, such efforts speak to a more substantive yearning for more life meaning that does not simply rest in the workings of political-economic frameworks. Such frameworks, however, based on the nature of dehumanization in the United States, must play a role – but they are placed in context, within the framework of a more expansive quest. As Jeffrey O. G. Ogbar (1999, p.167) remarks, 'many rap songs grapple with issues of contention in society, imploring listeners to assume higher levels of moral and spiritual consciousness, as well as social responsibility.' Again turning to Snoop Dogg:

> I paid the price to get myself free, from drugs and violence, from incarceration and intoxication, and from fear and death of every description. I paid the price so that maybe you don't have to, so that maybe when you read this book you can take a lesson from me, avoid my mistakes, and share my success. Like I said, I'm about elevating and educating. What I can teach comes straight out of my

life. What you can learn goes straight into yours. We're here to help each other. God taught me that. (1999, pp.3-4)

One might raise questions concerning issues of authenticity and the significance of selective memory that plagues personal narrative and our ability to access such stories. For example, Snoop Dogg speaks of inner-city realities as the paradigmatic structure for his work and life, but his lived context as a wealthy artist involves existential arrangements only impacted by such gritty realities to the extent he chooses. Yet I am not convinced that we, when speaking in terms of religious experience vis-à-vis conversion, can provide non-shifting and grounded responses. It is at this point, the pragmatic alternative is useful: conversion and religious experience are 'real' to the extent converts understand them as real. Suggested in the autobiographical reflections of Snoop Dogg is a particular way of life. In this regard, religious conversion and consequent life involve a certain mode of performance, an articulated posture toward the world acted out on the cartography of physical existence.

Tupac Shakur and Snoop Dogg, to a lesser degree, critique and jettison notions of conversion and religious life that require adherence to staid moralism through an embrace of doctrine with, at best, minor questioning and correction. In this way, religious conversion exposes the thick and often troubling dimensions of life without simple consolation and comfort. This is a posture foreign to many, and deeply troubling to most. But, those in the rap world who embrace this posture might respond by signifying a popular scriptural reference: the ways of God are foolishness to humans. Or, drawing directly from scripture: 'For it is written, I will destroy the wisdom of the wise, and will bring to nothing the understanding of the prudent' (1 Corinthians 1:19, King James Version). Such a perspective, however, does not amount to moral relativism in a strict sense in that religious conversion for Tupac and Snoop includes an awareness of the dilemmas and dangers of their undertakings (De Genova, 1995). I am not convinced gangsta rappers such as Tupac and Snoop offer only a modality of nihilism writ as good and, in light of this, I believe Nick De Genova raises an interesting point when saying, 'gangster rap can be found to transcend the mere reflection of urban mayhem and enter into musical debate with these realities, without sinking into didacticism or flattening their complexity' (ibid., p.114).

Final Thoughts

Rap artists such as Tupac and Snoop Dogg express a desire for a fuller sense of meaning through the felt reality of their bodies, as they take up time and space, as they force their recognition. It is through this forced recognition – involving a certain hold on the world – that they express the renewal of self that marks religious life. Traditional Christian conversion and religious life noted in the first part of this essay, often involves a dualism of vision – the gaze backward toward a spiritual legacy connecting the convert to God through Christ, and a gaze toward the future in which the Kingdom of God is proven. For rappers like Tupac or Snoop Dogg, the primary preoccupation is with the salvific nature of the present when properly understood and embraced. Here is a shift in religious aesthetics in that the look and workings of the body – from clothing, to tattoos, etc. – are recognized as vibrant, beautiful and a mark of wholeness.

Popular culture - in this case rap music - as a terrain for the articulation of religious struggle and conversion, forces a re-examination of the assumed cartography of religious engagement. It makes easier theological recognition of the historical nature of religion and the manner in which religious conversion and life are worked out not within non-troubled space, but rather within the midst of absurdity and angst. What is more, in addition to challenging staid notions of the locus of religious converstion and the shape of religious life, such attention to rap music also troubles all too easy depiction of this form of cultural production as degenerate and of no serious concern. In the language of rap, those bound to such reified notions of both religious experience and rap music 'betta recognize…'

Some Concluding Reflections

GORDON LYNCH

In drawing this book to a close, I want to offer some final thoughts in response to the discussion presented in the previous chapters. This is offered in the spirit of my own personal reflections on this material, and others will read this material in ways that highlights other questions and issues from the ones that I will explore here.

Firstly, (although this is hardly news to those working in this field) it is clear that there is a strong and sophisticated rationale for engaging in the study of religion, media and popular culture. Unlike the student mentioned at the start of Lynn Schofield Clark's chapter, the contributors to this volume have been very eloquent about the importance of this area of scholarly work. Tom Beaudoin is surely right to say that many of us who are drawn to the study of religion, media and popular culture because of our passions and concerns, the things we love to do and watch (or perhaps never got the chance to do when we were younger), and the particular forms of fandom with which we are bound up. But as Lynn Schofield Clark argues, the real value of this work lies in its ability to take us beyond the celebration of our own particular pleasures to an understanding of wider religious, social and cultural issues. This is not to de-cry Beaudoin's important proposal that this study is also work on the self – a point to which I shall return shortly. But Clark is surely right on this. I have sat through some presentations of research projects on religion, media and popular culture, only to be left with the question, 'so what?' – not an experience peculiar to me, I'm sure. When research in this field is little more than a thinly veiled attempt to indulge in an uncritical celebration and display of our curiosities and pleasures ('theologians talking about their record collections') then it can have a show and tell quality which may be entertaining, but ultimately unsatisfying in broader academic terms. The study of religion, media and popular culture has much more to offer than this.

In the preceding chapters, it is clear that a strong case can be made for the contribution of research on religion and popular culture to a broader understanding of religion, culture and society. As both I and Tony Pinn have suggested, the study of lived, popular cultures can inform our broader concepts of religion and the sacred themselves, making us more aware of unhelpful theological and ideological assumptions that may be bound up with the concepts of religion that we use in our work, and giving concrete examples of the nature and significance of sacred objects and religious experience in particular, lived situations. The study of religion and popular culture has the potential to generate better theorizing about religion and the sacred. As Jeffrey Mahan observes, the study of religion and popular culture can also help us to map the complex reconfigurations of religion and the sacred in late modern cultures that are neither wholly secular nor neatly definable in terms of neither traditional religious belief and ritual, nor the structures of traditional religious institutions. Studying religion, media and popular culture can also tell us more about how people make religious worlds for themselves. As a number of the previous chapters have suggested, people make use of media and popular cultural resources to construct religious identities, meaning, rituals, communities and experiences. Understanding more about how these cultural practices and resources contribute to the construction of these religious life-worlds can tell us much about the ways in which religion and the sacred are negotiated and reproduced in human societies, as well as the ways in which religion and the sacred can inspire and shape particular patterns of human relationship, belief and action. Interestingly, this volume demonstrates that such understanding is important both for religious 'insiders' and 'outsiders'. David Morgan's (1998, 2005) work on the sacred gaze and religious visual culture is an excellent example of an outsider's attempt to explore cultural forms of religion. But the chapters by Graham and Ward in this book also demonstrate that questions of how religious life-worlds are constructed are also interesting for theologians and religious insiders. The motivations behind such study are different. Morgan is interested in discovering more about the phenomena of religion so that the academy and wider society can become more thoughtful and literate about the nature and place of religion and the sacred in the lives of individuals, groups and nations. Graham and Ward are also interested in the cultural construction of religious life-worlds because they see such cultural work as performed theology, which should be the focus of on-going commitment and critical reflection, and which might inform a critical engagement with wider cultural patterns and resources.

So what questions and issues do the preceding chapters leave us with? I want briefly to highlight five. Firstly, several of the chapters (including Morgan, Mitchell, Mahan and Ward) emphasise the importance of the turn to the audience in the study of religion, media and popular culture. Whether for reasons of disciplinary inclination or practical convenience, scholars in theology and the study of religion have in the past often explored media and popular culture as ritual, text and symbol, subjecting it to theoretical readings or sometimes making unsubstantiated claims about the significance of these cultural resources and practices for particular individuals and groups. Whilst the recognition of the importance of understanding what people/audiences actually 'do' with media and popular culture in their everyday lives has grown – see for example the emphasis on the importance of audience reception studies in recent books on religion and film (Lyden, 2003; Marsh, 2004) – such research is still relatively underdeveloped. Whilst the importance of contributions by scholars such as Clark (2005) and Frykholm (2004) have been noted earlier in this book, there is still a long way to go for audience reception research in the study of religion, media and popular culture to catch up with the theoretical and methodological sophistication in studying audiences that has been developed more generally in media and cultural studies (see, e.g., Ang, 1994, 1995; Brooker & Jermyn, 2002). Importantly, though, as David Morgan and Pete Ward observe, this turn to the audience in the study of religion and popular culture should not become too strong an emphasis in its own right, but should be encouraged as part of the inter-disciplinary study of systems of cultural production and consumption. There is a remarkable consensus amongst many of the contributors to this book about the value of undertaking sophisticated work along these lines, and whether the next phase of research on religion, media and popular culture can deliver on this remains to be seen.

Secondly, the emphasis on reflexivity brought to this book by Beaudoin and Beckford is important and to my mind genuinely innovative within the previous literature in this field. Beaudoin's argument for seeing this field of study as a form of spiritual exercise is very stimulating, and simultaneously calls us to value the cultural contexts and experiences that bring us to this work, to engage critically with the discursive formations that shape our experience of our selves and our approach to our academic work, and to explore alternative ways of conceiving and living our lives. Beckford's chapter offers a concrete expression of such reflexivity. Using the gaze as a creative metaphor for our assumptions and orientations towards our academic and cultural practice, Beckford challenges us to respond to his gaze and to reflect on our own. Writing about the significance of a black gaze should also raise questions for many other researchers in this field (including myself) who have yet to ask what significance the 'whiteness' (Dyer, 2004) of their gaze has for their academic work and cultural life. This material on reflexivity is an important addition to the literature on religion, media and popular culture, and should serve as a useful reference point for future work in this field.

Thirdly, these chapters raise a basic question about the purpose of this area of research. Is it primarily to encourage understanding, as David Morgan suggests, or should it move beyond description and analysis to provide a framework for a normative critique of ourselves, our practices, our relationships and the wider communities, cultures and societies that we inhabit? My own view is that part of the exciting potential of research in this field is its capacity to contribute to wider discussions about the ethics of cultural life. We are living through an extraordinary period of technological, social, cultural and religious change, and, as many theorists of modernity have argued (e.g. Giddens, 1991; Bauman, 1993), this places an intensified focus on questions of our identities and values. In the context of these changes, new possibilities and uncertainties, the perennial question, 'how should we live?', becomes ever more pressing. Studying religion, media and popular culture becomes one means through which this question can be asked. By becoming more critically aware of the discursive and cultural formations within which we build our lives, it becomes possible to identify harmful assumptions, relationships, practices and structures that damage ourselves and the social and natural world, foreclose our grasp of the complexities of our existence, and hide the suffering of others from our sight. This is not to call for some unrelentingly joyless, ascetic scrutiny of our cultural lives – like the character 'Millie Tant' in the British cartoon book, *Viz*, who was ideologically incapable of finding any culturally innocent pleasure. Rather it is a quest that draws in both ethics and aesthetics in the pursuit of what it means to live a good, full and happy life. If the study of religion, media and popular culture can contribute to this wider quest, then its value will extend far beyond developing the academic and public understanding of religion. This is not to devalue that latter task, though. David Morgan's work, for example, strikes me as fundamentally ethical in its commitment to building religious and cultural literacy that can help us to live richer and more thoughtful lives as both scholars and citizens.

Fourthly, is the study of religion, media and popular culture really a single, coherent academic conversation? Talking in terms of the 'field' of religion, media and popular culture (as I have done too much in this book) could be seen as suggesting that scholars with interests in this area are engaged together in a seamless, academic project. The reality, as demonstrated by the chapters in this book, is clearly more complex than this. There are a number of fault-lines that can make communication and collaboration difficult. Aside from the different disciplinary backgrounds that scholars bring to work on religion, media and popular culture, there are also tensions between those who emphasise the importance of using particular theories as a basis for cultural analysis and between those who emphasise the importance of working on the basis on empirical work. There are tensions between those who see their research in terms of promoting academic and public understanding and those who see it as a framework for encouraging social transformation and the pursuit of social justice. There are also tensions between theologians who wish to analyse media and popular culture in the confessional language of their particular faith community, or for the purposes of developing particular missiological projects, and scholars adopting social scientific approaches to whom such religious language is irrelevant or unhelpful for the task of cultural analysis. This is not even to mention the tensions between those who differ on theological grounds, or on which cultural theorist is the most sure guide to wisdom. It is important not to skip over the challenges raised by the different assumptions, backgrounds, motivations, loves and hates of those drawn to studying religion, media and popular culture. But at the same time, it is important to recognize the value of this on-going field of research precisely because cross-disciplinary academic conversations are sustained within it despite these differences. In the context of the United States, in which the polarization between ('confessional') theology and the ('secular, rational') religious studies has become so great in many universities that constructive conversation between theologians and religious scholars is barely possible, it is important to celebrate the potential for the study of religion, media and popular culture to be a site for genuinely pluralist conversations. One of the dangers as the study of religion, media and popular culture becomes increasingly institutionalized and professionalized is that academic conferences, research centres and networks may retreat into smaller clusters of like-minded scholars, in which the complexities of inter-disciplinary conversations between theologians and religious scholars are avoided. If this is to be a rich field of study, particularly one that can make a useful contribution to the discussion of the ethics of cultural life, then the complexities of inter-disciplinary interactions need to be borne.

Finally, is it even helpful to talk about the field of 'religion, media and popular culture' at all? I would argue that the term 'media' is still useful, particularly if, as Jolyon Mitchell suggests, we ensure a broad definition of this which thinks in terms of systems of media and processes of mediation. But what about 'popular culture'? David Morgan's question, 'what's not popular?', is indicative of a growing dissatisfaction amongst some scholars (myself included) about defining our study in terms of 'popular culture'. Using the term 'popular culture' can have the implicit effect of reinforcing the ideologically-loaded binary of high/low culture and of perpetuating a sense of marginalization for scholars working in the area of cultures of everyday life. Perhaps the use of the term 'popular culture' may have been helpful at one stage in the academic study of religion in which it was important to focus attention more clearly on the significance of everyday cultural resources and practices in late modern society. And it is probably true to say that the term 'popular culture' still serves as an important role in conferences, academic associations and courses in conveying that interest in a particular range of cultural practices and resources are taken seriously there. But my sense is that the barriers and unhelpful assumptions generated by this term often out-weigh its value now. The turn to culture within theology and religious studies means that studying cultures of everyday life is no longer a niche area, to be valued and protected under the term 'popular culture', but is becoming increasingly mainstream. When we think that many of the leading contemporary writers on the study of religion – such as Leigh Schmidt (1997), Thomas Tweed (2006), Robert Orsi (2005) and Nancy Ammerman (2007) – use the study of lived, everyday, 'popular' cultures as an integral part of their analysis and theorizing, then it is clear that religion and popular culture has a key role to play in the future of this discipline. Thinking in terms of religion and cultures of everyday may serve us well in the next phase of research in encouraging communication and interaction between scholars interested in 'popular culture' and other researchers more generally interested in lived religion. Or better still, if we think in terms of religion and the sacred through lived cultural resources and practices, this will help to dissolve the unhelpful distinction of religion *and* popular culture, which implies that religion somehow exists in some pre-cultural Platonic world of ideas separate from actual cultural histories, resources and lives. Understanding religion and the sacred as culture, and through culture, forms an important future path-way for the study of religion. As Pete Ward observes, for those theologically committed to particular notions of transcendence, such a cultural turn need not involve reducing the transcendent to the cultural, but can instead be conceived of as the study of the ways in which the transcendent is mediated through culture. For both theology and the study of religion, the cultural turn has now broken beyond the confines of those interested in 'popular culture'. The questions and issues raised in this book therefore ultimately tell us not just about a particular sub-field of these disciplines, but give us an insight into some of the most important directions of study of religion and the sacred at the start of this new century.

Bibliography

Aichele, G. (2005). 'Artificial Bodies: *Blade Runner* and the Death of Man', In
Cinéma Divinité: Religion, Theology and the Bible in Film edited by E.C.
Christiansen, P. Francis and W.R. Telford. London: SCM Press, 137–148.

Akass, K. and McCabe, J. (2005). *Reading Six Feet Under: TV to Die for.* London: I.B.
Tauris.

Albanese, C. (1981). *American Religion and Religions.* Belmont: Wadsworth Publishing
Company.

Alexander, K. (2000). 'Black British Cinema in the 90s: Going Going Gone.' In
British Cinema of the 90s, edited by Robert Murphy, London: BFI, 110.

Althusser, L. (1971) *Lenin and Philosophy and Other Essays.* London: New Left Books.

Ammerman, N. (ed.) (2007). *Everyday Religion: Observing Modern Religious Lives.* New
York: Oxford University Press.

Ang, I. (1994) 'Understanding Television Audiencehood'. In *Television: The Critical
View.* Fifth edition, edited by Horace Newcomb, Oxford: Oxford University
Press, 367–86.

Ang, I. (1995). *Living Room Wars: Rethinking Media Audiences for a Postmodern World.*
London: Routledge.

Armstrong, B. (1979). *The Electric Church.* Nashville: Nelson.

Arnold, M. (1869/2006). *Culture and Anarchy.* Edited by J. Garnett. Oxford: Oxford
University Press.

Arthur, C. (1993). *Religion and the Media.* Cardiff: University of Wales Press.

Asad, T. (1993). *Genealogies of Religion: Disciplines and Reasons of Power in Christianity
and Islam.* Baltimore, MD: John Hopkins University Press.

Asad, T. (2003). *Formations of the Secular: Christianity, Islam, Modernity.* Palo Alto, CA:
Stanford University Press.

Asamoah-Gyadu, J.K. (2005). 'Anointing through the screen: neo-Pentecostalism
and televised Christianity in Ghana'. *Studies in World Christianity,* Volume 11.1,
9–28.

Askew, K. and Wilk, R. (eds). (2002). *The Anthropology of Media: A Reader.* Oxford:
Blackwell.

Astley, J. (2002). *Ordinary Theology: Looking Listening and Learning in Theology.* London:
Ashgate.

Badaracco, C. (ed.) (2004). *Quoting God: How Media Shape Ideas about Religion and
Culture.* Waco, TX.: Baylor University Press.

Bailey, R.C. (2000). 'Academic Biblical Interpretation Among African Americans in the United States.' In *African Americans and the Bible, Sacred Texts and Social Texture*, edited by Vincent Wimbush, London: Continuum, 696.

Baugh, L. (1997). *Imagining the Divine: Jesus and Christ-Figures in Film*. Kansas City: Sheed and Ward.

Bauman, Z. (1993). *Postmodern Ethics*. Oxford: Blackwell.

Bawden, D. & Robinson, L. (2000). 'A distant mirror? The internet and the printing press'. *Aslib Proceedings,* 52(2), 51–57.

Beaudoin, T. (1998). *Virtual Faith: the Irreverent Spiritual Quest of Generation X*. San Francisco: Jossey-Bass.

Beaudoin, T. (2003). *Consuming Faith: Integrating Who We Are Into What We Buy*. Lanham, MD: Sheed and Ward.

Beaudoin, T. (2004). 'In praise of young adult faith'. *Celebration: An Ecumenical Worship Resource* 33(6), 243–6.

Beaudoin, T. (2005). 'Believing what they need to'. *America* 193(7), 19 September 2005: 24–25.

Beckford, R. (1998). *Jesus is Dread: Black Theology and Black Culture in Britain*. London: Darton, Longman and Todd.

Beckford, R. (2000). *Dread and Pentecostal: A Political Theology for the Black Church*. London: SPCK.

Beckford, R. (2001). *God of the Rahtid: Redeeming Rage*. London: DLT.

Beckford, R. (2004). *God and the Gangs*. London: DLT.

Beckford R. (2005). *Jesus Dub: Faith, Culture and Social Change*. London: Routledge.

Begbie, J. (2002). *Sounding the Depths: Theology Through the Arts*. London: SCM Press.

Bernauer, J. (1990). *Michel Foucault's Force of Flight: Toward an Ethics for Thought*. Atlantic Highlands, NJ: Humanities Press International.

Bernauer, J. (1994). Michel Foucault's Ecstatic Thinking. In *The Final Foucault*, edited by James Bernauer and David Rasmussen, Cambridge, MA: MIT Press, 45–82.

Bernauer, J., and Rasmussen, D. (eds). (1994). *The Final Foucault*. Cambridge, MA: MIT Press.

Blythe, T., and Wolpert, D. (2004). *Meeting God in Virtual Reality*. Nashville, TN: Abingdon Press.

Boomershine, T. (1990). 'A new paradigm for interpreting the Bible of television'. In *Changing Channels - The Church and the Television Revolution*, edited by Tyron Inbody, Dayton, Ohio: Whaleprints, 59–76.

Bowie, F. (2005). *The Anthropology of Religion: An Introduction*. 2nd edition. Oxford: Blackwell.

Bradley, I. (2004). *You've Got to Have a Dream: the Message of the Musical*. London: SCM Press.

Bourdieu, P. (1984/2002). *Distinction: A Social Critique of the Judgment of Taste*. Cambridge: Harvard University Press.

Boylan, A. (1988). *Sunday School: The Formation of an American Institution 1790–1880*. New Haven: Yale University Press.

Branigan, T. (2004). 'Tale of rape at the temple sparks riots at the theatre', *The Guardian*. December 20 (online), available at:

http://arts.guardian.co.uk/print/0,,5089359-110427,00.html [accessed 16/12/06]

Brantlinger, P. (1983). *Bread and Circuses: Theories of Mass Culture as Social Decay.* Ithaca and London: Cornell University Press.

Brewin, K. (2004). *The Complex Christ: Signs of Emergence in the Urban Church.* London: SPCK.

British Broadcasting Corporation, (2006). *The Manchester Passion* (online), 13th April, available at:
http://www.bbc.co.uk/manchester/content/articles/2006/04/10
/140406_manchester_passion_event_feature.shtml [accessed 05/07/06]

Brooker, W. & Jermyn, D. (eds). (2002). *The Audience Studies Reader.* London: Routledge.

Burchell, G., Gordon, C. and Miller, P. (eds). (1991). *The Foucault Effect: Studies in Governmentality.* Chicago: University of Chicago Press.

Campbell, H. (2005). *We Are One in the Network: Exploring Religious Community Online.* Bern: Peter Lang.

Carlyle, T. (1993). *On Heroes, Hero-Worship, and the Heroic in History.* Berkeley: University of California Press.

Carson, D. (2005). *Becoming Conversant with the Emerging Church.* Grand Rapids, MI.: Zondervan.

Cawelti, J. (1976). *Adventure, Mystery and Romance.* Chicago: University of Chicago Press.

Chaddock, G. R. (2005). 'Bush Administration Blurs Media Policy.' *Christian Science Monitor.* February 17, 1.

Chadwick, O. (2001). *The Early Reformation on the Continent.* Oxford: Oxford University Press.

Chidester, D. (1996). 'The Church of baseball, The fetish of coca-cola, and the potlatch of rock-and-roll: theoretical models for the study of religion in American popular culture,' *Journal of the American Academy of Religion,* vol. LXI, Fall, pp.743-65.

Christian, M. (2000). 'Rap star Snoop Dogg talks about fame, fatherhood and family.' *Jet Magazine,* May 22nd 2000, downloaded from http://findarticles.com/p/articles/mi_m1355/is_24_97/ai_62364593 on 12th February 2007.

Clark, L.S. (2005). *From Angels to Aliens: Teenagers, the Media and the Supernatural.* New York: Oxford University Press.

Clark, L. S. (2006). 'Popular Culture.' In *Encyclopedia of Religion,* edited by David Morgan, New York: MacMillan.

Clark, L.S. (ed.) (2007). *Religion, Media and the Marketplace.* New Brunswick, NJ: Rutgers University Press.

Clark, L. S. (2007). 'Identity, belonging, and religious lifestyle branding (fashion Bibles, bhangra parties, and Muslim pop.' In Clark *Religion, Media, and the Marketplace,* edited by Lynn Schofield Clark, New Brunswick, NJ: Rutgers University Press, 1–36.

Cleague, A. (1968). *The Black Messiah.* Lanham, MD: Sheed & Ward.

Coakley, M. (1977). *Rated X: The Moral Case Against TV.* New Rochelle, New York: Arlington.

Cobb, K. (2005). *Blackwell Guide to Theology and Popular Culture.* Malden, MA: Blackwell.

'Colporteur Reports to the American Tract Society 1841–1846' (1940). Typescript prepared by the New Jersey Historical Record Survey Project, Newark, New Jersey, July, 1940. Library of Congress, Washington, D.C.

Cone, J. (1974). *God of the Oppressed.* New York: Orbis.

Cooper, C. (1995). *Noises in the Blood: Orality, Gender and the 'Vulgar' Body of Jamaican Popular Culture.* Durham, NC.: Duke University Press.

Couldry, N. (2003). *Media Rituals: A Critical Approach.* London: Routledge.

Cray, G. (ed.) (2004). *Mission-Shaped Church.* London: Church House Publishing.

Crockett, A. and Voas, D. (2006). Generations of Decline: Religious Change in 20th-Century Britain. *Journal for the Scientific Study of Religion* 45 (4), 567–584.

Davie, G. (1994). *Religion in Britain since 1945: Believing without Belonging.* Oxford: Blackwell.

Davis, R. (1997). *Lives of Indian Images.* Princeton: Princeton University Press.

de Chant, D. (2002). *The Sacred Santa.* Cleveland: Pilgrim Press.

De Genova, N. (1995). 'Gangsta rap and nihilism in black America: some questions of life and death.' *Social Text,* 43, 89–132.

DeLashmutt, M. (2006). 'The sexualisation of popular culture: towards a Christian sexual aesthetic'. *Crucible* July-Sept, 34–41.

Detweiler, C. and Taylor, B. (2003). *A Matrix of Meanings: Finding God in Pop Culture.* Grand Rapids, MN: Baker Academic.

Dogg, S. (1999). *The Doggfather: The Times, Trials and Hardcore Truths of Snoop Dogg.* New York: William Morrow & Co.

DuBois, W.E.B. (1903). *The Souls of Black Folk.* London: Dover.

du Gay, P., Hall, S., Janes, L., Mackay, H. & Negus, K. (1997). *Doing Cultural Studies: The Story of the Sony Walkman.* London: Sage.

Durkheim, E. (1912/2001). *The Elementary Forms of the Religious Life.* Oxford: Oxford University Press.

Dyer, R. (2004). *White: Essays on Race and Culture.* London; Routledge.

Dyson, M. E. (1996). *Between God and Gangsta Rap: Bearing Witness to Black Culture.* New York: Oxford University Press.

Dyson, M.E. (1997). *Race Rules: Navigating the Color Line.* New York: Vintage.

Dyson, M.E. (2001). *Holler if You Hear Me: Searching for Tupac Shakur.* New York: Basic Civitas Books.

Eisenstein, E. (1979). *The Printing Press as an Agent of Change.* Cambridge: Cambridge University Press.

Emerson, R. W. (2000). 'Man the Reformer.' In *Essays and Poems,* edited by George Stade. New York: Barnes & Noble Classics.

Fanon, F. (1967/1991). *Black Skin, White Masks.* London: Pluto.

Fiske, J. (1989). *Understanding Popular Culture.* London: Routledge.

Fitzgerald, T. (2003). *The Ideology of Religious Studies.* New York: Oxford University Press.

Flaubert, G. (1965). *Madame Bovary.* Norton Critical Edition. New York and London: W. W. Norton & Company.

Flory, R. & Miller, D. (eds). (2000). *GenX Religion.* London: Routledge.

Forbes, B. and Mahan, J. (eds). (2000/2005). *Religion and Popular Culture in America*. Berkeley: University of California Press.

Forbes, B. (2000). 'Introduction,' In *Religion and Popular Culture in America*, edited by Bruce David Forbes and Jeffrey H. Mahan, Berkeley, CA: University of California Press, 1–20.

Forshey, G. (1984). 'Studies in Popular Culture.' *explor*, Vol. 7, Fall, 17–27.

Foucault, M. (1978). *Discipline and Punish: The Birth of the Prison*, translated by Alan Sheridan. New York: Vintage.

Foucault, M. (1983). 'Preface', In *Anti-Oedipus: Capitalism and Schizophrenia*, edited by Gilles Deleuze and Felix Guattari, translated by Robert Hurley, Mark Seem, Helen R. Lane, xi-xiv. Minneapolis: University of Minnesota Press.

Ellul, J. (1985). *The Humiliation of the Word*, Grand Rapids, MI.: Eerdmans.

Foucault, M. (1990). *The Use of Pleasure*, translated by Robert Hurley. New York: Vintage.

Foucault, M. (2003a). *Society Must Be Defended: Lectures at the College de France, 1975– 1976*, edited by Mauro Bertani and Alessandro Fontana, translated by David Macey. New York: Picador.

Foucault, M. (2003). *Abnormal: Lectures at the College de France, 1974–1975*, edited by Valerio Marchetti and Antonella Salomoni, translated by Graham Burchell. New York: Picador.

Foucault, M. (2004). *Securite, territoire, population: Cours au College de France (1977– 1978)*, edited by Francois Ewald and Alessandro Fontana.

Foucault, M. (2005). *The Hermeneutics of the Subject: Lectures at the College de France, 1981–1982*, edited by Frederic Gros, translated by Graham Burchell. New York: Palgrave-Macmillan.

Friedmann, G. (1970). *La Puissance et la sagesse*. Paris: Gallimard.

Frith, S. (1996). Popular Culture. In *A Dictionary of Cultural and Critical Theory*, edited by Michael Payne, Cambridge, MA: Blackwell, 415–7.

Frykholm, A. (2004). *Rapture Culture: Left Behind in Evangelical Culture*. New York: Oxford University Press.

frenchification (2006). *Manchester Passion message 14* (online), posted April 15th, available at: http://www.bbc.co.uk/dna/england/ F2770282? thread= 2090395&phrase=Manchester [accessed 12/12/06].

Gallagher, M. (1984). 'Imagination and faith'. *The Way* 24: 115–123.

Gallagher, M. (1997). 'Theology, discernment, and cinema', In *New Image of Religious Film*, edited by John R. May, Kansas City: Sheed and Ward, pp.151–60.

Gallagher, M. (1997/2003). *Clashing Symbols: An introduction to Faith and Culture*. London: Darton, Longman and Todd.

Gauntlett, D. (1998). 'Ten things wrong with the "effects model" ', In *Approaches to Audiences: A Reader* edited by Roger Dickinson, Ramaswani Harindranath and Olga Linné, London: Arnold, 120–30.

Geertz, C. (1973). *The Interpretation of Cultures*. New York: Basic Books.

Geertz, C. (1980). 'Blurred Genres: The Reconfiguration of Social Thought.' *American Scholar* 49: 165–179.

Giddens, A. (1978). *Durkheim*. London: Fontana.

Giddens, A. (1986). *The Constitution of Society: An Outline of the Theory of Structuration*. Cambridge: Polity Press.

Giddens, A. (1991). *Modernity and Self-Identity: Self and Society in the Late Modern Age.* Cambridge: Polity.

Giggie, J. & Winston, D. (eds). (2002). *Faith in the Market: Religion and the Rise of Urban Commercial Culture.* New Brunswick, NJ.: Rutgers University Press.

Gilmore, L. & Van Proyen, M. (2005). *After Burn: Reflections on Burning Man.* Albuquerque: University of New Mexico Press.

Gilmour, Michael, (ed.) (2005). *Call Me the Seeker: Listening to Religion in Popular Music.* New York, NY: Continuum.

Gilroy, P. (1994). *The Black Atlantic.* London: Verso.

Goethals, G. (1981). *The TV Ritual: Worship at the Video Altar.* Boston. Beacon Press.

Goethals, G. (1993).'Media Mythologies'. In *Religion and the Media*, edited by Chris Arthur, Cardiff, University of Wales Press, 25–39.

Goethe, J. W. von. (1850/1984). *Conversations with Eckermann, 1823–1832*, translated by John Oxenford. San Francisco: North Point Press.

Gormly, E. (2003). 'Evangelizing through appropriation: toward a cultural theory on the growth of contemporary Christian rock music'. *Journal of Media and Religion*. Vol. 2, No. 4, 251–265.

Gorringe, T. (2004). *Furthering Humanity.* London: Ashgate.

Graham, E.L. (1996/2002). *Transforming Practice: Pastoral Theology in an Age of Uncertainty.* Eugene, OR: Wipf and Stock.

Graham, E.L. (2002). *Representations of the Post/Human: Monsters, Aliens and Others in Popular Culture.* Manchester: Manchester University Press.

Graham, E.L., Walton, H. and Ward. F. (2005). *Theological Reflection: Methods.* London: SCM Press.

Greeley A. (1988). *God in Popular Culture.* Chicago: Thomas More Press.

http://www.unomaha.edu/jrf/greinart2.htm [accessed 12/12/06].

Green, G. (1999). *Imagining God: Theology and the Religious Imagination.* Grand Rapids, MN: Baker Academic.

Greenberg, C. (1939/1961). 'Avant-Garde and Kitsch,' *Art and Culture: Critical Essays.* Boston: Beacon Press.

Greenberg, J. & Mitchell, S. (1983). *Object Relations in Psychoanalytic Theory.* Cambridge, MA.: Harvard University Press.

Greiner, K. (1999). 'The *Apostle*: A Psychiatric Appraisal'. *Journal of Religion and Film* (online), Vol. 3, No. 2. Available at:

Hadot, P. (1992). 'Reflections on the notion of the 'cultivation of the self'. In *Michel Foucault Philosopher*, edited and translated by Timothy J. Armstrong, 225–232. New York: Routledge.

Hadot, P. (1995a). *Philosophy as a Way of Life: Spiritual Exercises from Socrates to Foucault*, edited by Arnold Davidson. Cambridge, MA: Blackwell.

Hadot, P. (1995b). *Qu'est-ce que la philosophie antique?* Paris: Éditions Gallimard.

Hadot, P.. (2002a). *Exercices spirituels et philosophie antique.* Paris: Éditions Albin Michel.

Hadot, P. (2002b). *What is Ancient Philosophy?*, translated by Michael Chase. Cambridge, MA: Harvard University Press.

Halperin, D. (1995). *Saint Foucault: Towards a Gay Hagiography.* New York: Oxford University Press.

Hall, D., (ed.) (1997). *Lived Religion in America: Toward a History of Practice*. Princeton: Princeton University Press.

Hall, S. (1990). 'Encoding, decoding'. In *The Cultural Studies Reader*, edited by Simon During, London: Routledge, 507–17.

Hall, S. & Whannel, P. (1964). *The Popular Arts*. Boston: Beacon Press.

Hangen, T. (2001). *Redeeming the Dial: Radio, Religion, and Popular Culture in America*. Chapel Hill, NC.: University of North Carolina Press.

Heath, A., Martin, J. & Elgenius, G. (2007). 'Who do we think we are? The decline of traditional social identities.' In *British Social Attitudes: Perspectives on a Changing Society. The 23rd Report*, edited by Alison Park, John Curtice, Katrina Thomson, Miranda Philips and Mark Johnson, London: Sage, 1–34.

Heelas, P. (1996). 'On things not being worse, and the ethic of humanity'. In *De-traditionalization: Critical Reflections on Authority and Identity*, edited by Paul Heelas, Scott Lash and Paul Morris, Oxford: Blackwell, 200–222.

Heelas, P. (2000). 'Expressive spirituality and humanistic expressivism: sources of significance beyond Church and Chapel.' In *Beyond New Age. Exploring Alternative Spirituality* edited by Steven Sutcliffe and Marion Bowman,Edinburgh: Edinburgh University Press, 237–54.

Heelas, P. & Woodhead, L. (2004). *The Spiritual Revolution: Why Religion is Giving Way to Spirituality*. Oxford: Blackwell.

Hefner, P. (2003). *Technology and Human Becoming*. Minneapolis: Fortress.

Heidegger, M. (1993). 'Building, dwelling, thinking.' In *Basic Writings of Martin Heidegger* edited by D.F. Krell. 2nd Edn, San Francisco: Harper and Row, 343–364.

Hendershot, H. (2004). *Shaking the World for Jesus: Media and Conservative Evangelical Culture*. Chicago: University of Chicago Press.

Henry, W. (2006). *What the Deejay Said: A Critique from the Street*. London: Nubeyond.

Hervieu-Leger, D. (2000). *Religion as a Chain of Memory*. Cambridge: Polity.

Hills, M. (2002). *Fan Cultures*. New York, NY: Routledge.

Hobbs, S D. (1997). *The End of the American Avant Garde*. New York: New York University Press.

Hodgson, R. and Soukup, P. (eds). (1997). *From One Medium to Another: Basic Issues for Communicating the Scriptures in New Media*. Kansas City: Sheed and Ward.

Hohendahl, P. (1977). 'Introduction to Reception Aesthetics,' *New German Critique* 10 (Winter): 29–64.

Holm, R. (2005). ' "Pulling Back the Darkness": starbound with Jon Anderson. In *Call Me the Seeker: Listening to Religion in Popular Music*, edited by Michael Gilmour, New York, NY: Continuum, 158–171.

Hope, D. (2006). *Inna di Dancehall: Popular Culture and the Politics of Identity in Jamaica*. Kingston: University of the West Indies Press.

Hopkins, D. (1999). *Introducing Black Theology of Liberation*. New York: Orbis.

Hopkins, D. (2003). *Head and Heart: Black Theology – Past, Present and Future*. New York: Palgrave MacMillan.

hooks, B. (1992). Black Looks: Race and Representation. London: Turnaround.

Hoover, S. (1988). *Mass Media Religion: The Social Sources of the Electronic Church*. London: Sage.

Hoover, S. & Abelman, R. (eds). (1990). *Religious Television: Controversies and Conclusions,* Norwood, NJ: Ablex.

Hoover, S. & Lundby, K. (eds). (1997). *Rethinking Media, Religion and Culture.* London: Sage.

Hoover, S. & Clark, L.S. (eds). (2002). *Practicing Religion in the Age of the Media: Explorations in Media, Religion and Culture.* New York: Columbia University Press.

Hoover, S., Clark, L.S. & Alters, D. (2004). *Media, Home, and Family.* New York: Routledge.

Hoover, S. (2006). *Religion in the Media Age.* London: Routledge.

Horsfield, P. (1984). *Religious Television: The American Experience.* Longman: New York.

Horsfield, P. (2003). 'Electronic Media and the Past-Future of Christianity' In *Mediating Religion: Conversations in Media, Religion and Culture* edited by Jolyon Mitchell and Sophia Marriage, London: Continuum, 271–282.

Horsfield, P., Hess, M. and Medrano, A. (eds). (2004). *Belief in Media: Cultural Perspectives on Media and Christianity.* Burlington, VT: Ashgate.

Hulsether, M. (1999). *Building a Protestant Left: Christianity and Crisis Magazine, 1941–1993.* Knoxville, TN.: University of Tennessee Press.

Innis, H. (1950). *Empire and Communication.* Oxford: Clarendon Press.

Innis, H.(1951). *The Bias of Communication.* Toronto: University of Toronto Press.

James, W. (1902/2002). *The Varieties of Religious Experience.* London: Routledge.

Jantzen, G. (2004). *Death and the Displacement of Beauty: Volume 1: Foundations of Violence.* New York: Routledge.

Jensen, J. (1990). *Redeeming Modernity: Contradictions in Media Criticism.* Newbury Park, California: Sage.

Jewett, R. (1973). *The Captain America Complex.* Philadelphia: Westminster Press.

Jewett, R. (1993). *St. Paul at the Movies: The Apostles Dialogue with American Culture.* Louisville: Westminster/John Knox Press.

Jindra, M. (2005). 'It's about faith in our future; *Star Trek* fandom as cultural religion', in *Religion and Popular Culture in America,* 2nd edition, edited by Bruce Forbes and Jeffrey H. Mahan, Berkeley: University of California Press, 159–73.

Johnson, R., Chambers, D., Raghuram, P. and Tincknell, E. (2004). *The Practice of Cultural Studies.* London: Sage.

Johnston, R. (2000). *Reel Spirituality: Theology and Film in Dialogue.* Grand Rapids, MN: Baker Academic.

Kandinsky, W. (1912/1977). *Concerning the Spiritual in Art,* tr. M.T.H. Stadler. New York: Dover.

Katz, E., Peters, J.D., Liebes, T. & Orloff, A. (eds). (2003). *Canonic Texts in Media Research.* Cambridge: Polity.

Key, W. (1973). *Subliminal Seduction.* New York: Prentice-Hall.

King, R. (1999). *Orientalism and Religion: Post-Colonial Theory, India and the Mystic East.* London: Routledge.

Kopytoff, I. (1986). 'The Cultural Biography of Things: Commoditization as Process.' In *The Social Life of Things: Commodities in Cultural Perspective,* edited by Arjun Appadurai, Cambridge: Cambridge University Press, 64–91.

Leistyna, J. (2006). *Class Dismissed: How TV Frames the Working Class*. DVD produced by the Media Education Foundation.

Lelwica, M. (2005). 'Losing their way to salvation: women, weight loss and the salvation myth of culture lite', in *Religion and Popular Culture in America*, 2nd edition, edited by Bruce Forbes and Jeffrey H. Mahan, Berkeley: University of California Press, 174–194.

Lewis, G. (1977). *Telegarbage*. Nashville: Thomas Nelson.

Lincoln, B. (2006). *Holy Terrors: Thinking About Religion After September 11*. 2nd edition. Chicago: University of Chicago Press.

Lindbeck, G. (1984). *The Nature of Doctrine: Religion and Theology in a Post-Liberal Age*. Louisville, KY: WJK Press.

Livingstone, S. (2003/2006). 'The Changing Nature of Audiences: From the Mass Audience to the Interactive Media User', In *A Companion to Media Studies* edited by Angharad N. Valdvia, Oxford: Blackwell, 337–359.

Lonergan, B. (1990). *Method in Theology*. Toronto: University of Toronto Press.

Loughlin, G. (2005). 'Cinéma divinité: A theological introduction'. In *Cinéma Divinité: Religion, Theology and the Bible in Film* edited by E.C. Christiansen, P. Francis and W.R. Telford. London: SCM Press, 1–12.

Luckmann, T. (1967). *The Invisible Religion*. New York: MacMillan.

Lumby, C. (2004). ' "Cappuccino Courses": The truth.' *The Age*.(Australia), February 4, available online: http://www.theage.com.au/articles/2004/02/03/1075776057462.html?from =storyrhs, [downloaded 5/3/2007]

Lyden, J. (2003). *Film as Religion: Myths, Morals, Rituals*. New York: New York University Press.

Lynch, G. (2002). *After Religion: 'Generation X' and the Search for Meaning*. London: DLT.

Lynch, G. (2005). *Understanding Theology and Popular Culture*. London: Routledge.

Lynch, G. (2006). 'Exploring the research agenda for religion and popular culture: a report of a panel discussion at the American Academy of Religion, November 2005.' *Journal of Religion and Popular Culture*, available on-line at http://www.usask.ca/relst/jrpc/reports12.html

Lynch, G. (2007). *The New Spirituality: An Introduction to Progressive Belief in the Twenty First Century*. London: I.B. Tauris.

Mahan, J. H., (1980). 'The Hard-boiled Detective in the Fallen World.' *Clues* Fall/Winter, 90–9.

Mahan, J. H., (1984). 'Once Upon a Time in the West.' *explor*, Vol.7, pp.80–94.

Mahan, J. H. (2002). 'Celluloid savior: Jesus in the movies,' *Journal of Religion and Film*, Vol. 6: No.1, available for download at http://www.unomaha.edu/jrf/celluloid.htm

Manc-host2, *Manchester Passion message 1* (online) January 27, available at: http://www.bbc.co.uk/dna/ england/ F2770282?thread= 2090395 &phrase =Manchester (accessed 12/12/06).

Mander, J. (1978). *Four Arguments for the Elimination of Television*. New York: Morrow.

Marriott, R. (1996). 'Last testament'. *Vibe Magazine*, November 1996, 17.

Marsden, P. (2001). 'Religious Americans and the Arts in the 1990s.' In *Crossroads: Art and Religion in American Life*, edited by Alberta Arthurs and Glenn Wallach. New York: The New Press.

Marsh, C. and Ortiz, G. (eds). (1997). *Explorations in Theology and Film: Movies and Meaning*. Malden, MA: Blackwell.

Marsh, C. (1997). 'Film and theologies of culture'. In *Explorations in Theology and Film*, edited by Clive Marsh & Gaye Ortiz. Oxford: Blackwell, 21–34.

Marsh, C. (2004). *Cinema and Sentiment: Film's Challenge to Theology*. Milton Keynes: Paternoster.

Martin, J., and Ostwalt Jr., C. (eds). (1995). *Screening the Sacred: Religion, Myth, and Ideology in Popular American Film*. Westport: Greenwood Press.

May, J. (ed.) (1997). *New Image of Religious Film*. Kansas City, MO: Sheed and Ward.

May, T. (2000). 'Philosophy as a spiritual exercise in Foucault and Deleuze'. *Angelaki* 5(2), August 2000, 223–229.

Mazur, E. and McCarthy, K. (eds). (2001). *God in the Details: American Religion in Popular Culture*. New York, NY: Routledge.

McCloud, S. (2004.) *Making the American Fringe: Exotics, Subversives, and Journalists, 1955–1993*. Chapel Hill, NC.: University of North Carolina Press.

McCombs, M. and Shaw, D. (1992). 'The agenda-setting function of mass media'. *Public Opinion Quarterly*, 36 (Summer edition), 176–187.

McCutcheon, R. (1997). *Manufacturing Religion: The Discourse on Sui Generis Religion and the Politics of Nostalgia*. New York: Oxford University Press.

McCutcheon, R. (2003). *The Discipline of Religion: Structure, Meaning, Rhetoric*. New York: Routledge.

McDannell, C. (1995). *Material Christianity: Religion and Popular Culture in America*. New Haven: Yale University Press.

McDonnell, J. and Trampiets, F. (eds). (1989). *Communicating Faith in a Technological Age*. Slough: St. Paul Publications.

McEver, M. (1998). The Messianic figure in film: christology beyond the biblical epic. *Journal of Religion and Film* (online), Vol. 2, No. 2. Available at: http://www.unomaha.edu/jrf/McEverMessiah.htm [accessed 05/07/06].

McGushin, E. (2007). *Foucault's Askesis: An Introduction to the Philosophical Life*. Evanston: Northwestern University Press.

McLuhan, M. (1962). *The Gutenberg Galaxy*. Toronto: University of Toronto Press.

McLuhan, M. (1964). *Understanding Media: The Extensions of Man*. New York: New American Library.

McNulty, E. (2001). *Praying the Movies: Daily Meditations from Classic Films*. Louisville: Geneva Press.

Mercer, K. (1994). *Welcome to the Jungle: New Posititions in Black Cultural Studies*. London: Routledge.

Meyer, B. & Moors, A. (eds). (2005). *Religion, Media and the Public Sphere*. Indianapolis: Indiana University Press.

Miles, M. (1996). *Seeing and Believing: Religion and Values in the Movies*. Boston, MA: Beacon Press.

Miller, J. (1993). *The Passion of Michel Foucault*. New York: Simon and Schuster.

Miller, T. (ed.) (2006). *A Companion to Cultural Studies*. Oxford: Blackwell.

Miller, V. (2004). *Consuming Religion: Christian Faith and Practice in a Consumer Culture.* London: Continuum.

Mitchell, J. (1999). *Visually Speaking: Radio and the Renaissance of Preaching.* Edinburgh: T&T Clark.

Mitchell, J. (2002). 'Media', in *The New Dictionary of Pastoral Studies* edited by Wesley Carr, London: SPCK, 213.

Mitchell, J. and Marriage, S. (eds). (2003). *Mediating Religion: Conversations in Media, Religion and Culture.* Edinburgh: T&T Clark.

Mitchell, J. (2005a). 'Theology and Film' in *The Modern Theologians,* edited by David Ford, Oxford: Blackwell, 736–742.

Mitchell, J. (2007). *Media Violence and Christian Ethics.* Cambridge: Cambridge University Press.

Mitchell, J. and Plate, S.B. (eds). (2007). *The Film and Religion Reader.* London and New York: Routledge.

Mitchell, W. (1995). 'Interdisciplinarity and Visual Culture,' *Art Bulletin* 78(4): 540–44.

Mitroff, I. and Bennis, W. (1993). *The Unreality Industry: The Deliberate Manufacturing of Falsehood and What it is Doing to our Lives.* New York: Oxford University Press.

Moore, L. (1995). *Selling God: American Religion in the Market-Place of Culture.* New York: Oxford University Press.

Morgan, D. & Promey, S. (eds). (1996). *Icons of American Protestantism: The Art of Warner Sallman.* Yale: Yale University Press.

Morgan, D. (1998). *Visual Piety: A History and Theory of Popular Religious Images.* Berkeley: University of California Press.

Morgan, D. (1999). *Protestants and Pictures: Religion, Visual Culture, and the Age of American Mass Production.* New York: Oxford University Press.

Morgan, D. (2005). *The Sacred Gaze; Religious Visual Culture in Theory and Practice.* Berkeley: University of California Press.

Morris, C. (1984). *God-in-a-Box: Christian Strategy in the Television Age.* London: Hodder and Stoughton.

Morris, C. (1990). *Wrestling with an Angel.* Fount: Collins.

Mosala, I. (1988). *Hermeneutics and Black Theology in South Africa.* Grand Rapids: Wm. Eerdmans.

Moss, J. (ed.) (1998). *The Later Foucault: Politics and Philosophy.* Thousand Oaks, CA: Sage.

Muggeridge, M. (1977). *Christ and the Media,* London: Hodder and Stoughton.

Murray, A. (2001). *From the Briarpatch File: On Context, Procedure and American Identity.* New York: Pantheon Books.

Nelson, R. (2004). *Hagia Sophia, 1850–1950: Holy Wisdom Modern Monument.* Chicago: University of Chicago Press.

Naficy, H. (2002). 'Islamizing Film Culture in Iran'. In *The New Iranian Cinema,* edited by Richard Tapper, London: I.B. Tauris, 26–65.

Nickell, J., (with Beaudoin, T. and Lynch, G.) (2006). 'Meaning, spirit and popular culture: an interview with Tom Beaudoin, *Crucible* July-Sept, 17–23.

Niebuhr, H.R. (1951). *Christ and Culture.* San Francisco: Harper & Row.

Nord, D.P. (2004). *Faith in Reading: Religious Publishing and the Birth of Mass Media in America*. New York: Oxford University Press.

Nussbaum, M. (1986). *The Fragility of Goodness: Luck and Ethics in Greek Tragedy and Philosophy*. Cambridge: Cambridge University Press.

Nussbaum, M. (1990). *Love's Knowledge: Essays on Philosophy and Literature*. Oxford: Oxford University Press.

Ogbar, J. (1999). 'Slouching toward Bork: the culture wars and self-criticism in hip-hop music'. *Journal of Black Studies*, vol.33(2), 164–84.

Ostwalt, C. (1998). 'Religion and popular movies'. *Journal of Religion and Film* (online), Vol. 2, No. 3. Available at: http://www.unomaha.edu/jrf/popular.htm [accessed 05/07/06].

O'Brien, E. (1993). 'The Modern electronic era: 1920 to the present', In *Communication and Change in American Religious History*, edited by Leonard Sweet, Grand Rapids, MI.: Eerdmans, 472–3.

Ong, W. (1982). *Orality and Literacy: The Technologizing of the Word*. London: Methuen.

Pinn, A. (2003a). *Terror and Triumph: The Meaning of Black Religion*. Minneapolis: Fortress Press.

Orsi, R. (2005). *Between Heaven and Earth: The Religious Worlds People Make and the Scholars Who Study Them*. Princeton, NJ.: Princeton University Press.

Otto, R. (1917/1968). *The Idea of the Holy*. New York: Oxford University Press.

Pinn, A. (2003b). *Noise and Spirit: The Religious and Spiritual Sensibilities of Rap Music*. New York: New York University Press.

Pinn, A. (2006). 'Sweaty bodies in a circle: thoughts on the subtle dimensions of black religion as protest.' *Black Theology*, vol.4(1), 11–26.

Plate, S.B. (ed.) (2003). *Representing Religion in World Cinema: Filmmaking, Mythmaking, Culturemaking*. Basingstoke: Palgrave Macmillan.

Plate, S.B. (2004). *Walter Benjamin, Religion, and Aesthetics*. New York: Routledge.

Plunkett, J. (2005). 'Springer show not blasphemous, Thompson says'. *Guardian* (online), January 7, available at: http://media.guardian.co.uk/print/0,,5098341_105236,00.html [accessed 16/12/06].

Porter, J. & McLaren, D. (2000). *Star Trek and Sacred Ground: Explorations of Star Trek, Religion and American Culture*. New York: State University of New York Press.

Postman, N. (1985). *Amusing Ourselves to Death: Public Discourse in an Age of Show Business*. London: Heinemann.

Powell, K. (1995). '2Pac Shakur.' *Vibe Magazine*, April 1995, 50–55.

Pungente, J., and Williams, M. (2004). *Finding God in the Dark: The Spiritual Exercises of Saint Ignatius Go To the Movies*. Ottawa: Novalis.

Qibla Cola (2003). Homepage available at: http://www.qiblacola.com/index2.asp.

Rahner, K. (1990). *Faith in a Wintry Season: Conversations and Interviews with Karl Rahner in the Last Years of His Life*, edited by Paul Imhof and Hubert Biallowons, and translation edited by Harvey D. Egan. New York: Crossroad.

Real, M. (1977). *Mass Mediated Culture*. Englewood Cliffs: Prentice Hall.

Reed, A. (1989). 'Br'er rabbit and the briar patch.' In *Talk that Talk: An Anthology of African-American Storytelling*, edited by Linda Goss and Marian Barnes, New York: Touchstone Books, 30–1.

Reinhardt, A. (1953/1996). 'Twelve Rules for a New Academy.' In *Theories and Documents of Contemporary Art: A Sourcebook of Artists' Writings*, edited by Kristine Stiles and Peter Selz, Berkeley: University of California Press, 86–90.

'Report of Mr. D. H. S[mith].' (1854). *Twenty-Ninth Annual Report*. New York: American Tract Society.

Rich, A. (1987). *Blood, Bread and Poetry: Selected Prose 1979–1985*. New York: W.W. Norton & Co.

Rizzuto, A-M. (1981). *The Birth of the Living God: A Psychoanalytic Study*. Chicago: University of Chicago Press.

Rose, D. (2004). 'Pop and Politics: Celebrities Working Politics More Intensely Than Ever...But Will it Make a Difference?' *Watertown Daily Times* (NY).

Roth, W-M. (ed.) (2005). *Auto/Biography and Auto/Ethnography: Praxis of Research Methods*. Rotterdam: Sense Publishers.

Sanctus1. (2002). 'Who we are.' (online), available at: http:www.sanctus1.co.uk/whoweare.php [accessed 28–11–05].

Rothenbuhler, E. & Coman, M. (eds). (2004). *Media Anthropology*. London: Sage.

Schmidt, L. E. (1997) *Consumer Rites: The Buying and Selling of American Holidays*. Princeton, NJ.: Princeton University Press.

Schultze, Q. (1992). *Redeeming Television*. Downers Grove, Illinois: IVP.

Schwartz, T. (1983). *Media: the Second God*. New York: Anchor Books.

Scott, B. (1994). *Hollywood Dreams and Biblical Stories*. Minneapolis: Fortress Press.

Short, R. (1967). *The Gospel According to Peanuts*. Richmond: John Knox.

Smart, N. (1986). *Concept and Empathy: Essays in the Study of Religion*. Basingstoke: Macmillan.

Smart, N. (1999). *Dimensions of the Sacred: An Anatomy of the World's Beliefs*. Berkeley: University of California Press.

Smith, J.Z. (1988). *Imaging Religion: From Babylon to Jonestown*. Chicago: University of Chicago Press.

Spender, D. (1995). *Nattering on the Net: Women, Power and Cyberspace*. Melbourne: Spinifex Press.

Stern, R., Jeffords, C. and Demona, R. (1999). *Savior on the Silver Screen*. New York: Paulist Press.

Stout, D. & Buddenbaum, J. (eds). (2000). *Religion and Popular Culture: Studies on the Interaction of Worldviews*. Ames, Iowa: Iowa State University Press.

Stout, J. (2004). *Democracy and Tradition*. Princeton, NJ.: Princeton University Press.

Strinati, D. (2004). *An Introduction to Theories of Popular Culture*. New York, NY: Routledge.

Sullivan, R. (2005). *Visual Habits: Nuns, Feminism, and American Postwar Popular Culture*. Toronto: University of Toronto Press.

Sumiala-Seppänen, J., Lundby, K., and Salokangas, R. (eds). (2006). *Implications of The Sacred in (Post)Modern Media*. Nordicum: Göteborg.

Sweet, L. (ed.) (1993). *Communication and Change in American Religious History*. Grand Rapids, MI.: Eerdmans.

Swidler, A. (1986). 'Culture in action: symbols and strategies.' *American Sociological Review*, 15, 273–286.

Sylvan, R. (2002). *Traces of the Spirit: The Religious Dimensions of Popular Music*. New York: New York University Press.

Tanner, K. (1997). *Theories of Culture: A New Agenda for Theology*. Minneapolis, MN: Fortress.

Taylor, D., and Vintges, K. (2004). *Feminism and the Final Foucault*. Urbana, IL: University of Illinois Press.

Taylor, L. & Willis, A. (1999). *Media Studies: Texts, Institutions and Audiences*. Oxford: Blackwell.

Telford, W. (2005). 'Through a lens darkly: critical approaches to theology and film.' In *Cinéma Divinité: Religion, Theology and the Bible in Film* edited by Eric Christiansen, Peter Francis and William Telford. London: SCM Press, 15–43.

Teresa of Ávila. (1957). *The Life of Saint Teresa of Ávila*. Translated by J.M. Cohen. New York, NY: Penguin.

Thirty-First Annual Report. (1856). New York: American Tract Society.

Thomas, A. (2002). 'Reading the Silences: Documenting the History of American Tract Society Readers in the Antebellum South.' In *Reading Acts: U.S. Readers' Interactions with Literature, 1800–1950,* edited by Barbara Ryan and Amy M. Thomas, Knoxville: University of Tennessee Press, 107–36.

Thompson, J. (1995). *The Media and Modernity: A Social Theory of the Media*. Cambridge: Polity.

Thurman, H. (1979). *With Head and Heart*. New York: Harcourt Brace Jovanovich Publishers.

Tillich, P. (1959). *Theology of Culture*. New York: Oxford University Press.

Trachtenberg, A. (1989). 'Mirror in the Marketplace: American Responses to the Daguerreotype, 1839–1851.' In *The Daguerreotype: A Sesquicentennial Celebration*, edited by John Wood, Iowa City: University of Iowa Press, 60–73.

Tracy, D. (1975). *Blessed Rage for Order: The New Pluralism in Theology*. New York, NY: Seabury Press.

Tract Distribution Report. (1833). Richmond Street Congregational Vestry, Providence, Manuscript report, February, 5th Ward of Providence. American Tract Society, Mss 927, Box 1, Folder 1, Rhode Island Historical Society.

Tweed, T. (2006). *Crossing and Dwelling: A Theory of Religion*. Cambridge, MA.: Harvard University Press.

Twenty-Eighth Annual Report. (1853). New York: American Tract Society.

Vulliamy, E. (2006). 'Welcome to the new holy land'. *Observer* December 17 (online), available at: http://observer.guardian.co.uk/print /0,,329664634–102280,00.html [accessed 17/12/06]

Wagner, R. (2003). 'Bewitching the box office: Harry Potter and Religious Controversy'. *Journal of Religion and Film* (online), No. 7, No. 2. Available at: http://www.unomaha.edu/jrf/Vol7No2/bewitching.htm [accessed 12/12/06].

Walser, R. (1993). *Running with the Devil: Power, Gender and Madness in Heavy Metal Music*. Hanover, New England: Wesleyan/New England Press.

Ward, P. (2002). *Liquid Church*. Milton Keynes: Paternoster.

Ward, P. (2005). *Selling Worship: How What We Sing Has Changed the Church*. Milton Keynes: Authentic Media.

'Webstercat71' (2006). 'Manchester Passion message 10' (online), posted 14th April, available at: http://www.bbc.co.uk/dna/england/F2770282?thread=2090395&phrase=Manchester, (accessed 12/12/06).

West, C. (1991). 'The New Politics of Difference.' In *Out There: Marginalization and Contemporary Cultures*, edited by Russell Ferguson, Martha Gever, Trinh T. Minh-ha and Cornel West, Cambridge, MA.: New Museum of Contemporary Art and MIT Press, pp.10–29.

Williams, D. (1992). *Sisters in the Wilderness: Womanism and God-Talk*. New York: Orbis.

Williams, R. (1958). *Culture and Society 1780–1950*. London: Chatto & Windus.

Williams, R. (1992). *The Long Revolution*. London: Hogarth Press.

Winn, M. (1985). *The Plug in Drug*. New York: Penguin.

Winston, D. (2000). *Red-Hot and Righteous: The Urban Religion of the Salvation Army*. Cambridge, MA.: Harvard University Press.

Wuthnow, R. (2003). *All in Sync: How Music and Art are Revitalizing American Religion*. Berkeley: University of California Press.

Contributor Details

Lynn Schofield Clark is Assistant Professor and Director of the Estlow International Center for Journalism and New Media at the University of Denver. She is the author of *From Angels to Aliens: Teenagers, the Media, and the Supernatural* (Oxford University Press, 2003), co-author of *Media, Home, and Family* (Routledge, 2004), editor of *Religion, Media, and the Marketplace* (Rutgers, 2007), and co-editor of *Practicing Religion in the Age of the Media* (Columbia University Press, 2002). She is currently writing a book on young peoples' uses of digital media and the challenges these uses present to persons in positions of authority.

David Morgan is Professor of Religion and Visual Culture in the Department of Religion at Duke University. Prof. Morgan's major research interests are the history of religious images, American religious and cultural history, and art theory. He is the author and editor of a number of prize-winning books in the field of religion and visual culture, including *Icons of American Protestantism: The Art of Warner Sallman* (Yale University Press, 1996), *Visual Piety: A History and Theory of Popular Religious Images* (University of California Press, 1998), and *The Sacred Gaze: Religious Visual Culture in Theory and Practice* (University of California Press, 2005). Morgan has previously chaired the International Study Commission on Media, Religion and Culture, is co-editor of the 'Media, Religion and Culture' monograph series with Routledge, and is the co-founder and co-editor of the journal, *Material Religion*.

Jolyon Mitchell is Senior Lecturer in Communication, Theology and Ethics at Edinburgh University, having previously worked as a journalist and produced for the BBC World Service and BBC Radio 4. Dr Mitchell is author of *Media Violence and Christian Ethics* (Cambridge University Press, 2007); *Visually Speaking* (Edinburgh: T&T Clark, 1999); co-editor of *The Religion and Film Reader* (London and New York: Routledge, 2007); *Mediating Religion* (London: Continuum, 2003); and a co-editor of Routledge's monograph series on 'Media, Religion and Culture'. He was director of the Third International Conference on Media, Religion and Culture , Edinburgh, July 1999 and is director of the Fourth International Ecumenical Conference on Peacemaking in the World of Film: from Conflict to Reconciliation in Edinburgh, July 2007.

Jeffrey H. Mahan is Professor of Ministry, Media and Culture at the Iliff School of Theology, in Denver, Co. He currently serves as Academic Vice President and Dean of the Faculty. With Bruce Forbes he is the co-founder of the Religion and Popular Culture Group of the American Academy of Religion and co-editor of *Religion and Popular Culture in America* (University of California Press, Revised Edition, 2005.)

Elaine Graham is Samuel Ferguson Professor of Social and Pastoral Theology at the University of Manchester. Her publications include *Making the Difference: Gender, Personhood and Theology* (Augsburg, 1995), *Transforming Practice* (Continuum, 1996), *Representations of the Post/human: Monsters, Aliens and Others in Popular Culture* (Rutgers University Press, 2002) and numerous articles and reviews. She is the co-author, with Heather Walton and Frances Ward, of *Theological Reflection: Methods* (SCM Press, 2005).

Pete Ward is Senior Lecturer in Youth Ministry and Theological Education at the Centre for Theology, Religion and Culture at King's College, London. Ward was a founder member of the International Association for the Study of Youth Ministry, and has previously served as the Archbishop of Canterbury's youth advisor. He is the author and editor of a number of books concerning worship, missiology and contemporary culture, including *Liquid Church* (Paternoster, 2002) and *Selling Worship: How What We Sing Has Changed the Church* (Authentic Media, 2005), and is currently writing on practical theology and the cultural turn.

Tom Beaudoin is Assistant Professor of theology in the Religious Studies Department at Santa Clara University . He is the author of *Virtual Faith: The Irreverent Spiritual Quest of Generation X* (Jossey-Bass, 1998), *Consuming Faith: Integrating Who We Are With What We Buy* (Sheed & Ward, 2004), and many articles on theology and culture. His current research focuses on Foucault studies and psychoanalytic studies in dialogue with Catholic theology.

Robert Beckford is Reader in Black Theology and Popular Culture at Oxford Brookes University. Dr Beckford is one of the leading film-makers and television presenters on religion and contemporary social issues in the UK, having been involved in a number of high profile productions with Channel 4 television such as *God is Black*, *The Empire Pays Back*, and *God Gave You Rock*. He has been a pioneering writer in the field of black theology in Britain, with his previous books including *Jesus is Dread* (DLT, 1998), *Dread and Pentecostal: A Political Theology for the Black Church in Britain* (SPCK, 2000) and most recently, *Jesus Dub: Faith, Culture and Social Change* (Routledge, 2006). He is currently researching the interface between theology and documentary film-making.

Gordon Lynch is Professor in Sociology of Religion at Birkbeck College, University of London. He is the lead convenor of the UK Research Network for Theology, Religion and Popular Culture and co-chair of the Religion, Media and Culture Group within the American Academy of Religion. He is the author of a number of books on religion and contemporary culture including *Understanding Theology and Popular Culture* (Blackwell, 2005) and *The New Spirituality: An Introduction to Progressive Belief in the Twenty-First Century* (I.B. Tauris, 2007).

Anthony B. Pinn is the Agnes Cullen Arnold Professor of Humanities and Professor of Religious Studies in the Department of Religious Studies at Rice University. He is the author and editor of sixteen books, including *Why, Lord?: Suffering and Evil in Black Theology* (Continuum, 1997), *Varieties of African American Religious Experience* (Augsburg, 1998), *Terror and Triumph: The Nature of Black Religion* (Fortress Press, 2003), and *African American Humanist Principles: Living and Thinking Like the Children of Nimrod* (Palgrave Macmillan, 2004) . He is currently working on a book dealing with the aesthetics of black religious experience and a co-edited volume on theoretical and methodological considerations related to the study of religion in popular culture.

Index